BEST WALKS
IN THE CAPE PENINSULA

MIKE LUNDY'S
BEST WALKS
IN THE CAPE PENINSULA

STRUIK

ACKNOWLEDGEMENTS

First and foremost my thanks go to Jose Burman: although we never met, he was responsible, through his wonderfully descriptive books on hiking in the Western Cape, for getting me onto the mountain in the first place.

A book of this nature is not written without considerable help, and I would like to thank all those who so willingly assisted me in this task:

Marilyn Harcourt-Wood for typing the text and constantly correcting my spelling.

John Robertson and Paul Pigneguy, my regular companions on most of these walks.

Derick Louw of The Movie Studio, for his information on the Lion's Head Gold Mining Syndicate.

Ann Walton for her illustrations.

Amanda de Jongh of the Department of Surveys and Mapping in Mowbray for her cheerful helpfulness, and Zane Erasmus, former Forester at Cecilia Forest Station.

To experts in their various fields for their perceptive comments, in particular to Ernst Baard and Atherton de Villiers, herpetologists at the Department of Nature and Environmental Conservation, Jonkershoek; Dr Bill Borchers, retired geologist, and Dr Roger Smith, palaeontologist at the South African Museum; and Peter Steyn, well-known ornithologist.

Maps: Details from the maps have been reproduced under the Government Printer's Copyright Authority 9115 of 22nd August 1990.

Although the author and publisher have made every effort to ensure that the information in this book was correct at the time of going to press, they accept no responsibility for any loss, injury or inconvenience sustained by any person using this book.

Struik Publishers (Pty) Ltd
(a member of Struik New Holland
Publishing (Pty) Ltd)
Cornelis Struik House
80 McKenzie Street
Cape Town 8001

Reg. No.: 54/00965/07

First published 1991
Second impression 1994
Second edition 1995
Second impression 1997
Third impression 1997
Fourth impression 1998

Copyright © in published edition
Struik Publishers 1991, 1995
Copyright text © Mike Lundy 1991, 1995
Cover photographs © Mike Lundy 1991, 1995

Copyright maps © Euan Waugh 1991, 1995
Editor: Jan Schaafsma
Illustrator: Ann Walton
DTP conversion by Bellset, Cape Town
Reproduction of cover by Fotoplate
(Pty) Ltd, Cape Town
Printed and bound by National Book
Printers, Drukkery Street, Goodwood,
Western Cape

ISBN 1 86825 861 0

CONTENTS

Dedicated to my family

'When we reach the mountain summits, we leave behind us all the things that weigh heavily on our body and spirit. We leave behind all sense of weakness and depression. We feel a new freedom, a great exhilaration, and exaltation of the body no less than of the spirit.'

Jan Christiaan Smuts

FOREWORD

Among the many contrasts and nuances of beauty and mood that make up South Africa, those of the Cape Peninsula, with its marvellous combination of sea, sky and mountain, are outstanding. This is the environment that Mike Lundy has chosen to write about, presenting the reader with a choice of carefully selected walks, many of which traverse the slopes and heights of Table Mountain. Giving practical advice on such vital aspects as mountain safety and capricious local weather conditions, he skilfully guides his reader through an area that lies within one of the six great floral kingdoms of the world. Table Mountain alone, supporting more than 1 400 flowering plant species, is unparalleled in the enormous variety that occurs within so small a compass.

The potential reward for those seeking environmental and recreational inspiration is enormous. May they, like the author, hold fast to the idea that the pleasure we derive from our natural heritage must not blind us to our responsibility to conserve that heritage for future generations; may they also come to recognise that the environment is a pearl of great price. To protect this pearl mere talk of ecosystems, species and habitats is not enough. Instead we must live in awe of the senses, of light and shade and changing seasons, of life in an unspoilt environment. The author makes us aware of all these aspects. To those who tramp but do not trample underfoot, his message is an open invitation, not merely to visit but to climb and become involved.

I've had the privilege of exploring this great mountain system over a lifetime and the experience has been unbelievably enriching and a constant source of joy and inspiration to me.

The Table, a symbol of hospitality, invites you. Mike Lundy has prepared a fantastic menu of walks. A great feast awaits you.

KENT DURR

INTRODUCTION

Who can really say which are the best walks in the Cape Peninsula? When so many variables come into play, it is impossible to be objective, but I do believe that most of the ones I have chosen will appeal to most hikers most of the time.

The walks are extremely varied, as is Mother Mountain herself, and range from an easy walk along the beach to some real cliffhangers, though ropes are not required on any of the walks or climbs. There is something, I believe, to suit all tastes.

I have continued with the simple but descriptive grading system successfully introduced in *Twenty Walks Around Hout Bay*. When taken into account along with the duration of the walk, it should give you a fairly accurate picture of what to expect. The grading system makes allowance for people who suffer from a fear of heights – there seem to be a surprisingly large number of them.

I have measured the *effort* needed to complete the walk on a scale of 1 to 4 and combined it with a *fear of heights* (if the potential exists) on a scale of A to D.

All times given for walks include a suitable allowance for rests. They are also what I feel the average reasonably fit person should be able to achieve.

On the assumption that most people cannot read complex maps but can, hopefully, read precise instructions, I've kept the maps simple and the instructions detailed. I have tried hard to omit ambiguities, but no doubt I will still get complaints from people who got lost. As

GRADING

1. An easy stroll.
2. Tiring.
3. Strenuous.
4. Exhausting and only for the very fit.

A. No exposure to heights.
B. Some mild rock scrambling, but no worse than climbing a short ladder.
C. Moderately exposed. Those with a serious fear of heights should not attempt this walk.
D. Very exposed. Not for those with even a mild fear of heights.

my Dear Old Dad used to say: When all else fails, READ THE INSTRUCTIONS.

We are indeed fortunate to live in Cape Town, where Table Mountain's craggy but serene face towers protectively over the city. I can think of no other city in the world where such natural beauty is so easily accessible. All twenty-two walks described in this book are between five and thirty minutes' drive from the city centre. The magic of Table Mountain is that after many years of walking on it, I'm *still* discovering new treasures. I sincerely hope you discover a few while reading this book.

AN HISTORICAL PEEK

Seeing the faint purple mass of Table Mountain rise from below the horizon is one of the world's great sights. The first sailor on a Dutch East Indiaman to do so was rewarded with ten guilders and six bottles of wine; and to celebrate the prospect of fresh provisions, all hands were given a tot of brandy.

The first European to climb to the top of Table Mountain was the Portuguese admiral Antonio de Saldanha in March 1503 while he and his small fleet were on their way from Lisbon to India through largely uncharted seas. For a century after that, Cape Town was known as *Agoada do Saldanha* (The Watering Place of Saldanha).

Many years later the name found its way higher up the coast by mistake: the Dutch admiral Joris van Spilbergen made a landfall 100 km to the north and assumed the sheltered bay he found there to be *Agoada do Saldanha*. Thus Saldanha Bay got its name even though the Portuguese admiral had never been there, and his original watering place became *Tafel Baay*.

In 1620 an English seafarer, Humphrey FitzHerbert, landed at what he called the Bay of Soldania (Table Bay) and in the best British tradition promptly took possession of the area in the name of his king, James I. In a short ceremony on shore he sportingly presented the bewildered Khoi with an English flag, thus apparently making the exercise perfectly legitimate.

He then set about naming the surrounding mountains. First to be honoured was the present-day Signal Hill, which was christened 'King James His Mount'; what was later to become Lion's Head he dubbed 'Ye Sugar Loafe'. Not about to miss an opportunity to achieve everlasting fame, he named the present-day Devil's Peak 'Herbert's Mount'. Unfortunately, on his return to England, King James showed scant enthusiasm for his latest possession and it was left to the Dutch to move in.

When Jan van Riebeeck arrived in 1652 with a few more than a hundred souls, he landed at 'Leeuwenstaart' (Lion's Tail) – the present-day Granger Bay, which of course was attached to 'De Leeuwenbergh'. Herbert's Mount became Windbergh, but over five centuries and in many languages Table Mountain has always been and surely will always be Table Mountain.

SAFETY ON THE MOUNTAIN

A most revealing piece of research on mountain accidents was published in the 1987 edition of *The Journal of the Mountain Club of South Africa*. It analysed accident statistics on Table Mountain over almost the previous one hundred years, and revealed a strange paradox.

The classic rock climbs, such as Africa Crag, Africa Face, Slangolie Buttress and others, have not had one single fatality. And only one or two deaths in a hundred years have occurred on many of the other well-known difficult rock climbs. Yet it seems to be on the easy routes that people come to grief. Three deaths in Skeleton Gorge, three in Blinkwater Ravine, and even two in the almost – but evidently not quite – foolproof Platteklip Gorge.

To quote the leader article in the *Cape Times* of 8th August 1988 entitled *Easy but Deadly*, 'The lesson to be learnt from these high risk areas is the need for greater public awareness of the dangers involved. Lack of proper clothing, equipment and knowledge of the area can turn a so-called easy climb into a disastrous exercise.

The foolhardy seldom venture up cliffs, but they often commit themselves with irresponsible abandon to the kloofs and gullies which even a trained climber would not attempt before taking elementary precautions. The statistics show the penalty that has all too frequently been paid.'

On that note let it be said that the author and publisher take no responsibility for any accident arising from the breaking of the following commonsense rules, or as a result of any inaccuracies which may have inadvertently crept into walk descriptions. Proceed at your own risk!

THE TEN COMMANDMENTS
OF MOUNTAIN SAFETY
(Reprinted by courtesy of the Mountain Club of South Africa)

1. Never climb alone. Four is the ideal party.
2. Choose your route according to ability, fitness and experience of the party.
3. Go with somebody who genuinely knows the way, or use a map, guidebook, or description of the route by a person who has climbed it before. Allow plenty of time to get up and down in daylight.
4. Until you know your way around, stick to the recognized routes on well-used paths. Heed signs warning of danger and do not take short cuts or negotiate unknown ravines.
5. Tell someone exactly where you are going (up and down routes and expected time of return) and stick to this plan.
6. Every party should have a leader. Keep together and travel at the pace of the slowest. Never split up and go in different directions.
7. Always go prepared for bad weather and take proper weatherproof and windproof clothing. Carry everything in a rucksack to keep arms and hands free.
8. Always watch the weather and time and turn back as soon as bad weather threatens, or if the route is no longer easy to follow.
9. Stay put in case of trouble. Don't try to force your way down in darkness or mist. Find shelter, especially from the wind.
10. If you get lost or find yourself in an area that looks unsafe, retrace your steps. Do not push on into the unknown. If you can't find the path you left, look for a safe route – preferably down broad, open slopes – making sure at all times that you can retrace your steps.

BOTANICAL FOOD FOR THOUGHT

When discussing the indigenous flora of the south-western Cape, one important fact cannot be over-emphasised. We live in the richest floral kingdom in the world – and it's dying. Our grandchildren may never see fynbos.

The botanical world is divided into six 'floral kingdoms'. The largest is the Boreal Kingdom which covers virtually the whole of the Northern Hemisphere. The smallest in area is the Cape Floral Kingdom which stretches from Clanwilliam in the north to Grahamstown in the east along a narrow coastal strip. This tiny area is the richest of all the world's six plant kingdoms.

In the Cape Peninsula alone there are over 2 500 flowering plants – more than the whole of Britain. The whole kingdom boasts some 8 500 species – more than the entire Northern Hemisphere, three times the number of species of our nearest rival, the Amazon Basin.

Alien threat

This vast profusion of flowering plants is severely threatened by the invasion of aliens, not the least of which is mankind himself. Only 40 per cent of the fynbos flora found here in Van Riebeeck's time has survived.

Why are these aliens choking our indigenous flora? Unfortunately most have pyrophyllic seeds (pyro = fire, phyllus = love), and the intense heat of a fire stimulates the seeds to germinate, almost as if it were a signal to indicate a sudden absence of competition at ground level. Also, like any successful weed, the aliens are able to reach flowering maturity very quickly. With the exception of pines, most of the more threatening alien invaders come from Australia.

Cecil John Rhodes has been blamed for a great many things, including the introduction of Acacias to the Cape Flats in order to bind the sand, but in this case he's innocent, for there are records showing the importation of Acacia and Hakea species as early as 1833, before he was born. The blame can be laid squarely at the door of the resident botanist of the Cape Town Gardens during the 1830s, who felt there were not enough fast-growing shade trees in the Cape Colony at the time.

Unfortunately these aliens had no natural predators in South Africa and were not prone to local diseases. Being fast growers, they rapidly overcrowded the indigenous flora and in many areas replaced it with a monotonous, impenetrable green sea of one species only.

Much is done to combat the menace: for example, amateur conservation groups go out on weekend 'hacks' and cut down offending alien vegetation, but however well-meaning these groups are, I can't help feeling that they are merely scratching the surface. For every plant cut down, 100 000 seeds may be ready to germinate after the first fire. There is simply not enough manpower for 'hack groups' to succeed on more than a strictly local basis.

Nature has to be harnessed to tackle this immense threat to our environment, and this is indeed what scientists are trying to do. The invading plants are not a problem in Australia, their country of origin, because there nature provides a stabilising influence in the form of natural controls. Unfortunately when these plants were brought to the Cape, their biological governors were left behind. Currently biological control has been or is being introduced to fight the Port Jackson Willow (in the form of a fungus), Hakea (fungus and borer beetle), Long-leafed Wattle (gall-wasp) and Blackwood (snout-beetle). Rooikrans and others are also being tackled.

But there is no instant solution. Biological controls will take a hundred years to get on top – and don't forget the countless seeds lurking below the surface. Weekend 'hacks', though, will take forever.

Blister bush

One indigenous plant to beware of is the Blister Bush (*Peucedanum galbanum*) otherwise known as Mountain Celery because of its close resemblance and direct relationship to celery. This most interesting plant deserves healthy respect. Until very recently, little was known about the mechanism of its ability to inflict nasty blisters. Don't let anybody boast immunity because they've touched it and nothing happened – given the right set of conditions, they will blister just as badly as you and I.

Research done in 1985 by Dr Natie Finkelstein of the Cape Technikon's Department of Pharmacy has cast interesting light on this subject. It seems a combination of slight damage or bruising to the leaves, and strong sunlight, are the essential ingredients for blisters. The compound released from the plant on bruising is not in itself harmful, but when exposed to strong ultra-violet light a change takes place in its chemical composition, causing blistering after two days. To avoid these blisters, the affected area should be protected from sunlight.

Two experiments by Dr Finkelstein illustrate the point. In the first an untouched branch was brushed over the left arm. The right arm was similarly treated with a branch which had been roughly handled. Only the right arm was affected. In the second experiment both arms were rubbed with bruised leaves and one arm immediately covered to exclude light. Only the exposed arm produced blisters.

Blister Bush

BIRDS TO LOOK FOR

The rugged mountains of the Cape Peninsula, though rich in numerous plant species, do not support a wealth of birdlife. The barren rocky cliffs and exposed rocky outcrops provide little in the way of food or shelter, and it stands to reason that the few birds which are found here are well-suited to the harsh climate and habitat in which they live.

Here are the more common birds you are likely to find on your walks in the Cape Peninsula mountains. For a more complete picture and to help you correctly identify the birds, refer to *Roberts Birds of Southern Africa*; Ken Newman's *Birds of Southern Africa*; Ian Sinclair's *Field Guide to the Birds of Southern Africa*; or *Birds of the South Western Cape* by Joy Frandsen. A comprehensive list of birds recorded at Kirstenbosch is available free of charge from the National Botanic Gardens.

On the boulder-strewn upper slopes of the Table Mountain Range, look for the *Cape Rock Thrush* and the wary *Ground Woodpecker*, which abandoned life in the trees and lives on the ground. It lives in small groups and is the only terrestrial woodpecker in Africa, using tunnels excavated in earth banks in which to roost and nest.

The steep cliff faces above the contour path provide safe nesting sites for two prominent residents, the *Redwinged Starling* and the *Rock Pigeon*, which like many other starlings and pigeons have also become adapted to an urban environment. Large flocks of *Alpine* and *Black Swifts* are particularly noticeable in summer wheeling high in the sky or near the cliff faces where they nest in inaccessible vertical cracks under an overhang. These aerial birds feed on insects taken on the wing and rarely pause to rest except when breeding. The *Rock Martin*, a brown swallow-like bird, can be seen all year round in rocky and mountainous terrain where it builds its nest of mud pellets under an overhang.

Overhead look for the majestic *Black Eagle*. Although it is not all that common, there are at least four pairs resident in the Cape Peninsula. It is usually seen soaring high above the mountain crags in search of dassies which form its staple prey. Surprisingly this bird is not all black, but viewed from above it has broad white markings on the back and the rump, hence its Afrikaans name 'Witkruisarend'. Another bird of prey confined to mountainous areas is the chestnut-coloured *Rock Kestrel* which can be seen hovering in search of prey.

The *Whitenecked Raven* – a large, strong-flying bird of the mountains – is sometimes confused with the more familiar, but smaller *Pied Crow* or 'Witborskraai' as both birds have glossy black plumage with white markings. At most times of the year in the fynbos, you are likely to see the *Cape Sugarbird* which is attracted to the sweet nectar of the Protea flowers, but is also adept at hawking for insects which form an important part of its diet, especially during the breeding season. During its conspicuous undulating display flight, the male's long beak and streamer-like tail make it instantly recognisable. Another fynbos resident is the *Orangebreasted Sunbird*, which is found in stands of Proteas and Ericas in Kirstenbosch, on the top and along the western slopes of Table Mountain. The brightly-coloured male usually calls from a vantage point on a tall shrub. Other sunbirds resident in the Peninsula mountain chain are the *Lesser Doublecollared Sunbird* and the less common *Malachite Sunbird*.

Two other common residents of the fynbos and surrounding dense bush, are the *Cape Bulbul* and the *Cape Francolin*, a fairly large gamebird with mottled brown plumage and red legs. Not as easily identified is the *Grassbird* or 'lollipop bird' as it is sometimes known because of its plump chestnut-brown chest and longish tail. Look for it in long grass or skulking in bushes.

The small pockets of natural forest seldom harbour many birds. At the forest edge look for *Cape Batis, Sombre Bulbul, Olive Thrush, Dusky Flycatcher* and *Paradise Flycatcher.* In the forest canopy and in fruiting trees and large shrubs, especially along the contour path near Cecilia Forest and Kirstenbosch, the *Rameron Pigeon* is evident, while the shy *Cinnamon Dove* haunts the forest floor. A forest bird more often heard than seen is the *Redchested Cuckoo* or Piet-my-vrou, a summer migrant which mainly parasitises the nests of the *Cape Robin*.

Finally a word about LBJs – little brown jobs – which are those drab brown birds that are almost impossible to identify unless you are an expert birder. LBJs (or 'tinktinkies' as they are commonly called in Afrikaans) are generally beautiful songsters – how else can they hope to attract a mate? LBJs to look for include the *Cape Bunting, Cape Siskin* – a canary-like bird found in pairs or small parties feeding on seeds and insects, *Familiar Chat* – found on rock outcrops, *Greybacked Cisticola, Neddicky* and *Karoo Prinia.*

Cape Sugarbird

SNAKES IN PERSPECTIVE

Snakes must be among the most misunderstood and unfairly maligned of all God's creatures. They are commonly regarded as vermin which should be killed on sight, yet they occupy a most important niche in the ecosystem. The balance of nature would be severely upset without any control on the population of rats, mice and other pests.

While the danger of a small number of snake species must never be underestimated, I do believe that the threat of death from snakebite while walking on the mountain should be put firmly in perspective. In South Africa an average of 15 people die each year as a result of snakebite, with most fatalities occurring in Northern Zululand. Yet a survey in Natal in 1978 revealed that only one in

Cape Cobra

every 68 recorded snakebites resulted in death. By comparison over 200 people are struck dead by lightning every year; 10 000 people die in the carnage on our roads; and 29 000 die as a result of smoking-related diseases. If *you* are a smoker, you can stop worrying about being bitten by a dangerous snake. What you are doing is about 2000 times more likely to kill you!

There are some 23 snake species in the Cape Peninsula, of which only five are dangerous. There are about 130 species in Southern Africa, 14 of them deadly. It therefore follows that should you come across a snake on the mountain, as I do perhaps once or twice a year, the chances are that it does not deserve the fate you probably wish upon it. However, it would be foolhardy to regard any snake with contempt. In the Cape Peninsula the five that need to be given a wide berth are the Puff Adder, Berg Adder, Cape Cobra, Rinkhals and Boomslang.

The venom injected by most dangerous snakes falls into three categories. The Cape Peninsula's 'fearsome five' includes all three types:

Cytotoxic venom is a tissue-destroying poison which causes serious localised swelling, inflammation and eventual kidney failure due to fluid loss. Puff Adder venom is extremely cytotoxic.

Neurotoxic venom attacks the nervous system serving the diaphragm, chest and throat muscles and death is by asphyxiation. The Cape Cobra, Rinkhals and Berg Adder fall into this category.

However, to date no deaths have been attributed to the Berg Adder.

Haemotoxic venom contains enzymes which activate the body's clotting mechanism, resulting in minute but fatal blood clots throughout the body and consequently a great loss of usable blood. The Boomslang delivers haemotoxic venom, although fatal bites are rare due to its non-aggressive nature.

The deadliest of snakes in southern Africa is the Black Mamba of Northern Transvaal, the KwaZulu-Natal coast, and parts of Namibia. Fortunately it is not found in the south-western Cape. The Boomslang is a close second, but the incidence of fatalities accredited to these snakes is relatively low. More deaths result from Puff Adder bites than any other in southern Africa, not due to the strength of its venom, but rather to the high incidence of bites. In the Cape, it is the Cape Cobra which holds this dubious distinction.

SNAKE MYTHS

A few fallacies about snakes that need to be exploded are:

☐ Snakes do not travel in pairs. They are loners and only pair off briefly to mate.

☐ Snakes do not hypnotise their prey.

☐ Snakes are not deliberately aggressive. They strike in self-defence if trodden on or unexpectedly disturbed. They do not chase after people.

☐ Death from an untreated Black Mamba bite occurs within 7-15 hours, not five minutes as is commonly believed.

☐ Puff Adders do not strike backwards, nor do any other snakes for that matter.

☐ Most snakes will get out of your way first. Unfortunately this does not apply to the Puff Adder, which accounts for its high incidence of bites.

SNAKE BITE FIRST AID
DO'S AND DON'TS

1. Apply a firm pressure bandage over the bitten area and immobilise the limb. Do *not* use a tourniquet, as most venom is now thought to be carried by the lymphatic system and not in the bloodstream. The application of a tourniquet increases the possibility of gangrene, especially in the case of a Puff Adder bite.
2. Do not cut the bitten area; rather use an 'Aspervenin' suction pump kit, obtainable from most hiking shops.
3. Do not inject antivenom. This should be left to a doctor. Injection of the incorrect antivenom, or any antivenom at all if the victim hasn't been poisoned, could itself cause death.
4. Do not hunt down the snake and attempt to kill it, as a second bite would really complicate matters.
5. If the victim shows difficulty in breathing, apply artificial respiration until medical assistance is obtained.
6. Do not give the victim alcohol.
7. Above all, remember that snakebite deaths are extremely rare. Remain calm and reassure the victim – he could even have been bitten by a non-poisonous snake. Get the victim to medical care as soon as possible and treat symptomatically. Symptoms may not develop for 24 hours or more.
8. In the case of spitting snakes, such as the Rinkhals, do not rub the eyes, but flush with water, milk, beer, cooldrink, even urine and shade from bright light. The pain and inflamation usually subside within 24 hours.
9. Never assume that a snake is dead: a Rinkhals is an expert at feigning death and will even roll over onto its back. Adders will also remain motionless, even when provoked; therefore never pick up what at first sight appears to be a dead snake.

As in the case of mushrooms, stay well clear of snakes
if you are not an expert.

THE GEOLOGY OF
THE CAPE PENINSULA

The Cape Peninsula and its mountains are composed of three rock masses of different ages. Cape Town, Signal Hill and Sea Point constitute a mass of tilted *Malmesbury Slates,* which can clearly be seen along the Atlantic shoreline of this area. The upper cliffs of *Table Mountain Sandstone,* with some slate, form the mountain masses of the Cape Peninsula, and these rest on a solid foundation of *Cape Granite,* which can be most clearly seen as huge rounded boulders on the slopes of Lion's Head and on either side of the coastal road from Camps Bay to Hout Bay and below Chapman's Peak Drive. As each formation is geologically quite different from the others, it is interesting to note how each was formed.

The *Malmesbury Slates* represent the oldest formation in the Cape Peninsula. They were deposited as muddy sediments in a body of water over a long period about 800 million years ago. Subsequently, by the effects of heat and pressure, they were altered into slatey rocks which earth movements tilted steeply, as can be seen in the rock ridges jutting into the sea along the beachfront at Sea Point.

The *Cape Granite* is a rock mass which crystallised out from molten magma originating from the inner part of the earth. Granite is not uniform in appearance, but has three main components, namely large crystals of grey-white felspar, with lesser amounts of glassy quartz and black specks of mica. Incidentally, the predominant felspar decays to form clay, including the kaolin deposits being quarried between Fish Hoek and Noordhoek.

The *Table Mountain Sandstone* is sedimentary rock, meaning it was formed by millions of years of river-borne sediment which piled up on itself and was compressed by its own weight. If one looks carefully at sandstone cliffs, it will be noticed that they form large rectangular blocks. This is because the rock was laid down in horizontal beds which later became vertically fractured because of the horizontal movements of the earth's crust. The subsequent erosion of these rocks by wind, rain and glacial action resulted in the formation of ledges, vertical cliffs and flat table tops.Ever since they were lifted out of the primeval waters, the natural forces of weathering have been eroding at the Table Mountain Sandstone mass. What we see today is only the remnant of this great accumulation of sediments. Geologically speaking Table Mountain is in the winter of its life: the continued erosion will cause the mass to be flattened to the level of the present Cape Flats.

AGE OF TABLE MOUNTAIN

The rocks that make up Table Mountain are about 600 million years old, but as a raised geological feature the mountain is only a maximum of 60 million years old, compared to the age of the planet, which is 4 600 million years. The age of Table Mountain may be difficult to imagine, but it is easier to comprehend major events in relation to one another if we concertina these 4 600 million years into one calendar year.

☐ During the entire January and half of February the earth supports no life at all. It is an inorganic planet in the process of cooling.
☐ About 17 February simple microbes form.
☐ On 4 March the earliest known sedimentary rocks form.
☐ On 3 September the continents start drifting apart and the first mountains are formed by folding.
☐ On 13 November animals evolve hard shells.
☐ On 29 November vertebrates evolve and the earth is clothed in plant life.
☐ On 7 December coal is deposited.
☐ On 15 December oxygen reaches present levels.
☐ On 22 December dinosaurs rule the earth and the present-day continents begin to separate.
☐ On 25 December a cataclysmic event causes the extinction of many species, including the dinosaurs.
☐ On 26 December the precursor of Table Mountain, at least six times its present height, is formed.
☐ On 28 December the Himalayas begin to form.
☐ On 31 December at 20h00 primitive man first sets foot on the planet. Christ is born at 14 seconds to midnight and the Industrial Revolution begins a second before the year ends.
☐ Immense geological changes take place on the last day of our compressed year. As recently as 4 minutes to midnight on 31 December the whole of False Bay is dry land.

THE WEATHER

The climate of the south-western Cape is described in the geography books as 'Mediterranean'. By definition this describes long, warm summers and short, mild winters with the rainfall occurring mainly in winter. We share this climate with California and south-western Australia, apart from the Mediterranean region itself.

However, the south-western Cape and in particular the Cape Peninsula differs markedly from the other regions in that our weather is notoriously unpredictable: being a weatherman in Cape Town must be a most frustrating profession. There is only one fool-proof weathervane in the Cape Peninsula: when there is cloud on Lion's Head and nowhere else, rain is guaranteed within the next 12 hours.

I have often started up the mountain under clear blue skies and balmy weather, only to come down a few hours later in pouring rain accompanied by a chilling wind. Visitors to the Cape, in particular, should be warned never to underestimate the weather, as it can change dramatically in just half an hour. Locals should know better, but I have often found inexperienced hikers adrift in the cold wind and rain, dressed only in T-shirts and shorts.

Regardless of the weather when you start, always take raingear and warm clothes. It is also advisable to take a hat and a waterbottle.

Lion's Head

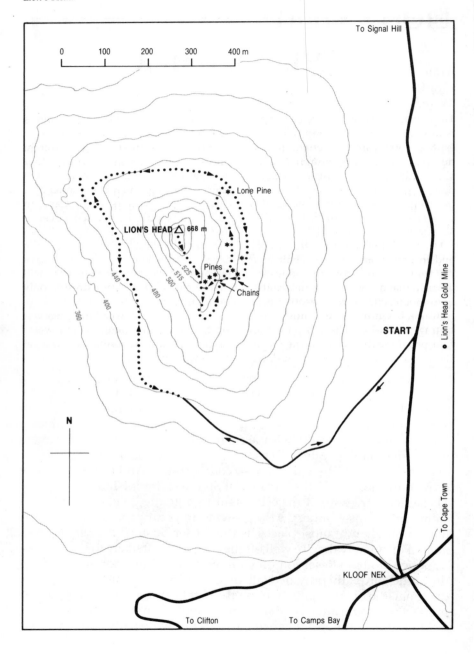

LION'S HEAD

Time: $2\frac{1}{2}$ *hours*
Grade: *2C or 2B, depending on the route*
Water: *None available*

This is probably the best value-for-energy walk in the Cape Peninsula. For the minimum of effort you are treated to a kaleidoscope of views as you spiral your way to the top.

I was fascinated to learn that Lion's Head, originally called Sugar Loaf, had its very own gold mine. Following so-called expert advice, a company, not surprisingly called the Lion's Head Gold Mining Syndicate, was formed in 1887 and actually sank a shaft some 30 m deep about 100 m below the tar road, at the beginning of this walk. This was no mere arbitrary scratching of the surface. Some gold quartz was said to have been found and in no time at all Lion's Head was teeming with prospective millionaires. Needless to say, the gold rush soon fizzled out when tests showed the quantities to be uneconomical. Imagine, though, if it had proved to be worthwhile. With beautiful scenery, wine, oil *and* gold, we Kaapenaars would perhaps have become even more arrogant and independent than ever in the eyes of our Vaalie friends!

But enough of this daydreaming, let's get on with our walk. If you do not have your own transport, take a bus to Kloof Nek. Once there, take the road up to Signal Hill and follow it for 600-700 m until you come to a parking area on either side of the road. This is your starting point up a gravel road closed off with a chain which passes through a most impressive stand of Silver Trees (*Leucadendron argenteum*). I can't think of anywhere else where they are so concentrated. And remember, they grow nowhere else in the world, but on the slopes of Table Mountain. These fickle trees are a majestic sight in a gentle breeze, their leaves shimmering and glinting. Also growing in great profusion here, perhaps more than in most places, is the Blister Bush (*Peucedanum galbanum*). Fortunately they're well off the road and not likely to bother you.

Notice Molteno Reservoir on your left as you start: not that long ago this little birdbath provided all of Cape Town's water supply. The diagonal line of large pine trees on the cliff face above you more or less marks your route after you have completed the first circuit.

After fifteen minutes the road narrows to a wide path, and you enjoy

23

a kaleidoscope of views as you spiral around the mountain: first the City Bowl, then Camps Bay, closely followed by Clifton and Sea Point and then the Mother City once again. You might be surprised at how green and tree-lined Fresnaye (upper Sea Point) is. One doesn't tend to notice it from ground level.

About 10 minutes after the road narrows to a path, you'll come to a fork. Keep to the upper right-hand path, as the left fork leads down to Lion's Rump (Signal Hill) and Sea Point. At this point, look down to the coast and notice two rocky outcrops forcing their way through the breakers off Clifton. These are called rather quaintly North Paw and South Paw (of the Lion).

Once around the corner, look down onto Lion's Rump and notice the kramat or Muslim tomb, one of many dotted around the Peninsula. This one is the final resting place of Hassan Ghaibe Sha Al Quadri, an Islamic leader. Soon you will come to a signpost giving you a choice of chains or no chains. Assuming you take the brave option, carry on along the level, and the path begins to climb slightly after a large pine tree to a second large pine. Just beyond it you will find the first set of chains that will help you to climb the rock face. You have now done a complete circuit of the mountain.

Don't be put off by the chains. The way up is not difficult, even if you do have a fear of heights. The chains are really cosmetic, rather like Linus' blanket for those who need reassuring. If, however, you have a serious fear of heights, see the end of this chapter, and the map, for an alternative route.

Kramat on Signal Hill

Scramble up the 8-m chain, then immediately up another, shorter chain. (Don't worry, they are well secured.) Now climb the steep slope immediately above to another rock face where a third and fourth chain will help you. Then follow the four pines diagonally up to the left. At the last pine, double back up the ridge, using a 3-m ladder. From the ladder it looks like heavy going, but it's only 10 minutes to the top. And when you get there – what a panorama! Looking down the length of Lion's Rump (Signal Hill), it is not too difficult to imagine the break-water being the lion's tail. At night under a full moon this climb is sheer magic. Try it around sunset and get the best of both worlds.

TO AVOID THE CHAINS (ALTERNATIVE ROUTE)

A few metres before the first large pine in the pathway going up Lion's Head, a path goes steeply up to the right. This traverses across the face between the second and third chains, continues around the ridge and up to just below the diagonal line of pines, and hence to the ladder. When returning from the top after climbing down the ladder, double back at the pines and turn sharp right at the third pine tree. It also makes a welcome change to come down this way.

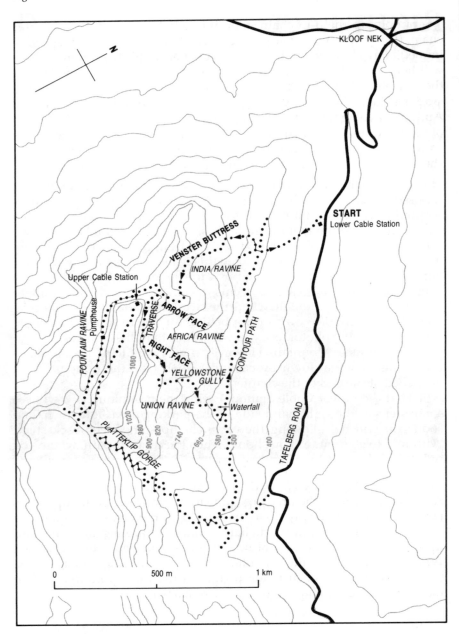

RIGHT FACE – ARROW FACE TRAVERSE 2

Time: $4\frac{1}{2}$ *hours*
Grade: *4D (This route is for experienced mountaineers only)*
Water: *Available on Africa Ledge only*

This is surely the most remarkable walk on Table Mountain: extremely exposed on the traverse, yet still just a walk with a couple of tricky rock scrambles. It's really no more difficult than walking along a narrow pavement, excepting that the gutter is about a hundred metres below!

If you have a fear of heights, stay away from this one; but if you are fit and can handle the exposure, then this walk presents you with a stiff but interesting slog up, followed by an exhilarating traverse along a ledge which on two occasions seems to come to a dead end – only to continue *inside* the mountain where the face of the mountain has literally shifted forward to leave a corridor behind for you to squeeze through.

If you study the photomap, you will notice that this climb doesn't go to the top of Table Mountain. However, if you want to do this, perhaps preferring to come down by cable car, then take the optional extra described at the end of the chapter.

Start at the Lower Cable Station. Facing the mountain, you will see some steps at the right-hand side of the parking area. Take them and soon you will be following the cable car up some steep rock steps. Within 15 to 20 minutes you should reach the contour path, where you will be confronted by a notice announcing 'This route is considered dangerous. Inexperienced climbers should use Platteklip Route'.

Disregard this ominous sign (though you have been warned) and cross straight over the contour path. Take the right-hand option where the path forks 10 m further on. (The left fork follows the route of the cable car up India Ravine, which is a more difficult alternative to the one we are following.) Your way up is called India-Venster Route. India Ravine is the one the cableway follows up and Venster Buttress is to the right of it. Your route is a combination of both. India Ravine gets its name from the fact that, viewed from the city, it takes on the outline of a map of India. Venster Buttress has a picturesque 'venster' (window) in the rocks, which we shall see some 10 to 15 minutes after leaving the contour path. If you wish to make a slight detour to the window, keep an eye open for a pile of boulders on the skyline 100 m to the left and 10 to 15 minutes above the contour path, whilst in a narrow gully. Get above the line of the boulders, then leave the path to get to the 'venster' about 100 m to the left. It frames Devil's Peak beautifully from one side and Lion's Head from the other.

Once back on the path, continue the upward slog for another 10 minutes before emerging from the gully. Ahead and to the left you will see the top of India Ravine. Your route traverses the top of India Ravine and goes diagonally up to the top left-hand corner, after which a short rock scramble (more or less straight up) is necessary. Follow the path, and keep a sharp eye open for cairns and foot-worn rock.

Once over the rock scramble, follow the cairns in the direction of the Upper Cable Station. You will reach a spot where the path takes you to almost directly below the cable station; at the same time there is a short, sheer cliff face on your right. This is an important junction. On the face of Table Mountain in front and to the left of you are three bushy ledges. The middle one is Africa Ledge and the lower one Right Face – Arrow Face Traverse. Just as the path starts climbing steeply up to Africa Ledge, a faint path goes down to the left. This is your way.

If you decide to take the optional extra (see end of chapter) to the Upper Cable Station, then this is the point to which you must return, so as to ascend to the higher level of Africa Ledge.

For the time being, however, you descend slightly to Right Face – Arrow Face Traverse. After about 7 minutes the precipitous path apparently comes to an abrupt end. Closer inspection of the rock face will reveal a narrow crack: get into it and walk 8 m behind the face of the mountain. On emerging into the sunlight again, immediately turn right and scramble 2 m up onto a higher ledge. After walking 25 m along this ledge, you again run out of space. Squeeze through a narrow crack into another tunnel which is closed overhead for 20 m and then becomes an open corridor for another 30 m. At this point scramble down 3 to 4 m at the very end of the ledge near a rocky cairn.

Now follow the clear path for about 100 m, but don't let it take you to a rocky corner: you must drop down to a lower level about 25 m before reaching the corner. Cairns mark the down route to a level some 10 m below. This lower path will now lead you safely around the corner into the top of Yellowstone Gully. Follow the cairns down.

Once over a short rock scramble, turn left and head straight down. Do not continue the traverse. Keep a sharp lookout for cairns, because

if you lose them, then you are lost! If this happens, retrace your steps to the last cairn and look again. Yellowstone Gully goes straight down for a distance, then turns sharp right into Union Ravine. Traverse halfway across Union Ravine to reach the river bed, and then continue on down. Beware, however: 5 minutes down Union Ravine you need to cross the river, allowing the path to take you the 100 m across and to the other side before descending to the contour path. If you were to continue down the river bed, you could just walk off into space!

About 15 minutes' walk along the contour path will complete your circuit under the cableway. Continue down to the Lower Cable Station to complete this exciting walk.

In case you have any misgivings about the cableway, it was officially opened on 4 October 1929, and at the time of writing has carried some 8 million passengers with not a single accident. I once told this to a rather nervous overseas visitor, who accused me of tempting fate! The cable is visually inspected and lubricated once a month, and once every six months an electromagnetic rope test is done.

Had the Cape Town City Council carried out their plans before World War I, a funicular railway would have been built up Fountain Ravine. However, the sterling work of Norwegian engineer Trygve Stromsoe gave us the very safe and highly successful cableway which carries up to 28 passengers to the summit in only 5 minutes.

AFRICA LEDGE TO THE UPPER CABLE STATION (Optional Extra)

Time: *45 minutes one way*
Grade: *2C*
Water: *Available*

Having returned to the spot mentioned earlier, climb up to the level of Africa Ledge and take the path around the corner to the right overlooking Camps Bay. Five minutes further on you will come to a rock scramble which goes straight up (the path will no longer continue its traverse to the right). About 50 m higher up, the path continues its right traverse at the higher level. Some 5 minutes after reaching the top of the rock scramble, the narrow path passes centimetres away from the highest sheer drop on Table Mountain. You are now entering Fountain Ravine, which may be picturesque, but is narrow and pretty hairy.

Soon a concrete pumphouse will come into view. After stepping over a metal water pipe which takes water from the pumphouse to the restaurant on the mountain, scramble up the rock face opposite on the left: the route is clear. Alternatively carry on up Fountain Ravine (the 'fountain' is where the pumphouse gets the water it pumps). The pumphouse was built in 1928 to raise water the last 60 m to the construction site of the Upper Cable Station. The top of Fountain Ravine meets up with the back of Platteklip Gorge, which is the gap in the middle of the table as seen from the city.

Either way, the route to the Upper Cable Station is obvious. Refreshments await you in the restaurant, if you can fight your way through all the tourists!

THE PIPE TRACK *3*

Time: *3 hours*
Grade: *1A*
Water: *None available in summer*

This is a most pleasant stroll and not at all strenuous, although in summer it is recommended that you do this walk in the early morning when most of it is still in shade. It will take about $1\frac{1}{2}$ hours to get to Slangolie Ravine where the Pipe Track ends, and slightly less time getting back. It is one of the best-known hikes in Cape Town, and certainly one of the oldest, for the Pipe Track was constructed in 1887 to lay the pipeline from the proposed reservoirs on Table Mountain to Kloof Nek. Work began in the same year on the Woodhead Tunnel to which the track leads.

The start of this walk is at Kloof Nek, next to the fire hazard board. Follow the steps up alongside the neatly trimmed hedge surrounding the waterworks' cottage. I wonder if anyone has bothered to tell the occupant that the hedge is Australian myrtle, a dreaded alien invader!

At the top of the steps you'll see Camps Bay and get a first look at the pipe where it crosses a small ravine. This first aqueduct is known as the Blockhouse Aqueduct after a long since demolished blockhouse and gun battery built in 1781 by the French. Believe it or not, the French occupied the Cape for about eighteen months to protect the Dutch settlers against the English. The French it seems, would travel half the world to have a pot shot at the Poms.

Note the occasional benches at strategic viewpoints. You are so close to the city and yet the feeling of unspoilt nature and raw mountain are all around you. I've been fortunate enough to have travelled widely, but can think of no other large city with such easy access to nature and breathtaking views. Rio de Janeiro, Sydney and Vancouver might not agree, but they don't hold a candle to Cape Town.

The second aqueduct is appropriately named Granite Aqueduct. Discourage your children (and some adults) from trying to do a tight-rope act on the pipe. It could spoil your entire day!

Ten to fifteen minutes after starting you will find yourself below the Kloof Nek Filtration Plant. Built in 1938 to treat the water from Wood-head Reservoir, it gave Cape Town its first crystal-clear water. Prior to

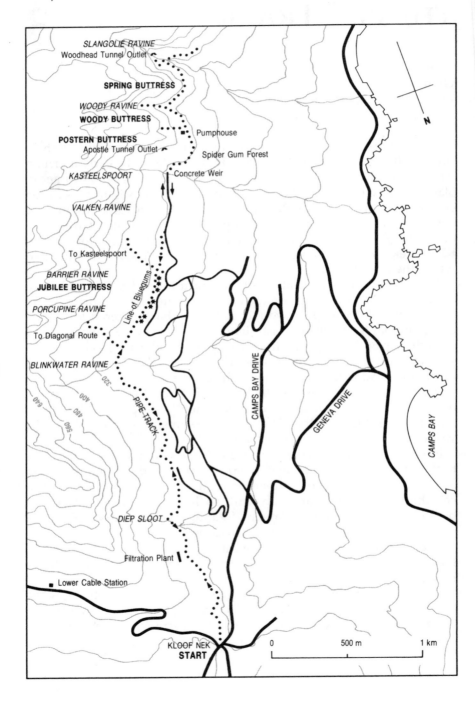

1938 the water that came from Cape Town taps was brown. Looking up at the imposing building, notice the cannon, probably a relic from the French visitation.

Beyond the filtration plant the Pipe Track plunges down into Diep Sloot, giving you some work to do getting up the other side. This is really the greatest effort you have to put in on the whole journey, which generally follows a level contour for most of the way. Every so often you will come across a small brick-and-cement housing containing a valve. They have recently been numbered, which makes a description of the route easier. At 'Air Valve 7' (about 25 minutes after leaving Kloof Nek) look up at the Upper Cable Station, an imposing structure built in 1929. The big gap to the right is Blinkwater Ravine. At 'Air Valve 12' look up and see the deep cut immediately to the right of the cable station. This is Fountain Ravine. It's difficult to imagine that there is a path up there (see Chapter 2), coming across from the left where the cable cuts across the skyline. It is even more difficult to think that the Cape Town Municipality contemplated routing a track railway for tourists up there before the cableway method was finally settled on.

You should reach the bottom of Blinkwater Ravine 40 to 45 minutes after leaving Kloof Nek. After a serious rockfall a few years ago the ravine was closed to the public. A fence closing off the original path can be seen at the end of another aqueduct crossing the Blinkwater Stream. Its original name was Stinkwater, but now it seems to have been upgraded, even if it is closed.

Two minutes beyond the base of Blinkwater Ravine, a rocky cairn marks the start of Diagonal Route, which goes up to the left. This is covered in Chapter 4. Carry on along the Pipe Track past weatherbeaten and fire-ravaged bluegums until, 10 minutes beyond Blinkwater Ravine, you reach a signpost indicating another important route up to the Back Table, namely Kasteelspoort (meaning Castle's Gateway). Again keep on the level. Five minutes later a jeep track joins your path from the right-hand quarter. This is a relic from the construction of the Apostles Tunnel in 1964. Remember this jeep track, for it is an alternative route down provided you have left a car at the top of Camps Bay, thus saving you 45 minutes on the return trip.

Beyond 'Air Valve 17' look past the three large pine trees ahead and pick out a straight scar going directly up the mountain for about 100 m. This leads to the outlet of Apostles Tunnel, which replaced Woodhead Tunnel in 1964.

About one hour after starting you should cross a concrete weir which in winter is usually overflowing with water cascading down Kasteels-poort. Look up and see the 'Castle's Gateway'. A sign decrees that there shall be no overnight camping, which is a classic bit of Councilese bureaucracy. I cannot imagine anything more uncomfortable than camping on a concrete weir.

The road peters out here as there is no further need for it. The gravel path ascends gently and on the hilltop the trig beacon atop Slangolie Buttress comes into view, as well as an exceptionally solidly built pumphouse which looks more like a mausoleum. Fifteen metres beyond the mausoleum-like pumphouse is the turn-off up Woody Buttress, a very popular and easy rock climb. Five minutes on will bring you to the base of Woody Ravine, a steep and narrow route to the top. A further 5 minutes will take you around the corner and into Slangolie Ravine. Your path is up a series of steep steps clinging to the side of the ravine. Note the very loose scree high up in the ravine: only the indigenous forest at the top seems to be keeping the rest of the rocks from tumbling down.

A rusty notice a little further on warns of a 'Dangerous Ascent'. About a minute beyond the rusty notice the path is hemmed in on both sides by Buchu bushes. Take the tiny leaves between finger and thumb and crush them: the pleasant smell will remain with you all day.

Soon you'll come to a second but much newer notice, once again warning of a 'Dangerous Ascent'. This one is much more relevant than the first. I have climbed up Slangolie Ravine, but it is a case of two steps forward and one back, as the loose rock is indeed dangerous. At this new 'Dangerous Ascent' notice, a path goes upwards and downwards. Go down if you need water and up if you insist on going to the very end of the Pipe Track 5 minutes further along. The up bit isn't dangerous as long as you stop when you reach a small cave and gate marked 'Danger'. Beyond this you need ropes to get to the opening of the Woodhead Tunnel. Do not proceed beyond the gate. The tunnel is closed off with iron bars anyway, so it is not worth the risk.

Despite its lurking dangers and ominous name, Slangolie Ravine is peaceful and tranquil, and is also a haven for indigenous trees.

Perhaps returning the same way doesn't appeal to you, but somehow it is different. Anyway, you should be able to do it in about 15 minutes less than the outward journey.

VALLEY OF THE RED GODS

4

Time: $3\frac{1}{2}$ hours (add an hour extra to the Valley of Isolation)
Grade: 3C
Water: Available

This is one of my favourite walks up one of the most popular routes on Table Mountain (Kasteelspoort) and down a cliffhanger with spectacular views (Diagonal Route). At the terminus there are a couple of lush box canyons to choose from for your rest and tea break.

Start by driving to the very top of Rontree Estate, above Camps Bay. Turn off Camps Bay Drive into Fiskaal Road, which leads into Francolin Avenue and eventually to Theresa Avenue. At the highest point of Theresa Avenue a little side road leads to a gate and a Table Mountain Nature Reserve signpost. Park your car here, being careful not to block anyone's driveway.

Walk up the concrete strip road beyond the gate for about ten minutes, after which time you will come to a fork. Keep right at the fork. You want to reach the line of tall bluegums above you, as these mark the contour of the Pipe Track. A hundred paces past the fork, leave the strip road up some rock steps to the left heading directly upwards towards the bluegums. On reaching the Pipe Track (and the bluegums), you should be confronted by a metal signpost pointing the way up Kasteelspoort. You should have reached this point within about 15 minutes of leaving your car. If you run out of concrete strip road, you have overshot the mark. Remember the bluegums.

The signpost marks the beginning of one of the most popular routes up Table Mountain, leading to the Back Table, Mountain Club huts and the reservoirs. Kasteelspoort (meaning Castle's Gate) is affectionately known to aficionados simply as 'KP'. From here it should take $1\frac{1}{4}$ to $1\frac{1}{2}$ hours to reach the top of KP, depending on how fit and keen you are.

The path starts climbing gradually, becoming steeper and steeper as it cuts diagonally up across the slope for about half an hour before traversing along the level for 100 m. Then comes a sharp incline before you reach a large, wide slab, which is a welcome spot for a rest despite the marks left by the sick graffiti brigade.

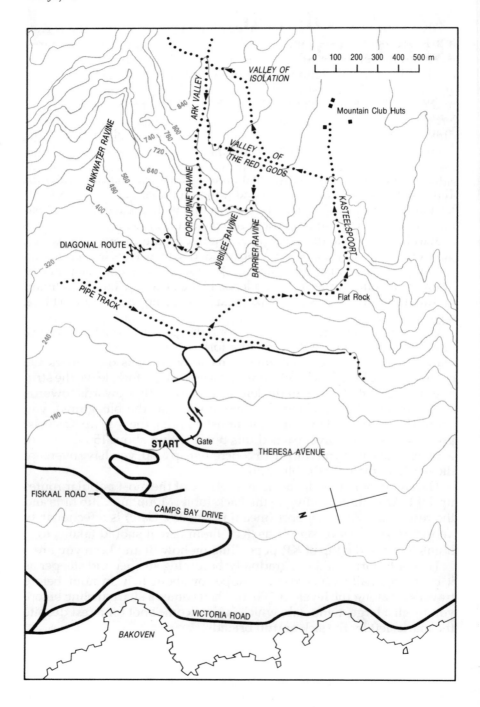

After your rest, you start the steep climb up and around the corner into Kasteelspoort itself, and should soon see how appropriate the name is. About half an hour after leaving the 'slab' you are finally at the top, marked by a metal signpost showing you two ways: Skeleton Gorge and Maclear's Beacon straight ahead (both a long way off) and Spring to the left. The 'Spring' referred to is in the Valley of the Red Gods, so left is your route. You need to head for the gap in the mountains in the direction indicated by the Spring sign. Keep left at a slight fork, 50 m from the sign. Five minutes later you should be over the ridge and into the Valley of the Red Gods, a small but pretty valley closed in on all sides. In the middle of it you will come to another metal sign pointing to the right, indicating the direction of Platteklip Gorge.

This is the point at which you have a choice. Depending on how much time you have left, you can either start for home, or be a little more adventurous and return to this spot via two adjoining valleys. These are the Valley of Isolation and Ark Valley. The former is particularly pretty, with a waterfall which disappears into a cavern in the ground, and at the end of Ark Valley, one of the most spectacular views on Table Mountain awaits you. Your return journey from here to your car will take about $1\frac{1}{4}$ to $1\frac{1}{2}$ hours without the optional extra which is described at the end of this chapter.

From the Platteklip Gorge sign, you need to reach the western lip of the valley in order to take the Diagonal Route back down towards home. It is so named because it traverses diagonally across three ravines and three buttresses before depositing you back onto the Pipe Track. Once at the lip on the seaward side of the Valley of the Red Gods, the path descends steeply down Barrier Ravine. Just before the 'barrier' – a sheer drop preventing further descent – the path swings to the right, drops down a bit and then traverses across the top of Jubilee Ravine along a precipitous path.

It then continues into Porcupine Ravine, a deep gully through which you follow the steep path down, once again swinging to the right before running out of terra firma. Enjoy the spectacular view of Bakoven framed by Jubilee and Porcupine buttresses. The path skirts around Porcupine Buttress along a wide bushy ledge, then drops 4 m down a mild rock scramble. Just at the end of the bushy ledge and 20 m before the down scramble, note Porcupine Cave on the right. It hardly justifies the 'cave' description, for it is really no more than a rock overhang. At the base of the rock scramble turn right, even though a path seems to go off to the left. After this part the path zigzags all the way down to the Pipe Track. Once on the Pipe Track, turn left and proceed for 5 or 6 minutes to a point where you are well into the line of bluegums at which you started. You don't need to go all the way back to the start of Kasteelspoort; instead take a shortcut down at a fire hydrant point marked by a black-and-yellow striped pole. Fifty metres below the Pipe Track you will come across a gravel road. Turn left and soon you will be on the concrete road on which you came up. Your car is just a few minutes away.

VALLEY OF ISOLATION (OPTIONAL EXTRA)

This is well worth an extra 45 to 60 minutes if you have the time.

Leave the Platteklip sign in the Valley of the Red Gods and proceed in the direction it indicates along a path which heads up the valley just *before* the sign (backtrack a few metres). An upward climb of 10 to 15 minutes will get you to the lip between the Valley of the Red Gods and the Valley of Isolation. The latter is a deeper and more 'boxed in' valley which, apart from befitting its name, is rich in unspoilt fynbos, especially King Proteas, Geelbos and Volstruisies. Its main feature is a grotto which for most of the year has a modest but pleasant waterfall cascading into it. As a youngster, I used to camp in this superb little spot but, alas, overnight camping is no longer permitted on Table Mountain.

After you have sampled the crystal waters of the grotto, continue on the path to about halfway up the far side of the valley, before it swings northward, passing some interesting caves on the left, and leads over the top and into Ark Valley. At the top of Isolation, look back and see Hout Bay Harbour in the distance with the Sentinel towering protectively over it. And beyond that, Kommetjie Beach and the Lighthouse.

The path drops gently into Ark Valley, a shallow and narrow cutting which runs in an East/West direction. At its base, cross the perennial stream and about 5 m on, turn left. Were you to carry straight on and up, you would finish up at Platteklip. But that is not your way.

To the left down Ark Valley will take you through wet marshy ground – especially in winter – for about 5 minutes. Just as the path starts to descend gently, an indistinct path branches off to the left through Restios or thatching reeds and up through the weathered grey rocks. If the path starts to descend steeply down Porcupine Ravine, and you can see the coastline of Camps Bay, you have gone too far. Retrace your steps about 100 m and look for that indistinct way through the rocks.

Just a few metres up, above the rocks, on the ridge, you will find a path heading westwards towards the sea. Follow it for 3 minutes almost to the end of the buttress, and you will find a clear path going down to the left, following a firebreak, back into the Valley of the Red Gods. The view from this point is quite breathtaking. Five minutes down the firebreak will bring you back to the Platteklip sign at which you started this worthwhile detour.

View of Lion's Head

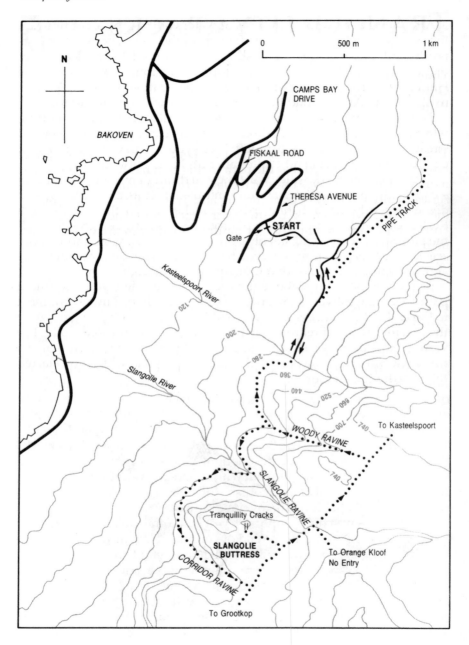

TRANQUILLITY CRACKS 5

Time: *4 hours*
Grade: *3C*
Water: *Available on the lower slopes*

This was one of Table Mountain's best kept secrets. In recent years, however, I have noticed that the path to this gem has become more and more well used. The 1987 issue of the *Journal of the Mountain Club of South Africa* finally let the cat out of the bag and Tranquillity Cracks were on the map. Also known as Yellowwood Cracks and The Underground Forest, it is a fascinating trick of nature which from above looks like metre-high fynbos – but what you're seeing from above is the tip of the iceberg, so to speak. Below the tip is a veritable forest of Yellowwoods growing from a crack in the skull of Table Mountain.

Situated on the crest of Slangolie Buttress, Tranquillity Cracks are best reached by going up Corridor Ravine and returning via Woody Ravine. Start by driving to the very top of Rontree Estate, above Camps Bay. Turn off Camps Bay Drive into Fiskaal Road, which leads into Francolin Avenue and eventually Theresa Avenue. At the highest point of Theresa Avenue a little side road leads to a gate and a Table Mountain Nature Reserve signpost. Park your car here, being careful not to block anyone's driveway. Walk up the jeep track beyond the gate, keeping to the right all the way until you reach the Pipe Track (see Chapter 3). Now you're on the level, and soon the track narrows to a path and ascends gently. At the hilltop, notice the trig beacon atop Slangolie Buttress. This marks the spot very close to your destination. You soon pass a pumphouse which looks like a mausoleum but which more than anything is a lasting monument to the skill of the Scottish stonemasons who constructed the reservoirs on Table Mountain over a century ago.

Five minutes past the pumphouse you will come to a notice indicating Woody Ravine. This marks the end of your down route. Keep following the Pipe Track and soon you will round the corner into Slangolie Ravine. The path climbs some steep steps clinging to the side of the ravine. A rusty notice soon proclaims 'Dangerous Ascent'. Ignore it, because you are not, for the time being anyway, going up. Soon you'll come to a second but much newer notice, once again warning 'Dangerous Ascent'. This time take it seriously and go down to the river bed. Cross over the stony rivercourse (dry for most of the year) and follow the path which continues on the other side of the ravine. After passing under a rock face, it picks its way steeply up the slope under dense indigenous trees. Five minutes after leaving the Slangolie river bed, the path levels out into a rock overhang. From here on the path is quite precipitous, but well defined.

About 15 minutes beyond the rock overhang the path turns a corner and starts climbing up the slope. Now you're into Corridor Ravine, and the top is about half an hour away. This is probably one of the gentlest slopes up Table Mountain, but just to balance things out, you'll be going down one of the steepest descents: Woody Ravine!

After a rest at the top, turn left onto the main Twelve Apostles path, and after 5 minutes you should come to the crest of Slangolie Buttress. Keep a sharp lookout for a path off to the left, just 5 m short of the crest. Follow this path for 3 or 4 minutes through waist-high fynbos to a clump of rocks on the right. When the path reaches the rocky outcrop, go straight in through a crack in the rocks marked by a small, stunted Yellowwood Tree. The crack goes some 20 m in and then turns sharp left and over a hump. Suddenly you're into Tranquillity Cracks, a labyrinth of natural corridors with Yellowwoods reaching up to the strip of sky above.

Pristine, tranquil, serene – Tranquillity Cracks is all of these things. Rest here and leave the other world behind for a while ...

Retrace your steps to the main path and turn left towards Table Mountain. Five minutes later you will reach a cliff edge. Either take the easy rock scramble straight down, or the longer way around to the right. Either way you finish up at the top of Slangolie Ravine. Continue up the other side and on the main path for about 5 minutes until you see a weird rock formation on the left eroded by wind and rain over many thousands of years. It's known as the Saucy Dog, because from the northern aspect it resembles a dog sitting up and begging.

Some 25 m beyond the Saucy Dog there is a cairn marking the path down Three Firs Route, which is not recommended as a descent due to erosion. Seven or eight minutes further on you will reach the top of Woody Ravine, clearly marked with a metal sign. The down trip to the Pipe Track is only about 20 – 30 minutes from here – the same time it took you to climb up Corridor Ravine. Although it is very much steeper, the steps are well spaced all the way down. It's like running down the Eiffel Tower, which I was once crazy enough to do. After a rest on the Pipe Track to get rid of the knee wobbles, retrace your steps to your car.

SUIKERBOSSIE CIRCUIT

Time: *6 hours*
Grade: *3C*
Water: *Available*

This is another of my favourite walks even though it is more lengthy than it is strenuous. A large portion of it is on the flat, but parts also wind through some magnificent ravines. The ravine you climb up, in particular, is unequalled anywhere on Table Mountain and the Cape Peninsula for its pristine beauty.

The route takes you from near the Suikerbossie Restaurant on the nek between Llandudno and Hout Bay in an easterly direction below Geel-klip Buttress to Myburgh's Waterfall Ravine. This magnificent ravine is deep and narrow and endowed with some huge indigenous trees of which the Knysna Forest would be justly proud. The route goes up the ravine, then across the top, past Judas Peak, and down again via Llandudno Ravine.

There are only a few sections which warrant the 'C' grading: first a steep climb around the actual waterfall in Myburgh's Waterfall Ravine, then the trickiest bit, a climb up a 45- to 60-degree cascade at the top of Myburgh's Waterfall Ravine. I hesitate to call it a waterfall, as it's more of a steep rocky slope down which, in winter anyway, the water cascades. For this reason I would recommend you walk this route in summer when this section is relatively dry. I have done it in winter without too much difficulty, but some people might feel a little uneasy on the wet rocks. Late December to early February are recommended when the Red Disas abound in Myburgh's Waterfall Ravine.

To get to the starting point, turn off the main coastal road between Llandudno and Hout Bay, about 200 m on the Hout Bay side of the top of the hill. Here you will find a signboard to Suikerbossie Restaurant. It was from the Suikerbossie Restaurant parking area that this walk used to begin. However, in August 1990 extensive fencing was erected, effectively cutting off access to the mountain from this convenient starting point. Even worse, the adjoining Ruyterplaats, for centuries a sprawling private estate, has fallen to the property developers, and has likewise been fenced off. However, thanks to sympathetic developers, hikers still have access to the mountain at this point, albeit temporarily.

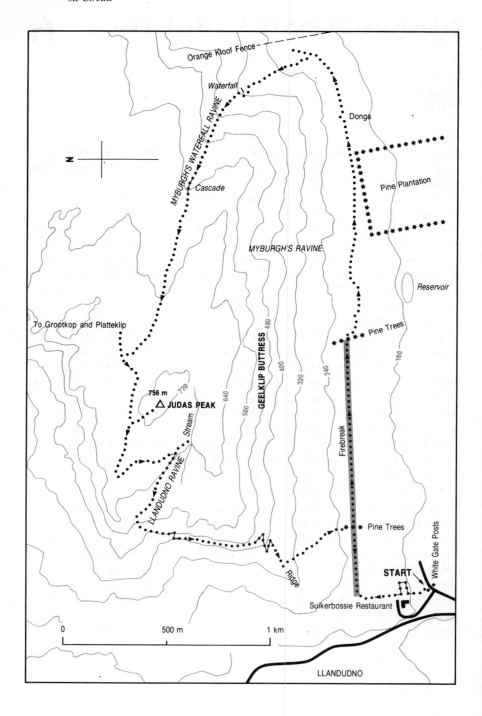

LLANDUDNO

Park your car on the verge, near the stone pillars of the Ruyterplaats Estate entrance, some 200 m after the main road turn-off. Explain to the guard that you are a hiker and sign the hikers' register.

Walk through the gates and turn half left to go up a path, which 50 m further on leads you to some staff cottages, from which you are separated by a fence. Follow this fence around to the right for about 50 m. The fence encloses an underground reservoir, which supplies some of the water to Hout Bay. You need to follow the fence around three sides of the reservoir's perimeter. Having completed three sides of the square, you should continue up the avenue of pines to the wide firebreak near the top of the hill.

Once on the open firebreak, get onto a clear path running down its central spine. It will soon lead you over a rise, and a north-south line of pine trees will come into sight directly ahead. The path passes straight through the pines and continues on towards the next line of pines ahead in the distance. About 200 m after the first line of pines, look up to your left and see Judas Cave at the base of a series of black streaks high up on the buttress above, and don't miss the charming view to the right of Hout Bay nestling between the mountains like a Swiss lake.

As you pass through the second row of pines, the path turns to the right for 10 m before straightening out again. Notice the bad infestation of Stinkbean (wattle). The path is much narrower now, but keep heading in an easterly direction towards a koppie with a remarkable resemblance to Lion's Head. Soon you step over a water pipeline and the path dips down into Myburgh's Ravine (not to be confused with Myburgh's Waterfall Ravine, which is the next one). Cross over Myburgh's Ravine and continue in the same direction for another 15 minutes, after which you will reach a thickly wooded ravine. This is Myburgh's Waterfall Ravine and it is your route up the mountain. It should have taken you about one hour to this point.

Do not follow the path down into the ravine, but look for a path going sharply off to the left at the edge of the indigenous forest. Follow this path for a few metres before it plunges under the forest canopy and down to the stream. Your aim is to climb the left bank of the stream for about 15 minutes before the waterfall. The path stays high up on the bank and then descends to alongside the stream. Keep to the left bank all the way.

This exceptionally beautiful waterfall was rather spoilt in January 1986 when a 20-m-high rooiels crashed down from above. Since then heavy rains have caused even more trees to come unstuck from the cliffs.

After a rest at the waterfall, follow the base of the cliff face on the Hout Bay side of the waterfall until you come to a point about 30 m further along where it is possible to climb up the steep embankment. The path clings to the steep face of the bank and care should be taken not to dislodge loose rocks. Suddenly you find yourself above the canopy of the forest. When you are almost above the top of the waterfall, keep a sharp eye open for a path diving down to the right. This is the way down to the head of the waterfall. Continuing on the more obvious upward path will only lead you into dense wood.

From here on you need no directions, for you have no alternative but to follow the river bed. You are now in a naturalist's heaven where majestic Yellowwoods reach for the narrow slit of sky and literally hundreds of Red Disas flower in the summer season. Water trickles down off fine moss, like the strings of a harp. It is a very special ravine, reaching back in time to another era when the earth was young and unscathed by civilization. The higher up you go, the narrower it becomes, until you reach a point where the two cliff faces are a mere 5 m apart, yet they reach perhaps 40 to 50 m up.

Shortly after the narrowest section you will come to the base of the second waterfall, or cascade in this case. The easiest way up is straight up the waterfall itself. Stay on the right-hand side, at least for the first half. If there is too much water, there is an alternate route up the steep earth embankment. Five metres beyond the beginning of the rocky cascade, turn sharp right up the embankment. It's very steep and not recommended unless the alternative is too wet. In any event, it joins the cascade again halfway up, but takes you past the wettest parts.

Pause to observe the superb view, over the treetops in Orange Kloof, of the Cape Flats and False Bay through the gap of Constantia Nek.

You will reach a point about three-quarters of the way up the cascade where you need to cross over to the left bank, and here you will find a steep path which will take you to the top, following the general direction of the river.

Once near the top, the path gradually moves away from the river on the left bank. At this point, look around you. On the far right is the huge massif of Grootkop. Ahead is a rocky ridge with what appears to be a cave near its right end. On your left is an unnamed ridge. You should be aiming for the main gap between 'left' ridge and 'cave' ridge. If you haven't found the path at the top left of the cascade, beat around until you find it: it's your ticket home! The path skirts the extreme left-hand side of the valley formed between 'left' ridge and 'cave' ridge. As long as you keep to the left-hand side of the valley, you can't go wrong. The path is hidden in dense bush, but it's clear enough once you're on it. Finding it in the first place is the trick.

About 20 minutes after leaving the top of the cascade you'll start running out of ridge on the left, then suddenly the trig beacon on Judas Peak pops up in front of you on the left. The path then swings right, through a marshy area before it reaches a region of large, flat rocks, level with the ground. Look out for a cairn which marks the point where you join the main north-south 'highway' from the Back Table to Hout Bay: the junction is not very clear because of the rocky surface. At the cairn turn sharp left towards the Judas Peak beacon. The path should soon become clear and you'll pass Judas Peak on your left. The detour to Judas Peak is well worth the view and it will take you about 10 minutes to get there. Remember, you are still $1\frac{1}{2}$ hours from your car. Don't turn off to Judas Peak until the beacon is 45 degrees behind you.

After your detour to this splendid viewpoint (there is a lean-to cave under the beacon on the Hout Bay side), return to the main path which immediately begins to descend towards the sea. Suddenly Sandy Bay and Klein Leeukoppie come into view. Notice, above Klein Leeukoppie, the old army barracks for the radar station near the top of Karbonkel-berg. On the way down the path swings to the left. If uncertain, look for cairns to guide you.

After about 10 minutes of gradual descent in the direction of Hout Bay, the path does a sharp right turn at a cairn perched on a metre-high rock. It almost doubles back on itself. This turn is easily missed and occurs about 100 m before you reach a stream at the foot of the valley. The path carries on to the stream: if you get that far, you will know that you need to retrace your steps. You should not have to start climbing up again, and whatever you do, don't follow the stream down.

The sharp right turn will, within a few hundred metres, bring you to the top of Llandudno Ravine. The northerly descent is steep and narrow. Near the bottom keep right to get to a short 4-m rock scramble. Now the path doubles back on itself and heads in the direction of Hout Bay again, soon to begin a zigzag descent to a lower ridge. At one point you may be tempted to go up, but don't do this.

Note the green gun battery below, just above the coastal road. This forms part of the Apostle Battery, which was officially closed down in December 1943. Its guns were never fired in anger, but it is said that nearly all the windows in Llandudno were broken during its one and only practice shoot.

Cross under a small waterfall (in winter). You are now on a contour path which continues at the same level on a wide bushy ledge for a few hundred metres (about 12 minutes) towards Klein Leeukoppie. Confetti Bush, a type of Buchu, grows on this ledge in great profusion. Take the tiny leaves and crush them between forefinger and thumb: the pleasant smell will linger with you right until your bath. In spring this shrub lives up to its common name when it is covered with tiny white flowers.

At the corner of the mountain you will see a prominent cairn on a rock. On reaching it, look down in the direction of Klein Leeukoppie, and on a lower level you will notice another cairn on a rock. Beyond that a path runs along the top of a ridge. This path is your next destination, and leads you down the slope to the line of pine trees you passed through earlier in the day, thus completing the circuit. Beware, however, not to attempt a straight-line approach to the path on the ridge below. The path first zigzags down to the left, but don't be misled into going too far left. Always come back to the right, remembering your objective. Once down to the line of pines, you should get back to your car in a little over 10 minutes.

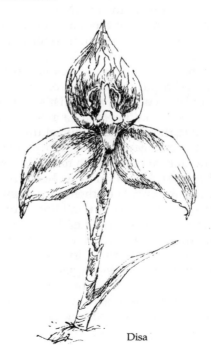

Disa

KAPTEIN'S PEAK

7

Time: $2\frac{1}{2}$ *hours*
Grade: *2B*
Water: *None available*

When I was writing *Twenty Walks Around Hout Bay*, I overlooked this little gem. I had not even bothered to climb it, thinking it was insignificant and too close to civilization. Just how wrong can you be? It offers a charming bird's-eye view of Hout Bay, and on the way an utterly breathcatching 'long drop' a mere 100 m away from a point past which I had walked for years, totally oblivious of this remarkable sight.

Start by driving past Mariner's Wharf at the northern end of Hout Bay Harbour. Take the first major turn right and then turn right again beyond the Sentinel School. Turn right once again beyond the community hall and library and make your way to the top right-hand corner of the housing development. You need to get to the very top end of Bay View Road, where you will find a locked gate closing off a gravel track. Leave your car here, being careful not to block anyone's driveway. This road leads to the old radar station on Karbonkelberg.

Technically you need permission from the SA Navy to use this road, but, as you're not going to the radar station, I trust that they won't mind too much. Take a note of the time when you leave your car. After about 15 minutes you'll come to a second gate. Squeeze around to the side of it and start to enjoy the unfolding parorama. Kommetjie Lighthouse has popped out from behind the Sentinel, the broad stretch of Noordhoek Beach flanks Chapman's Bay (the oldest English name on the South African coast), and Hout Bay Harbour lies below, a glistening jewel in the crown of the Fairest Cape.

Just around the second corner beyond the second gate you'll see the radar station on the skyline ahead of you. Built during 1944, it was the first such installation in South Africa and indeed one of only a few in the world. Its height above sea level gave it quite exceptional performance and probably made it unique at the time.

About 30 minutes after you leave you car, the road widens and comes out into the open. Look for a cutting in the bank on the right. It is the point where you leave the road and go up the dead straight firebreak path, up the slope. As you climb and look back, you will see

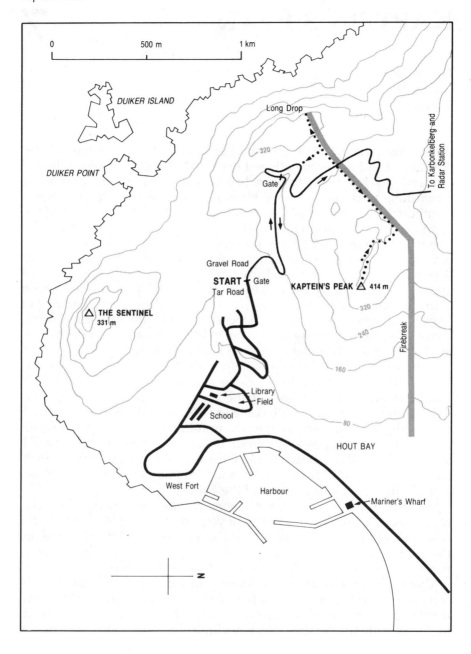

the firebreak path continues down and across the road you have just left. The downside of the firebreak path leads to the 'long drop' which we'll visit on the way back. A 10-minute climb up this firebreak will take you to the crest of the hill. About 50 m before the firebreak starts descending again, look out for a rocky beacon indicating a faint path off to the right. You should now be heading straight towards Kaptein's Peak in an easterly direction. Just before the path comes up against a rocky ridge, bear right and follow the clear path which traverses the Sentinel side of the ridge. Just as it begins to appear impassable, the path does a sharp 90-degree upward left turn into a little gully. Once up the gully and on the crest, turn right towards the Constantiaberg mast, and follow the path winding its way between large boulders.

Shortly before reaching the trig beacon atop Kaptein's Peak you walk into a tranquil milkwood grove with interesting rock overhangs and crags. You need to scramble up the last couple of metres. Surely this is one of the finest views in the Cape Peninsula: to the north lies Judas Peak (the 'pimple'), Grootkop and the back of Table Mountain. If you look carefully, you can see the chimney of the restaurant on top of Table Mountain, just to the right of Grootkop. The slight nick in the flat table is the top of Platteklip Gorge. The whole of the 'Republic' of Hout Bay is spread out before you. To the east lie Constantiaberg and Chapman's Peak Drive, and to the south see how the peak of the Sentinel fits like a jigsaw piece into the sweep of Chapman's Bay and Noordhoek Beach. At your feet lies the picturesque Hout Bay Harbour with its compatible blend of commercial and pleasure craft.

Once you've taken in the scene, rested and uplifted your soul, retrace your steps to the gravel road (at the point where the firebreak crosses it). For maximum surprise at the 'long drop', cross the road directly and stick to the firebreak over a rocky outcrop, without crossing over to a parallel firebreak. Follow it, but don't run as it comes to a very sudden end! This staggering drop must be all of 300 m without touching sides. I have no fear of heights, but I caught my breath when I first saw it. Way below the path around Karbonkelberg (described in *Twenty Walks Around Hout Bay*) can be seen. Don't be tempted to throw stones from any mountain. There might well be people below.

About halfway back along the firebreak to the road, a path goes off down to the right. Follow it as a pleasant alternative: it will take you back onto the road further down. The easy lope back to your car should complete a pleasant and eventful walk.

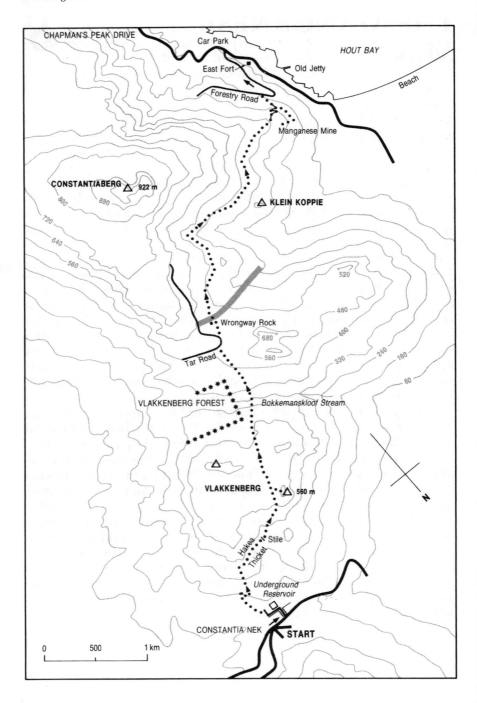

THE MANGANESE MINE

8

Time: $4\frac{1}{2}$ hours
Grade: 3A
Water: *None available in summer*
Remember to take a torch

This walk is strenuous only as regards its duration and affords some of the most splendid land and sea views in the Peninsula. In addition you can explore a fascinating old mine which penetrates all of 84 m into the mountainside. It is inadvisable to enter the shafts in winter, as they are often wet and slippery.

If you are in a hurry and are prepared to skip the views, you can reach the mine and walk back in about 2 hours, provided you start at the Chapman's Peak Drive end of this walk (*see* map). By far the better alternative, though, is to use two cars. Leave one at the end of the forestry road just beyond East Fort on Chapman's Peak Drive and the other under the trees at Constantia Nek. Walk down from Constantia Nek about 150 m in the direction of Hout Bay until you reach a sign indicating a footpath to Vlakkenberg. Go through the fence at this point and follow the road around the reservoir. Another sign shows the way through the fence at the top left-hand corner of the reservoir area. Now turn left and follow the fence for about 75 m, after which the path veers away and starts to climb first down then up the slope. At the top of the slope it swings sharply to the right after skirting around a fenced off area. The path is very clear, as it has only recently been cut through the dense wattle and hakea infestation. The Long-leafed Wattle (*Acacia longifolia*) on the way up the slope is showing highly encouraging evidence of successful biological control (see page 77).

About half an hour after starting out you will reach a stile and river crossing where there is a notice stating that you need a permit. Don't be too concerned – hordes of hikers use this route every weekend without anybody seeming to bother very much.

Cross over the stream and head for the gap to the left of the beaconed peak high on the skyline. This is Vlakkenberg Nek. You should reach the top within an hour of leaving Constantia Nek.

If you're in this area in spring or summer, once over the nek you'll be amazed at the breathtaking display of wild flowers, particularly the white Everlastings. Now make your way down to the Vlakkenberg Forest, where you need to cross another stream. In winter this stream tends to be a bit slushy, and you may have to cross higher up. Once across, continue on the path up the other side of the valley. After ascending for about 15 minutes, the path suddenly deposits you onto a tarred road – the service road to the Constantiaberg mast.

Follow this road for about 2 minutes to where it turns to the left. At this point leave the road again, following a clear, narrow path to the right (south) which seems to be heading for a point just to the right of the Constantiaberg mast.

Soon the Sentinel comes into view, and along with it a superb view of Hout Bay harbour. You will shortly reach a 2-m high rock next to the path and to the left of it which marks a 4-way intersection. Carry straight on, resisting the temptation to go down to the right. Years ago I was tempted and ended up in impenetrable bush. Ever since, I have known this landmark as 'Wrongway Rock'.

From here it's an easy and pleasant walk, mostly on the level or downhill. Some 15 minutes beyond Wrongway Rock the path takes you into a deep ravine where (in winter) you will find the last source of water on this walk. From the other side of this deep ravine, look back and note the strange rock formation with its vertical rather than horizontal strata. Meantime, below you, Hout Bay continues to present its many varied and beautiful faces.

About 25 minutes later, just before the path descends on a zigzag route down to Chapman's Peak Drive, you'll come across the first of the manganese ore dumps. Continue past them and begin tackling the zigzags down towards the sea. Beyond the fourth bend, and only a few metres before reaching the fifth, a path doubles back. One could almost mistake it for the fifth bend, except that it does not carry on down. Instead it takes you to a gaping hole – No 7 shaft – a couple of hundred metres around the corner in the direction of Hout Bay. Of the eight shafts that make up the Manganese Mine, this has the most impressive entrance by far. It must be all of 15 m high and 3 m wide. However, don't judge this shaft by its entrance: somewhat disappointingly, it penetrates only some 20 m into the mountain. You don't even need a torch.

To reach the deepest shaft (No 4), scramble up to the left of No 7. The shaft you are heading for is about 100 m above and directly in line with No 7. The entrance is large although partly hidden by undergrowth. In the entrance there are three holes, but two of these go straight down to

No 6 shaft below and should be avoided. The third hole is No 4 shaft – at 84 m the longest of them all. You will need a torch to explore it. Even though at the time of writing there were no hidden holes to fall into in the dark, you do enter at your own risk. Considering the primitive tools available in 1909, when the shaft was sunk, it is quite a remarkable feat of tunnelling.

As the manganese was found rather high up on the mountain, an economical means of transporting the ore down to the waiting ships below had to be devised. To get the ore down to the jetty below, the remains of which can still be clearly seen, a chute of corrugated iron was built. This primitive and often rather ineffective construction was over 750 m in length and must have been quite impressive. However, all didn't go as the designers would have liked, because the steep gradient often caused the ore to go out of control.

A popular Hout Bay legend has it that the first load of ore went careering down the chute and straight through the bottom of the waiting ship. Alas, while colourful and amusing, it is simply not true. An examination of the angle of the jetty and its construction shows up the story for what it is – a local myth. Early photographs show that the ore was transported along the jetty in cocopans, quite apart from which there is the notable absence of a wreck to substantiate the tale.

The manganese content of the ore varied greatly. In some cases the iron content (which occurs together with manganese) made a mockery of any reference to a manganese mine. One assay in the largest shaft revealed ore with 43 per cent iron and no manganese at all. A combination of transport problems and the decreasing grade of ore caused the mine to close down in 1911, after only two years' operation.

Find your way back to the zigzag path by which you came down. It will soon lead you to the gravel forestry road below, and to your waiting car parked on Chapman's Peak Drive.

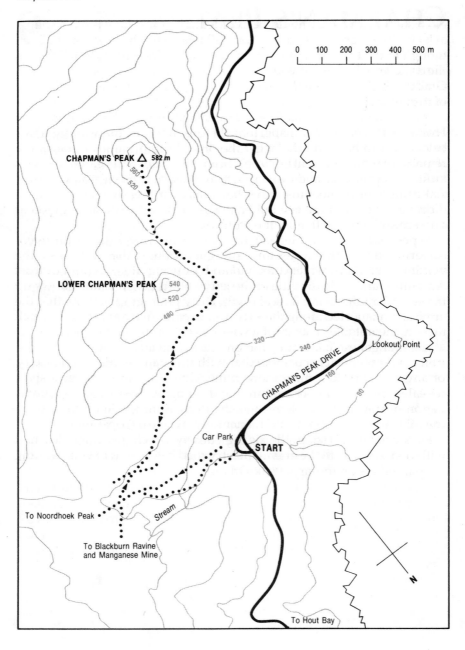

CHAPMAN'S PEAK 9

Time: $2\frac{1}{2}$ *hours*
Grade: *2A*
Water: *Available on lower slopes only*

This walk is much easier than it looks. To reach the top requires less than an hour and a half, and the path takes you through some dense stands of proteas whilst presenting you with some breathtaking views. The rocks on top of Chapman's Peak afford protection from the wind and make this an ideal spot to enjoy a late breakfast.

Leave your car at the last big bend before reaching the top of Chapman's Peak Drive, 750 m on the Hout Bay side of the lookout spot.

Log steps lead from the left-hand side of the picnic area, and three minutes later cross the stream. Just beyond the stream you are confronted with a fork. A left turn would follow the river's course along its right bank; a pleasant but not very well-trodden route (*see* map). The right-hand option takes you straight up the slope for 25 m before turning left at a clear T-junction. This more strenuous but clearer of the two routes will take you straight up the side of the ravine for another 20 minutes before depositing you on to a flat plateau at the top.

Here you will reach a parting of the ways (*see* map) and a good place for a rest. You need to turn sharp right, in the direction of Chapman's Peak. The path crosses over a firebreak path and then dives into dense stands of proteas on the way to your destination, which is still almost an hour distant. In the early morning or late afternoon you may be treated to delightful song as birds of all descriptions tell of their pleasure in this forest of proteas – mainly Blackbearded Protea, which flowers in winter, and a smattering of Yellow Pincushions.

The path takes you around and to the right of the first peak. Now you can see round the corner of the Sentinel and view the wild Karbonkelberg coastline. Then, suddenly, Chapman's Peak pops up in front of you and Hout Bay slips from view as the path makes its way down through more proteas, across the saddle between 'Lower' Chapman's Peak and Chapman's Peak itself.

As you climb from the saddle to make the final assault, Fish Hoek unexpectedly appears on your left. Now it is an easy scramble to the survey beacon at the top, and the panorama which unfolds from here is well worth all the effort. Not only can you see Hout Bay nestling peacefully below you, but Gordon's Bay in the far distance as well!

Allow 45 minutes to get back to your car on Chapman's Peak Drive (originally known as the 'Hout Bay – Noorde Hoek Road'). Contrary to popular belief it was not built by Italian prisoners-of-war. This would have been rather awkward, as Italy fought on the side of the Allies during World War I, the period during which it was built. (The confusion probably arises from the use made of 5 000 Italian POW's to make a start with the construction of Du Toit's Kloof Pass between 1943 and 1945 during World War II.)

Chapman's Peak Drive was built with the help of convict labour, of which some 700 in all were provided by the newly formed Union Government. Construction started in 1915 from the Hout Bay end, and more than a year later also from the Noordhoek end. In September 1919 the relatively easy stretch from Hout Bay to the lookout was completed, but it was more than 2 years before the Noordhoek stretch caught up. The great day arrived on 6 May 1922, when this magnificent scenic drive was opened by the Governor-General, Prince Arthur of Connaught.

According to the *Cape Times* of Monday 8 May 1922, 'Amongst those present were the Administrator of the Cape, Sir Frederic de Waal, the Archbishop of Cape Town, Dr Carter, Colonel Metz, Colonel Reitz and many members of Parliament, as well as a large number of ladies.' The news reporter makes it sound as though the ladies had been let out for the day!

Prince Arthur drove through a silk ribbon followed by '160 to 170 motor cars and charabancs conveying the invited guests' who were later 'regaled with refreshments'.

Sir Frederic de Waal (who was the main driving force behind this scenic drive and after whom De Waal Drive is named) predicted, 'The day will come when people will get tired of Egypt and other parts of the world and they will come to South Africa to spend two or three months here, when there is winter in England.'

Alas, that day has come and gone. The pace of life is such today that long colonial winter sojourns are very much a thing of the past.

LONG BEACH AND A SHIPWRECK

10

Time: *2 hours*
Grade: *1A*
Water: *None available*

This is a walk for the entire family, including the dog. Along the beach between Kommetjie and Noordhoek you'll be accompanied by the call of gulls and the crash of the waves. The highlight of this walk, apart from the fact that it is totally different from a mountain walk, is a fascinating shipwreck. Depending on which option you choose, this is encountered either at the midpoint or at the end of the walk. The wreck of the *Kakapo* is in fact the midpoint between Kommetjie and Noordhoek, so you can do one of two things: either walk from Kommetjie to the wreck and return the same way, or go the whole hog and walk the roughly 6 km or so to Noordhoek. However, unless you want to walk all the way back again, this latter option requires that a car be left at the end, which is a time-consuming business in itself.

From Kommetjie (or Noordhoek) to the wreck is about 45 minutes' walk. Give yourself half an hour at the wreck for exploring and refreshments, plus 45 minutes back, which totals 2 hours. It would still be 2 hours if you continued to the other end, but then allow an extra 45 minutes for shunting cars back and forth.

If you're going to walk the full length of the beach, or for that matter the 'half return', then I suggest you start at Kommetjie and not Noordhoek. There are three reasons for this: The view walking north is far more interesting and if the inevitable south-easter is blowing, rather let it push you, than struggle against it. Lastly, the beach is more interesting and varied at the Kommetjie end. A further word of advice is to choose low tide for your walk, as the going is much easier on the firm sand of the intertidal zone.

Start by driving to the quaint little village of Kommetjie. The name Kommetjie refers to the 'little basin' formed in the rocks of the shoreline which is surrounded by many splendid Milkwoods. Once you reach the outskirts, take the third turn to the right into Kirsten Avenue, and follow the signs to Long Beach, where you will find a parking area adjacent to

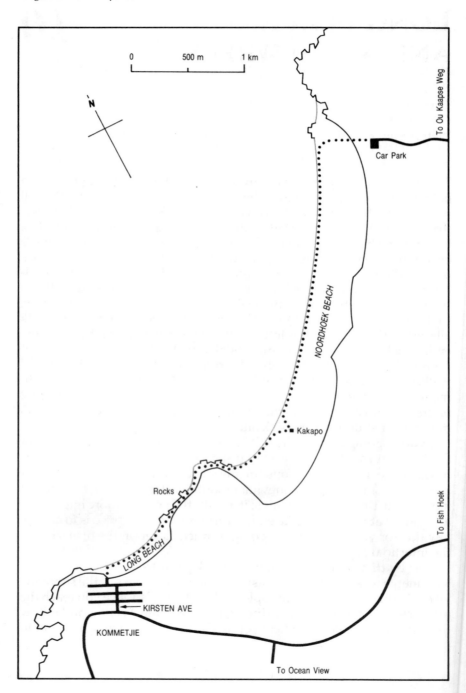

the beach. Leave your car here and walk down to the water's edge: Noordhoek looks a long way off. Soon after you start your walk, you wouldn't be blamed for thinking you were at Arniston, with its quaint thatched and whitewashed beach cottages. The architectural style is so 'Cape Beach' that it almost begs to adorn a calendar.

Ahead you will see the glorious sweep of Hout Bay, from Karbonkelberg on the left (the little pimple on top is the old World War II radar station) through the Sentinel, Klein Leeukoppie, Judas Peak, Grootkop and the flat table top of Table Mountain as seen from behind to Chapman's Peak in the foreground. Provided you have the necessary permit, the rocks on your left are home to tasty black mussels just waiting to be plucked at low tide. Once you get around the rocky corner, about 25 minutes after starting, you'll get a glimpse of the wreck of the *Kakapo*, set back about 100 m above the high-water mark. It will first be seen as a black cylinder with a 'pole' sticking up to the right. The 'cylinder' is the ship's boiler and the 'pole' is the rudder post.

Forty to forty-five minutes from the start and you're there. Notice how the rudder is still in the 'hard-a-port' position, as a lasting reminder of the moment nearly a century ago when the captain desperately tried to correct his unfortunate error. This steamship came ashore under circumstances that were most embarrassing for its master. The vessel was on its way from Table Bay to New Zealand one foul and stormy night in May 1900 whilst on its maiden voyage. As there was no Kommetjie lighthouse in those days (more correctly known as the

Wreck of the Kakapo

Slangkop lighthouse), the captain mistook Chapman's Peak for Cape Point and did a sharp left turn. With engines at full ahead and the assistance of a gale force following wind and high spring tide, the ship was driven so high and dry onto the beach that the crew were able to walk off at low tide without getting their feet wet. Try explaining that to the shipowners and cargo underwriters back in London!

The lighthouse incidentally was completed in 1914, just a few days before the outbreak of the First World War. This provided the authorities with a dilemma; for right next door was a military radio station, built in 1910. To light the lamp would have perfectly pinpointed a military target. So there stood this non-shining edifice, utterly useless for nearly five years before the lamp was finally turned on in March 1919.

The ribs of the vessel still stick defiantly out of the sand and give an indication of the *Kakapo*'s size. Some of the plates forming the sides of the vessel were removed at one time and were used to prevent sand from blowing over the railway line at Fish Hoek. The boiler is quite fascinating. The three large holes at beach level are the furnaces into which the coal was shovelled: two of them are still exposed enough to climb into. It's not often you can claim to have had tea in the furnace of a ship's boiler! It was a fire-tube boiler and the fire tubes, long since corroded away, connected the battery of holes you see.

Have you ever wondered where a steamship at sea for a month or two got fresh water to feed its boilers, not to mention the crew? I suspect the upright cylindrical structure to the forward starboard side of the boiler is the remains of the ship's evaporator. This used to boil and distil seawater to produce fresh water.

Your walk back to Kommetjie, or on to Noordhoek, will take you about 45 minutes. If you choose to continue to Noordhoek, leave the beach from a point almost directly below the tip of Chapman's Peak. Another car should be waiting for you at the Noordhoek Beach parking area. On your return to Kommetjie, remember that the local hotel serves an excellent crayfish in season at a very reasonable price.

ELSIE'S PEAK

11

Time: *2 hours*
Grade: *1A*
Water: *None available*

This is a short, easy hike with pleasant views and includes a wonderful example of fynbos triumphing over alien invaders. Drive to Fish Hoek or take the train and make your way to the three-way traffic circle at the end of Fish Hoek's Main Road. Turn right towards Kommetjie and immediately on your left, just before a church, is a large off-road parking area. Leave your car here and go up some steps named 'Ravine Steps' leading off the left-hand corner of the parking area. These will take you to the top line of houses, where a path continues the upward climb as an extension of the steps. Cross over a firebreak and soon you will come to a T-junction where there is an old signpost which used to announce that you were about to enter the Fish Hoek Municipality Mountain Reserve. Bear half right here. The path traverses to the right, and about 100 m further along doubles back on itself to a higher level. Up to this point you are still surrounded by alien shrub, but this soon gives way to a superb variety of fynbos, which is a credit to the Fish Hoek Alien Vegetation Control Group, a volunteer organisation who have laboriously hacked back the invading hakea and rooikrans and allowed the indigenous fynbos to re-establish itself, all in the last ten years. As you reach a higher level, look back to your right and see the clearly marked battlefront, indicated by a huge green wall of wattle.

Keep to the left at a faint fork, and some 35 minutes after leaving your car you will arrive at the back of a quarry, which can be clearly seen from Fish Hoek as a pile of loose stones high on the mountainside. You will recognise it from the loose scree on your left. Just before and just after this point you need to keep your eyes open for forks in the path. Keep left all the way up. The idea is to go up the left-hand fork and return via the right-hand route after visiting the summit.

Some 8 minutes after taking the left-hand fork you'll come to a 2,5-m-high rock pinnacle at the edge of the path. Bear right here just before you find yourself between two koppies. The path then climbs up and behind the koppie on the right. About 20 minutes after taking the left-hand fork, you'll find that the other path joins yours again from the

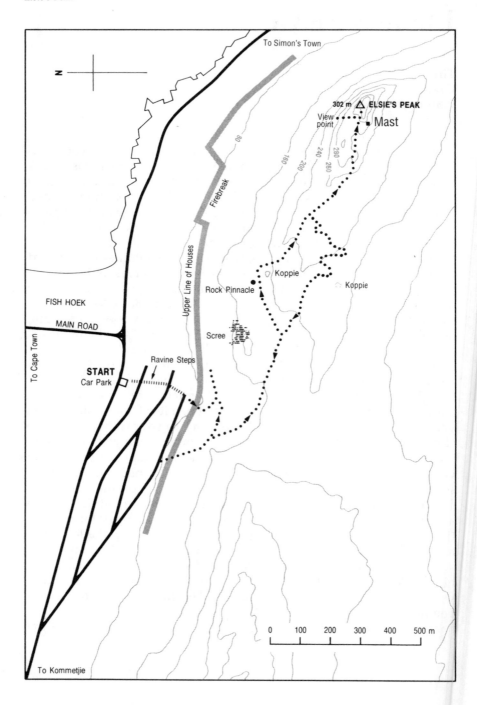

right. Soon you'll see the beacon on Elsie's Peak and the Simon's Town Naval Base will ease into view, nestling peacefully in the lee of the mountain. A peppering of small craft completes the picture.

You pass a communications mast just before you reach Elsie's Peak about one hour after starting. Glencairn is just below you on one side, while on the other side Fish Hoek, Kalk Bay and Muizenberg lie at the beginning of a majestic sweep all the way around False Bay to Hangklip. From this point you can clearly see two oceans, as the Atlantic peeps through Noordhoek valley. While looking in that direction, notice the hump in the middle of the Fish Hoek valley on which Peer's Cave is situated. This is the site of many remnants of early man. If you are up Elsie's Peak in late September or early October, you may be lucky enough to see Southern Right whales with their calves in False Bay. They return year after year to the bay during spring, and, although their numbers were reduced rapidly in the past, it is encouraging to see that they are slowly increasing. A large whaling station was built at Kalk Bay in 1806 but was forced to close five years later because the whale population had declined so dramatically.

It will take you about 30 minutes to get back to the parking area. Remember to go left at the fork 5 minutes after leaving the top to give your return some variety.

Yellow Pincushion

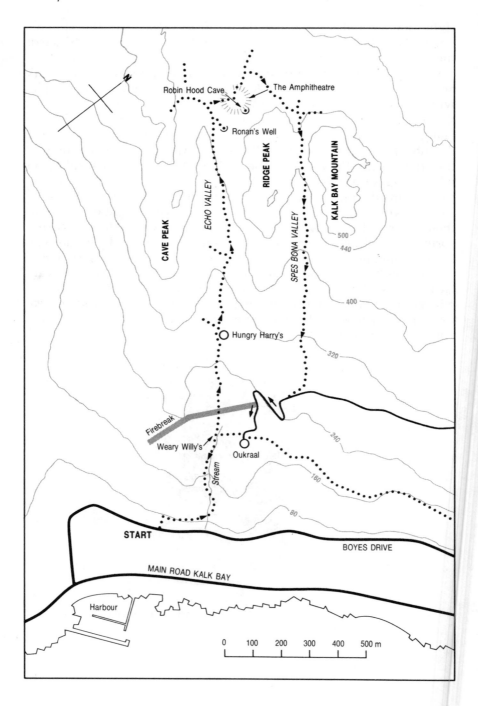

THE AMPHITHEATRE 12

Time: *3 hours (allow extra time if you wish to explore the caves)*
Grade: *2A*
Water: *Available*
Remember to bring along a torch

Two delightful indigenous forests and a number of interesting caves are features of this walk.

I was amazed that an old friend of mine who has lived in Cape Town most of his life and is a keen hiker, wasn't aware that the mountains above Kalk Bay and Muizenberg are riddled with caves. In fact there are 67 in all, with names ranging from Devil's Pit to Musical Drops Cave, not to mention such interesting-sounding appellations as Aladdin's Cave, Surprise Grotto, Commemoration Hall and Spookgrot. With as many as 67 caves to choose from, I shall resist the temptation to turn this and the next chapter into a detailed description of them. If you are interested in more than just hiking, then get hold of the detailed guide to the Kalk Bay and Muizenberg caves from the Parks and Forest Branch of the Cape Town City Council.

Begin your hike from Boyes Drive up some steep steps marked by a Silvermine Reserve signpost. The steps are directly opposite and in line with the Kalk Bay Harbour entrance. At the top of the short flight of steps turn right and climb steadily towards Muizenberg. As you ascend the well-worn path, you might hear the clickety-clack of a passing train, or look down onto the picturesque fishing harbour while stopping for a rest. Kalk Bay got its name from the days of Simon van der Stel when kilns were used to burn seashells to produce lime (kalk) for mortar for buildings throughout the Peninsula. The limestone origins of the caves might also have had some say in the matter.

A few hundred metres on, the path turns sharp left up the mountain, up some well-placed stone steps and over a few wooden foot bridges. About 20 to 25 minutes after starting, you will arrive at Weary Willy's, a small clearing with a 'sitting stone' in the middle of it. Your return route brings you back to this point from across the stream on your right. Continue the path upward, heading for a large clump of rocks ahead of you at the base of Echo Valley, which is bounded on the left by Cave Peak and on the right by Ridge Peak. The large clump of rocks should be reached about 35 to 40 minutes after starting and is known as Hungry Harry's Halfway Halt. It is indeed about halfway between the start and your tea stop and terminus, The Amphitheatre. Hungry Harry's, also known as Cavern Rocks, is a good spot for a rest, as it provides shelter from all kinds of weather.

A mere 15 m beyond the short turn-off to Hungry Harry's a path breaks off to the left. Do not take it. Merely note, for a future adventure, that it goes to the south face of Cave Peak, which is rich in interesting caves, in particular Boomslang Cave, which penetrates 150 m right through the mountain. Your way is straight on and up Echo Valley. A few minutes later you'll see another path breaking off to the left. This comes down from the northern exit of Boomslang Cave after it has gone through Cave Peak. This cave, one of the finest on the mountain, is not recommended in winter as it is too wet.

Look back and see Hangklip framed between Ridge and Cave peaks. This is a good growing area for South Africa's national flower, the King Protea (*Protea cynaroides*). Soon the path dives into a magnificent Yellowwood and Milkwood grove which must surely bring back childhood memories of Walt Disney's Magic Forest. You almost expect to see Bambi, Snow White and other characters frolicking here. You emerge from the magic forest all too soon at the head of the valley.

Two minutes after emerging from the dense forest, as the path climbs up the right slope for a short distance, another path turns off the main one sharply to the right. Take this slight detour upwards for 10 m and another 10 m to the right to bring you to the opening of Ronan's Well. This is not a cave for amateurs, but is interesting to look into, and it always has water. The entrance to the cave proper is near the ceiling at the far end of the cavern.

At the ripe old age of 14, I was convinced that my days had come to an end when I got stuck in this cave, well beyond what was then the official limit! Since then it has been opened up and at 400 m is the longest cave in these mountains. It is also one of the most dangerous, so don't even think about exploring it!

Return to the main path. A few minutes later the path forks. Take the right-hand fork, which will lead you into The Amphitheatre within a couple of minutes. The Amphitheatre can best be described as a box canyon. It's an ideal spot for a rest. In the far right-hand corner a clump of trees hides Robin Hood Cave (also not recommended for beginners).

After resting and refreshing yourself, your way out is up the far left-hand corner as seen from the point where you came in. This path

King Protea

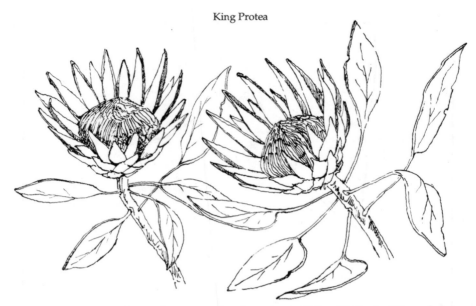

takes you past a few other caves in the area and finally forks 25 m short of the top of the ridge. Take the right-hand fork in the direction of a very weathered rock on the horizon. Once past the rock, head back towards False Bay. Suddenly Simon's Town Naval Base pops into view.

The white trig beacon you see is atop Kalk Bay Mountain. Keep heading in its general direction. Shortly after it disappears from view, you will come to a four-way junction. Turn right towards Spes Bona, and on reaching the crest of the valley descend into another lovely indigenous forest, this time mainly Yellowwoods. In some places they are so intertwined with Milkwoods that different leaves seem to be growing on the same tree. Nature has painted the rocks green with moss and the trees assume the most contorted shapes: nothing seems to grow straight up in this fascinating forest.

Five minutes after emerging from the Spes Bona forest, you will see a gravel road below you. On reaching the road, head towards Simon's Town, following the winding gravel road down for about 500 m to where it narrows to a broad path at a green City Council rubbish bin: this is Oukraal. Now take the path straight down into the kloof and back to Weary Willy's, from where you retrace your steps to Boyes Drive.

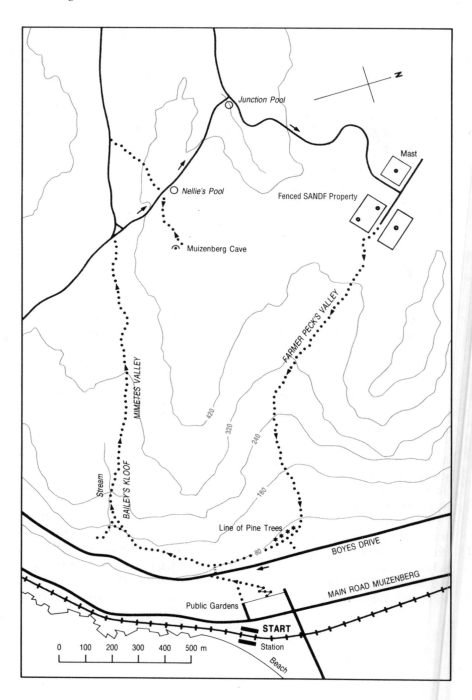

MUIZENBERG CAVE 13

Time: *3 hours*
Grade: *2A*
Water: *Available*
Remember to bring a torch

Where else in the world can you get on a train, travel a relatively short distance (in this case to Muizenberg), and get off at a station where the sea and a length of beautiful beach stretch far into the distance from one platform – and towering above the other platform is a mountain which takes little more than an hour to climb to the top. Just to add to all this, history surrounds you, and the views, as well as the plant and bird life en route, are magnificent.

Even if you haven't travelled on a train for years, why not take a trip to Muizenberg this weekend, and do a circular hike around the mountain above Muizenberg station? It's called St James' Peak. (Just to confuse you, Muizenberg Peak is the one above False Bay station, and your destination, Muizenberg Cave, is on St James' Peak. Work that one out if you can.)

Start from Muizenberg station and turn right towards the very pleasant public gardens on the slopes below Boyes Drive. School Road runs up the left-hand side of the public gardens to the police station at the top. Once at the top of School Road, keep going up across a short stretch of grass until you reach a gravel path that runs from right to left. Walk up this path until you finally reach Boyes Drive above. Almost directly opposite, but perhaps some 15 m to the right, some crude steps go straight up the mountain. You should by now be opposite the clock tower on the station.

After leaving Boyes Drive, three minutes of uphill slog will bring you to a T-junction where you turn left towards Simon's Town. Ten minutes later you'll reach a fork. Keep right for three minutes until you come to a barbed wire reclamation fence 25 m below the path. Opposite the fence steep steps ascend sharply to the right. Take these steps, and you're on your way up Bailey's Kloof. Look down on Bailey's Cottage, a thatched-roof abode almost in the sea. It once belonged to Abe Bailey (1865–1940), who featured prominently as a mining magnate and politician around the turn of the century. It is at this very spot that the Battle of Muizenberg took place nearly two centuries ago. It's hard to imagine that this peaceful little corner of False Bay could have been the scene of such conflict. Picture eighteen English warships with sails set like bulging chests pounding the Dutch troops on the shore. The Dutch fell back and dug in at a place now called Retreat! This battle was of no small significance, for it changed 150 years of Dutch occupation to 150 years of British domination.

However, history is not the only thing of interest on this easy hike around the mountain. Flowering during spring from August to December is an uncommon species of Erica called *Erica urna-viridis* (the Latin name meaning 'resembling a green urn'). It's a very pretty, almost white-greenish Erica, sticky to the touch. What is so special about it is that it occurs only on this mountain above Muizenberg and nowhere else in the world. On one occasion I saw this extremely rare plant in three separate locations, and I wasn't even looking for it.

But let us tear ourselves away from history and botanical rarities, and continue the slog up Bailey's Kloof. Rest occasionally on the steep stone steps (which in themselves represent a labour of love) to see the full sweep of False Bay from Hangklip to Cape Point. After some ten minutes up these steep steps, you meet various paths. Just remember you need to go up, and straight, along the gently sloping valley which begins to open up before you. This is where Bailey's Kloof leads into Mimetes Valley. Keep straight ahead and just to the right of and parallel to a small stream. A short wire fence spanning the stream shows the way. Mimetes Valley is named after a member of the Protea family, *Mimetes fimbriifolius*, a stout, dense shrub or small tree which flowers between June and November in a brilliant splash of red.

The path veers gently away from the stream to the right-hand side of the valley. After about half an hour of easy walking up Mimetes Valley (pronounced My Meetees) from the top of Bailey's Kloof the path spills out onto a gravel road, which immediately presents you with three possibilities. Take the right-hand fork up. After 200 m, keep a sharp eye open for a path off the gravel road to the right, turning half back. Five minutes' walk up this path will bring you to Muizenberg Cave, to the right of the path at the top of the ridge.

Within the large, gaping entrance to the cave, there are two smaller entrances on the right-hand side of the main chamber. Take the first and larger of these, provided you have a torch. This leads, within a few metres, to a 6-m deep well. Care should be taken here, as the rocks can be slippery. At the well, turn sharp left and walk for another few metres until you come to a T-junction. A left turn will lead you back to the main entrance chamber. A right turn will take you 40 m through the mountain on hands and knees to emerge on the southern side of the ridge.

Leave the cave the same way you came up and return to the gravel road. On reaching it, turn right and continue up the slope. Within a few metres you will pass Nellie's Pool on the right. The gravel road takes you over the rise and downhill to Junction Pool. On the way down, notice the Ou Kaapse Weg in the distance as a reminder that civilization isn't far away. Junction Pool is a pleasant grassy picnic spot where there's always water. Cross the river and at the T-junction turn right. Now follow this road through fields of indigenous Geelbos which at times of the year are such a brilliant yellow as to be almost loud!

Some 15 minutes beyond Junction Pool the road runs alongside the fence guarding an SANDF mast. (The vertical wires of varying lengths are the aerials, and not the mast structure itself.) On the far side of the mast area the road forks to the right and three or four minutes later you reach a corridor between two more fenced-off areas, after which the gravel road stops abruptly and becomes a track. You are now at the top of Peck's Valley, named after the brothers Peck who ran the well-known and popular Farmer Peck's Inn, which in the early to mid-1800s stood on the the site now occupied by a tall block of flats.

Suddenly Muizenberg Corner pops into view. Hopefully you will notice the quaint and colourful bathing boxes so well known from postcards and calendars: a legacy from a by-gone era. These were knocked down shortly after the first edition of this book was published, and, at the time of going to print on this second edition, the authorities had promised to replace them, following a public outcry. If you thought the steps on the way up were a labour of love, what about those going down Peck's Valley? A great deal of sweat and toil must have gone into making your journey down more comfortable.

Near the bottom of the valley the path veers to the right. Halfway along a line of pine trees and opposite an old ruin, take the steps down to Boyes Drive. Some 150 m along Boyes Drive to the south you should find the path on which you came up from the station.

Silvermine Circuit and Elephant's Eye Cave

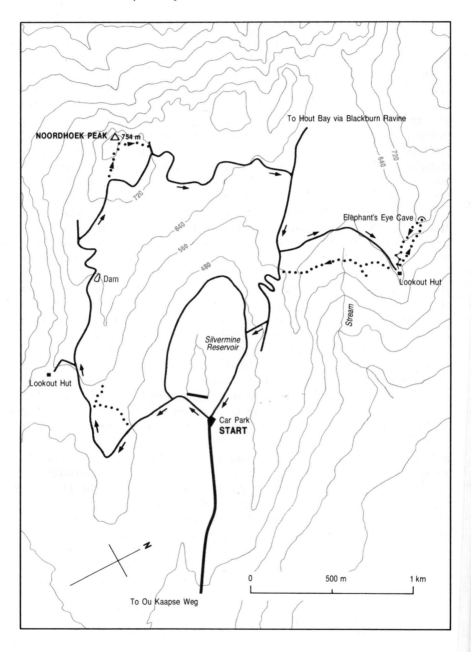

Silvermine Circuit and Elephant's Eye Cave

14

Time: *3 hours; allow 1 hour extra to get to and explore the cave*
Grade: *2A*
Water: *Available only at the beginning and the end*

This walk is almost entirely along gravel roads, which makes it easy going. There are two glorious viewpoints en route.

The name Silvermine is complete misnomer; although shafts were sunk in the area between 1675 and 1685, not one ounce of silver was discovered. Drive to the top of Ou Kaapse Weg from the direction of Cape Town and turn right into the western half of the Silvermine Nature Reserve. You'll be required to pay a modest fee at the gate, immediately beyond which you have a choice of taking a left turn or going straight ahead. Follow the tarred road straight ahead for 2,4 km until you reach a parking area just to the right of Silvermine Reservoir wall.

Leave your car here, note the time and take the gravel track which cuts across the valley below the reservoir wall. Once you have reached the end of the wall, bear left, following the gravel road on its gentle ascent. The reservoir was built in 1898 by the old Kalk Bay Municipality to supply water for its residents, but is now used solely for the purpose of watering the Westlake golf course. When the reservoir is full and the surrounding pines are reflected in the quiet waters, one is instantly reminded of a tranquil Canadian lake. Keep to the main road and ignore the side roads to left and right. However, you might wish to take a short cut to the right marked 'Noordhoek Peak'.

If you take this option, be sure to turn left at the T-junction near the top of the ridge, to get back onto the gravel road. It's perhaps safer to stick to the road, being easier and only about 100 m longer. Assuming you stay on the road, it soon sweeps round a sharp right-hand curve and the Noordhoek lookout hut comes into view. What appears to be a fork in the road further on is merely a side track to this hut. The 3-minute detour is worth it just for the view: Fish Hoek, Simon's Town and Noordhoek look great from here.

From the fork, the road climbs steadily for some way before it negotiates three sharp bends. Soon after the third bend you'll reach another fork, with a sandy track off to the left. Ignore it and keep half right along the gravel. Approximately 6 to 8 minutes further on, you will come to a fairly substantial stone pillar built to the left of the road. It proudly announces 'Footpath', and at first glance it seems such a grandiose sign for such an insignificant pathway. However, when you see the view to which it leads you, the pillar seems quite inadequate, for this path is a must: it leads you to a stone pyramid a few hundred metres up ahead which marks Noordhoek Peak. It has probably taken you about an hour to reach the peak.

Surely this is the most photogenic view in all of the Western Cape? This is a matter of opinion obviously, but on a clear day it is quite superb. For the best photographs make sure you get there by late morning, otherwise you'll be looking into the sun.

On leaving Noordhoek Peak, don't retrace your steps, but rather fork to the left, which will lead you back to the gravel road further down. The road now descends gently for about half an hour before sweeping to the right, into the home stretch. At this point another road joins in from the left and behind, coming from the top of Blackburn Ravine above Hout Bay. This is the 'Old Road to Hout Bay', and you are on it. It went from the Tokai forest, along this road and down Blackburn Ravine into Hout Bay. It could only have been used by pack mules and horses, as I can't imagine oxwagons making their way down the steep slopes of Blackburn Ravine.

After walking along the 'Old Road' for about 8 minutes, you will come to a T-junction, just before the road dips down and is reinforced with a double concrete strip. A metal pole marks the T-junction: presumably it was a signpost pointing the way to Elephant's Eye Cave. At this point you need to decide whether or not you have time to divert to Elephant's Eye Cave. It's situated just around the corner from the Lookout Hut you can see on the ridge. It will take you 15 minutes to reach the hut and a further 10 minutes to the cave, so allow an hour for the diversion.

Once at the Lookout Hut, you can't miss the cave, as it's a gaping black hole in the cliff face. From most parts of Tokai this bit of mountain takes on the shape of an elephant's head, with the cave in just the right place for an eye. From this substantial cave you have a sweeping view of False Bay all the way to Hangklip. Pick out the Rondevlei bird sanctuary as well as Zeekoevlei, Sandvlei and Marina da Gama.

Silvermine Reservoir

You can get back to the Lookout Hut and the Old Road via an alternative and more interesting route. Leave the cave at the highest level possible against the rock face, traverse above the point where you came up, then climb down some log steps. Once on the road, cross over it, aiming for the white sandy path skirting the right-hand edge of the pine forest below, then cross over the river (the only source of water on this hike). On the left, after crossing the river, you might notice the results of some fascinating biological control. Long-leaf wattle (*Acacia longifolia*) appear to be covered in large green and brown berries. These 'berries' are in fact the result of a wasp (imported from Australia, like the wattle itself) that lays its eggs in the ovary of the flower. The flower aborts, and grows a wart-like growth around the invaders. If you were to take a penknife and carefully cut one of these in half, you'll find two or three wriggling grubs inside, but only if the berry is green. If it's brown, look for the minute holes on the outside where the grubs burrowed their way out to repeat the cycle. Perhaps this kind of biological control is the only way in which we will be able to eradicate this serious alien invasion.

Once back on the gravel road you zigzag down to the level of the reservoir. Don't be tempted to cut corners and add to soil erosion. You need to get to the darker of the two parallel roads you see below you (the one nearer the dam). It will lead you straight back to your car. This is a popular braai spot during summer. With proper planning you could even arrange to have some hot coals and a cold beer waiting for you!

77

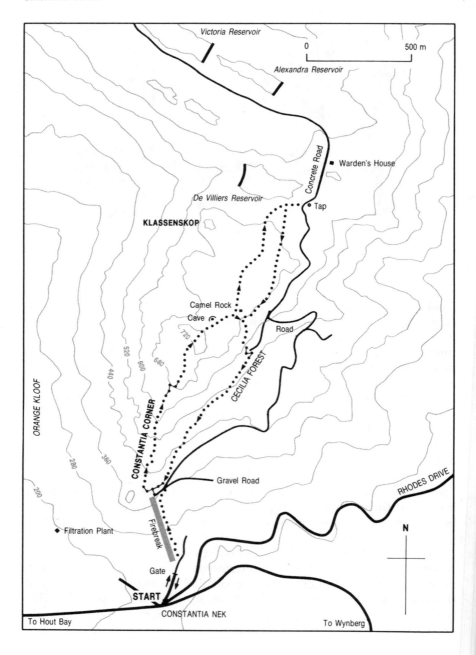

CONSTANTIA CORNER 15

Time: $3\frac{1}{2}$ *hours*
Grade: *3C*
Water: *None available*

This is another of my favourite walks. It is relatively short, fairly strenuous and offers magnificent alternating views of Orange Kloof and the Cape Flats. An added bonus is that you'll be in shade for most of the way up, provided you start by 09h00.

Leave your car in the parking area on the north side of Constantia Nek. Take the narrow tarred road leading up alongside some houses (not the one leading into Orange Kloof). Three minutes up this road, you will come to a gate across the road. You have just walked up the last remaining section of the original Rhodes Drive, which was built for Cecil John Rhodes to travel through his vast estate. Go through (or around) the gate and, about 25 m beyond it, on the edge of a pine forest, you will find some steps ascending to the left. The well-cut log steps will take you up a steady climb more or less along the inside edge of the forest. Some quarter of an hour later they will deliver you onto a gravel road. At the gravel road, turn right and follow it to its end, a mere 100 m away. At the end of this road, take the footpath that goes up to the right. This will take you 50 m up to a cliff face, where it turns sharp left. On the way up to the cliff face you'll be tempted by a few left turns, which do not matter since they all end up at the same spot anyway. It is just easier to go right up to the cliff face.

Traverse around to above Orange Kloof and Hout Bay on a clear path through what were once dense stands of Protea bushes, devastated by fire in February 1990. If in doubt, keep right. Eventually it will lead you into a ravine about 35 to 40 minutes after leaving your car. At this point turn upwards into the ravine. A rocky cairn will show you the point where you should turn upwards. Keep to the right-hand side of the ravine and avoid the scree in the middle.

You will soon be on the ridge known as Constantia Corner, which separates Cecilia Forest and Orange Kloof (the one planted by man and the other by nature). The path then zigzags up this ridge, giving you wonderful alternating views of Constantia and Hout Bay. Shortly you'll zigzag back into the top part of the ravine you started up. The path should always be perfectly clear and well defined: if not, retrace your steps. Sometimes on the zigzag you'll be faced with a choice of two clear paths. Take either, as they soon join again.

At the top of the ravine the path eases to a gentle slope, taking you to the base of a cliff face. You should have reached this point more or less an hour after starting. Look down over the burgeoning, but still beautiful, Hout Bay Valley. I have lived there since 1970, and still find it as enchanting as ever. Don't let the cliff face intimidate you as the path finds an easy scrambling route up it. Only those with a severe fear of heights might experience some difficulty. Soon a trig beacon comes into sight, followed by a flat stretch of about 100 m which leads to another cliff barrier. This time the path leads you through a gap in the cliff, over and down into a superb spot for a rest. Here two huge rock overhangs form a welcome stop and provide shelter from the wind and the weather, be it hot or cold.

When rested, cross the valley floor in front of the 'cave' and look up to see Camel Rock, one of many bizarre weather-beaten rocks in this little valley. It doesn't have much of a hump, but its neck is certainly better defined than the one at Scarborough. It is an important landmark, because here you have a choice of paths at the bottom of the valley it overlooks.

Turn right if you're in a hurry. This is a shortcut, and as long as you keep going right, it will eventually bring you back to where you started. Your second choice is to carry on up to the base of Camel Rock and on to the Back Table. This route is only an extra 25 minutes walking time, and is well worth the trouble.

From Camel Rock the path continues north for 5 minutes until the forester's cottage and concrete road pop into sight. At the last moment the De Villiers Reservoir comes into view. This is the southernmost of the five reservoirs on the Back Table. About 50 m before reaching the concrete road, you're faced with another decision. If you want to take the easy but less interesting way down to Constantia Nek via the road, do just that. If, on the other hand, you want to try a path which skirts above the road and is much more pleasant but somewhat precipitous in places, then look for the right-hand turn back up the koppie about 50 m before reaching the road. It is a clear path, almost a firebreak, and does not peter out. This path affords superb views of False Bay and the southern Peninsula which you will miss on the concrete road as it winds through dense pine plantations.

After 10 minutes along the upper path you'll meet the path coming down from Camel Rock. Continue along it down to lower levels. From here the path plunges steeply down and crosses the end of a gravel road before continuing its plunge down and to the right. You can't lose your way from here. Just follow the path until it comes to a fairly abrupt end at the cliff face you first encountered just above the gravel road. Retrace your way down the log steps for the last few minutes.

Constantia Nek

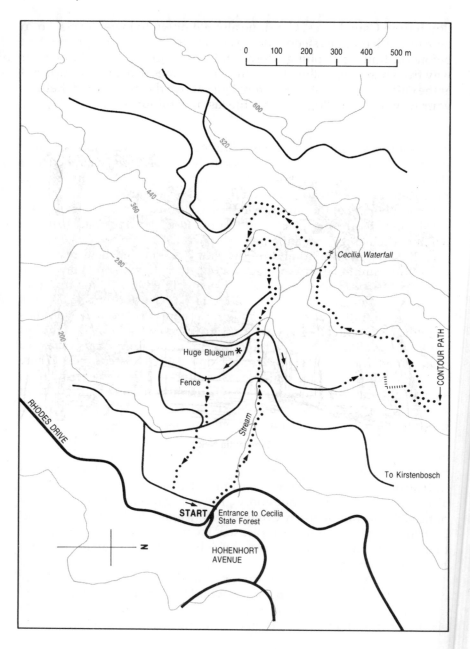

CECILIA WATERFALL 16

Time: *2 hours*
Grade: *2A*
Water: *Available*

This is a great walk if your time is limited and you want to work up a good sweat. The waterfall is well worth the sweat, for it is surely one of the loveliest in the Cape Peninsula. Covered in thick green moss, it is probably at its best when reduced to a trickle in mid-summer.

Leave your car at the entrance to the Cecilia State Forest (named after Cecil John Rhodes) opposite Hohenhort Drive on the road between Kirstenbosch and Constantia Nek. Hop over the wooden fence where it ends at the main road and follow the wire fence in the direction of Cape Town until you cross a stream about 100 m further on. A faint path goes up the side of the stream, mostly on its right bank (going up). Five minutes up the stream you pass a crude wooden footbridge. Do not cross over it, rather continue up the right bank for another 5 minutes until the clear path takes you over a forestry road. Cross over to the left bank and continue up for yet another 5 minutes until you come to a point where three forestry roads and some more log steps meet. There is a huge bluegum at the confluence of all four. Take the narrow road sharp right: this is the Contour Path which starts at Constantia Nek and ends at Kloof Nek (see Chapters 20, 21 and 22). You'll come back to this meeting of the ways at the end of your circular route.

Soon the road peters out into a narrow path. Notice that the pine trees are of a particular type (*Pinus radiata*). They are commercially viable because all the knots appear at regular intervals where the branches radiate out from one point on the trunk. Also the main trunk is straight, as opposed to the pine commonly grown in gardens and particularly noticeable on Rondebosch Common, *Pinus pinaster*, which sends out branches in all directions as it pleases. Try making straight poles out of that. Further on you'll reach some huge bluegums; they may be aliens, but they are majestic.

The path makes a U-bend around a little ravine and immediately climbs nine log steps. Fifteen paces beyond the top step turn off the path and climb up another more substantial set of steps to the left. On emerging from the Kirstenbosch edge of the bluegums, a sign directs you to the left (Cecilia Ravine). Ten metres past the sign a path leaves the Contour Path sharply up to the left. Take this log staircase, stopping every now and again to admire the view. Below lies the Kirstenbosch Dam, used to irrigate the world-famous Botanical Gardens. This is one of the more pleasant 'up' climbs I can think of: hard work, but rewarding. In no time at all, thanks to well-placed and carefully maintained steps, you are high up, and lovely views begin to unfold. Notice the indigenous Cape Cypress on either side of you, which is often mistaken for Hakea, an alien invader.

Five or six minutes after leaving the Contour Path up the log staircase, you will reach your first high point. Thereafter it descends through a tight ravine overgrown with indigenous vegetation and ascends the other side for more splendid views, with a bird's eye view over the canopy of Cecilia Forest. Also notice Wynberg Hill beyond.

About a quarter of an hour after leaving the Contour Path, you will reach the second high point. This is a good spot to rest and admire the view for a short while. Not too long though, for just around the corner is the reward for all your effort. You will be looking into two ravines merging into one. The zigzag path on the far side is on the slope of Spilhaus Ravine (your down route), and the nearer, dense indigenous forest grows in Cecilia Ravine. The waterfall is reached some 7 minutes after leaving your rest place at the second high point.

It is a lovely spot, full of peace and tranquillity. About 18 m high and covered in moss, the waterfall almost always has water. There is a faint path up the right-hand side of the waterfall, but don't be tempted to climb up this path, as you'll only contribute to soil erosion and it doesn't go anywhere. Any attempt to get to the top of the waterfall is fraught with danger, so remain at peace and admire it from below.

After you have refreshed your body and soul, climb up and out of Cecilia Ravine and see your zigzag route down. About 6 minutes after leaving the waterfall, the path reaches its highest point. At this spot log steps go up and off to the right. This is not your route, but it does mark the top of your climb. These steps join the Bridle Path back to Constantia Nek (see the rock cutting above and ahead of you). Your way, thankfully, is now all down, and a gentle down at that.

About 15 minutes of descent will bring you to some concrete settling tanks which must once have been used for water purification. Don't follow the jeep track you now see, but rather step over the plastic water pipe to the left and follow the path down to the river. Although this is known as the Old Picnic Site, a regular climbing friend of mine

Cecilia Waterfall

prefers to call it 'Bacon-and-Eggs Corner', because we have detected that gorgeous aroma from 100 m up! Five minutes down the river from 'Bacon-and-Eggs Corner' brings you back to the four-way intersection with its huge bluegum you passed earlier.

From here you can either return the way you came up, following the river, or for variety take a different but equally rewarding route back to the car. If you choose the latter, follow the road down in the direction of the foresters' cottages, around and to the left of the bluegum. Close on 300 m down, you will see a fence and the foresters' accommodation. Leave the road and go down the side of the fence until you reach another gravel road, then turn right. Just after the hairpin bend the path again leaves the road and wanders down through pine forest straight back to your car.

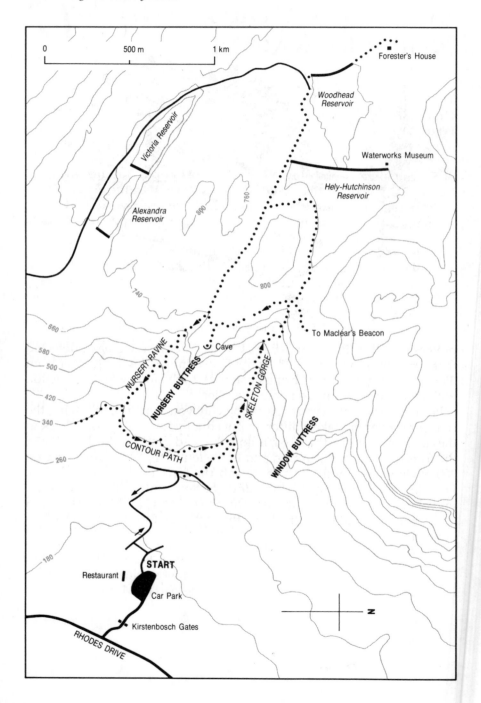

Skeleton Gorge and Nursery Ravine 17

Time: $3\frac{1}{2}$ *hours*
Grade: *3B*
Water: *Available*

Skeleton Gorge is probably one of the most popular routes up Table Mountain. The other two routes that carry heavy traffic, namely Kasteelspoort above Camps Bay and Platteklip Gorge above the City Bowl, are not nearly as pleasant, as they are much more exposed to the sun and the more inclement weather.

Skeleton Gorge on the other hand is an excellent climb on a hot summer's day as it is almost entirely in the shade at all times. Furthermore this is not just any old shade, but the kind provided by majestic Milkwood, Red Alder, Wild Peach, Yellowwood, Assegaaibos and other indigenous trees.

Drive through the main entrance gates to Kirstenbosch Botanical Gardens (a modest charge is levied, so have your cash ready). The road leads to a large parking area where you leave your car. At the far end of the parking area is the Botanical Society's Bookshop, and lower down the Tea Garden and Restaurant. Your starting point is the top left-hand corner of the parking area. Facing the mountain, turn left into a gravel walkway clearly marked 'Skeleton Gorge, Smuts' Track and Contour Path'. Another three such signs will lead you past a rectangular concrete reservoir after about 10 minutes. Notice the interesting float control on top of it, indicating the level of the water. About 3 minutes beyond the reservoir you'll come to another sign saying 'Dogs should be kept on a leash at all times'. At this point leave the gravel road and go up the log path. You will cross over the road again, as it doubles back on itself.

Another sign leads you on to the Contour Path, Skeleton Gorge and the Back Table. The log staircase in front of you is neatly spaced. The sounds of running water and the chirping of insects, a gentle breeze and luxurious shade, all combine to make this a most pleasant setting. No wonder it was General Jan Smuts' favourite part of Mother Mountain. There's no mistaking the Contour Path when you reach it. Where you cross over it on your upward stroll, there is a metal plaque on a rock where the great statesman used to take a breather. You might like to do the same. This is the point back to which you'll be coming after descending Nursery Ravine.

Continue your upward climb along what must be the best maintained path on all of Table Mountain. It keeps to the left side of the gorge for about half the way up, then leads you to a 2-metre ladder which makes it much easier to scramble up the rock face at this point. It then continues up the river bed in a deep, narrow section of the gorge to a gabion (a loose stone wall held together with wire mesh) damming up the river above: the gabion probably helps to make this section passable in winter. At the gabion turn right and cross the river onto a zigzag path which winds its way up through gorgeous ferns, their rich greenness shimmering in the filtered sunlight. Ignore a path going off to the right – this leads to a small overhang cave.

Near the top of the narrow zigzag path are some huge Red Alders (Rooiels or Butterspoon Trees). The path crosses over the gorge again and from here you can look down on your car way below. Just beyond a spot where you cross over back onto the left bank there is a spot against the dripping rock face where Red Disa (*Disa uniflora*, also justifiably named The Pride of Table Mountain) grow. Keep a sharp eye open for them in January and February. I recently saw no less than forty here in an area of no more than three square metres.

On reaching the top you'll be confronted by a huge boulder. Some call it 'Breakfast Rock', but I never seem to get there early enough. The path continues for a few metres to the right and beyond Breakfast Rock to a metal signpost with three direction pointers on it. Skeleton Gorge points the way you've just come, Maclear's Beacon indicates the direction of the path to the right and Kasteelspoort is straight ahead. Oddly enough you need to turn left at this point in the only direction that isn't indicated! The path picks its way faintly up the slope and in a few short minutes you'll be at the top. Look back at the sheer drop of Hiddingh Buttress above Newlands, and nearer at hand at the startlingly bright red Crassula growing out of seemingly inhospitable cracks in the rock from January to March.

Once over the top you start to descend into Nursery Ravine, but after about only 50 m look out for a path going off sharply to the left. This is an extremely worthwhile 3-minute detour to a substantial cave with superb views and excellent shelter from the sun or rain.

Retrace your steps to the main path, which will soon bring you to the top of the steep Nursery Ravine. From here down to the Contour Path

it is a steep, bone-jarring descent, made worthwhile by some of the best stands in the Peninsula of King Protea (*P. cynaroides*), our national flower, from February to April. Such steep descents need to be done either slowly, one step at a time, or on the trot. I prefer the latter, which gets me down to the Contour Path in a mere 20 minutes.

Once you reach the Contour Path and have given yourself enough time for the Shaking Legs Syndrome to disappear, turn left to get back to Kirstenbosch. It's mostly on the level and looks down on the lovely gardens and rolling lawns interspersed with footpaths and patches of indigenous bush. Ten minutes' walking along the Contour Path will bring you to the metal plaque you saw earlier, and a right-hand turn takes you down and back to your car. A welcome cooldrink or tea at the restaurant might not be out of place.

Doing this walk the other way round is not recommended. Nursery Ravine is too steep for comfort on the way up, and doesn't provide nearly as much shade.

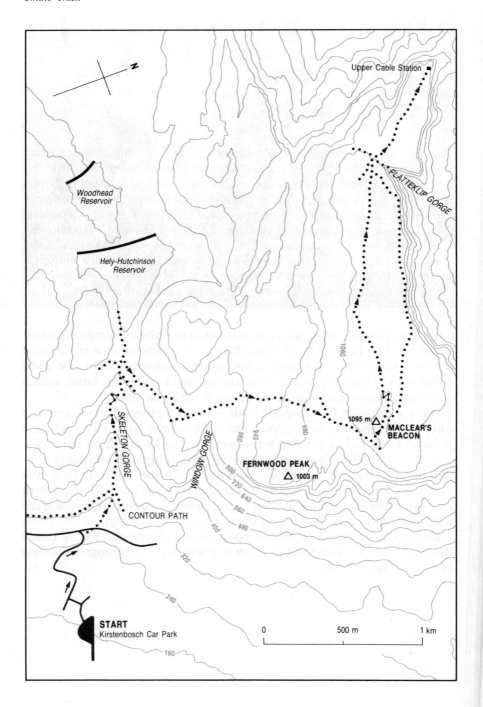

SMUTS' TRACK

18

Time: $4\frac{1}{2}$ *hours (one way)*
Grade: *4B*
Water: *Available*

This classic walk is surprisingly strenuous considering it was named after a man who regularly walked this route even when well into his seventies. It starts from Kirstenbosch, ascends Skeleton Gorge and ends at Maclear's Beacon, the highest point on Table Mountain, at the opposite end of the table top to the Upper Cable Station. For the purpose of this walk, we will carry on to the Upper Cable Station so as to take the easy way down in the cable car. This means that you need to have a car at each end. Check first that the cable car is operating, and take enough money with you for the fare, otherwise you'll have to get down via Platteklip Gorge, for which you will need to add another hour.

Jan Christiaan Smuts (1870-1950) left an indelible mark on South African history and made no small contribution to international events of this century. At Yalta he sat shoulder to shoulder with Stalin, Eisenhower and Churchill, and he was one of the architects of the United Nations. He walked this route for 50 years, more times than you and I have had Sunday dinners. Think of this remarkable man as you climb. I have a strange idea I may have met him, but more of that later on.

Having left another car at the Lower Cable Station, park your car in the parking area of Kirstenbosch Botanical Gardens. (There is a small charge to enter the gardens.) Start from the top left-hand corner of the parking area, where you will find a signpost showing you the way to Smuts' Track and Skeleton Gorge. Wherever there is a junction in the gravel road that follows, you will find another signpost pointing you in the right direction to Smuts' Track and Skeleton Gorge. After 15 to 20 minutes of upward stroll along the gravel road, you will reach a point where log steps lead straight up, with the usual helpful signpost. Leave the road at this point and start the strenuous but tranquil walk up Skeleton Gorge. Most of the way up, the path is well maintained and is characterised by comfortably positioned log steps.

Keep an eye open for nameplates on the indigenous trees. These carry various bits of information regarding the trees. First the family to which it belongs, then the Latin name, followed by its Afrikaans and English common names and finally the tree number. This reference can be looked up in any national tree index, thus making all the previous information unnecessary!

About 100 m after leaving the gravel road you might notice one nameplate in particular which rather tickled me. There's nothing unusual about the Common Turkey-Berry, except its Afrikaans name. *Gewone bokdrol* describes the fallen berries perfectly.

Most times the river flowing down Skeleton Gorge is a babbling brook but occasionally, after heavy rain, it gives out a thunderous roar. At times like this, this walk should rather be left for fair weather, as a short section near the top of Skeleton Gorge runs up the river bed.

Ten minutes after leaving the gravel road you will reach the Contour Path (Chapters 20 and 21). At this point a bronze plaque set into a rock announces 'Smuts' Track', and you know you are on the right path. After a brief rest continue the upward slog through this magnificent indigenous forest. Half an hour later you will reach a couple of ladders that help you over a tricky part. Shortly beyond the ladders the route is forced into the river bed by the surrounding cliffs. You then reach a gabion (a wall of loose stones held together by wire mesh).

At this point the path zigzags up the right-hand slope, passes below a cave and finally emerges from the forest to reveal a superb view of the Cape Flats. The trees now below you are Rooiels (Red Alder). These huge and ancient specimens are quite the finest examples of these indigenous trees I have seen. Another name for Rooiels is Butterspoon Tree, named after the shape of the apical leaf at each growing tip.

About $1\frac{1}{2}$ hours after your start you should reach the top of Skeleton Gorge. Here you will find a metal signpost, where you will no doubt wish to rest. A few metres further on are the upper reaches of the Hely Hutchinson Reservoir. That is not your way, however, and you'll get a much better view of it from on high. Turn right and follow the sign to Maclear's Beacon. The path is well defined, and as long as you keep heading in a northerly direction you can't go wrong. From the top of Skeleton Gorge the path climbs steeply for 6 or 7 minutes before levelling out for a while. Notice Junction Peak on your left, and the imposing hulk of Fernwood Peak dead ahead.

Twenty minutes after leaving Skeleton Gorge you reach the top of Window Gorge, an area where Red and Mauve Disas abound in summer. After crossing the Window Gorge stream the path ascends the slopes of Fernwood Peak. Some way up, notice the aqueduct over to the left. Follow the cairns on the upward scramble and 10 – 15 minutes later you will see ahead of you a pointed pinnacle on the left and a weirdly shaped overhanging block on the right. The path finds its way between these two landmarks.

Immediately beyond the overhanging block the path veers sharp right for a few metres, and then straightens out again to reveal another signpost. A sharp left turn would take you to Kasteelspoort, but your way is straight on, despite the fact that the signpost is a bit askance: the way is clear enough. About 8 minutes beyond the signpost you come to some simple rock scrambles. Just before these, look out for a rocky cairn almost hidden in the bush on the right which marks a faint path off to the right through waist-high fynbos. It leads to Carrell's Ledge, a sensational traverse along a narrow ledge which eventually brings you to the same spot you are headed anyway. This is the crazy alternative, however, and only for those who have absolutely no fear of heights and are full of the-devil-may-care. Ropes are not necessary.

Normal people should continue up the rock scramble at the top of which there is a fork. Take the more obvious left-hand alternative, and you're almost there. Two minutes later there is another signpost, and 50 m further on the stone pyramid of Maclear's Beacon itself. Read all about it on the bronze plaque on the beacon. Near the beacon, 15 m to the north of the signpost, is the Mountain Club War Memorial, which was dedicated on 25 February 1923 by General (later Field Marshal) J.C. Smuts.

When I did this particular walk for the purposes of writing this account, I was pressed for time due to publishers' deadlines, and was obliged to do it in the foulest of weather, by myself, which was foolish on at least two counts, but could not be avoided. It was absolutely pouring with rain, the wind was howling and visibility was down to about 20 m. Suddenly, out of the mist, came an old man dressed in rain gear, so that I could only see his eyes and nose and grey beard through his anorak. I called out to him and said, 'I thought I was the only one crazy enough to be on the mountain today'. He stopped and looked at me and said, 'Surprisingly mild, actually,' and then he turned and disappeared into the mist. As I write, I wonder about that old man. Was he real, or was I affected by the extreme weather conditions, or could it be that he was ...? No, surely not!

From Maclear's Beacon follow the yellow-and-white footprints painted on the rocks in reverse (in other words, walk against the direction of the footprints). This will bring you, within about half an hour, to the head of Platteklip Gorge (the 'nick' in the middle of the otherwise flat table top). On the way notice the superb view of the Table Mountain reservoirs, the two main ones built nearly a century ago. At that time they supplied all of Cape Town's needs, but today the combined capacity of all five reservoirs when full to the brim would provide Cape Town with water for only about five days.

The path descends into the 'nick' of Platteklip Gorge and then ascends again onto the Western Table. The Upper Cable Station and Restaurant are about ten minutes' walk from the top of Platteklip Gorge.

Maclear's Beacon

CONTOUR PATH: CONSTANTIA NEK TO KIRSTENBOSCH

20

Time: $1\frac{3}{4}$ *hours one way*
Grade: *1A*
Water: *Available*

This is a leisurely stroll through forest and fynbos and is suitable for the whole family. If you're wise you'll have a friend's car waiting for you at Kirstenbosch, and remember that the restaurant there serves an excellent breakfast or brunch. This is also a gentle walk that can be done at any time of the day or year, as it is mostly in shade so a hot summer's morning or sunny winter's afternoon can be equally pleasant. In fact you could even do it dressed in your Sunday best. Not that this form of attire is recommended, but I have seen numerous overly well-dressed people on this walk, so it must be all right.

Start at Constantia Nek. A narrow tarred road leaves the Wynberg side of the picnic area and travels up for about 200 m before coming to a closed gate. A few metres beyond the gate log steps ascend to the left, but ignore them and continue along the gravel road for about 4 minutes until you come to a fork in the road. Take the left fork up. After a further 8 minutes or so, the road doubles back on itself opposite a steel road barrier. Don't double back, but rather carry on. (To turn sharp left would take you to the dams and the Back Table along the so-called Bridle Path – actually a road.) Carrying on along the straight, you'll soon come out into the open, with splendid views of the Cape Flats and False Bay. A little koppie on the right offers a grandstand view. At this point the road does a sharp 90-degree left turn and about 10 minutes later the black-tiled roofs of the Cecilia Forest Officer's home come into view, as does a giant bluegum at a fork in the road. It's hardly necessary to say keep right at the fork, as the left alternative is obviously less used. Keep right then, and soon you'll come to a major intersection. At this intersection three roads and a set of log steps all come together. One road is behind you, one doubles back 180 degrees to the right to the foresters' cottages, and one goes 90 degrees to the right. The steps on the left come down from Cecilia Waterfall (see Chapter 16). The way you need to go is the road going 90 degrees to the right.

Soon the road narrows to a path and shortly after it does a little U-bend around a small ravine, and then climbs nine log steps. Some fifteen paces on turn sharp left up some more steep log steps. At this point you seem to be leaving the Contour Path, but you're not. You're just getting back up to the right level. This is the point where most people go wrong, so read carefully!

Having climbed up the steep log steps, you'll soon come to a notice at a fork in the path. Right and down will take you to the southern outskirts of Kirstenbosch Gardens. You need to keep left to continue on the Contour Path, but beware. Having taken the left fork up, it almost immediately doubles back on itself. **Do not** double back, but rather carry on along the less obvious straight path. If you take the more obvious route up, you will eventually reach Cecilia Waterfall (see Chapter 16). Remember that you are on a contour path which, as the name implies, means you should remain more or less on the same level.

Now you are out of the forest and into the fynbos. A few minutes further on you'll meet a path coming up from Kirstenbosch. Ignore it and continue a few more metres to the bottom of Nursery Ravine (a sign set into a rock tells you that you have arrived there). Keep going along the Contour Path, now delightfully wrapped in indigenous forest. Ten minutes later you will reach the point where the Contour Path crosses Skeleton Gorge, and here another plaque announces 'Smuts' Track'. At this point turn down the well-marked path which will lead you to the Kirstenbosch restaurant some 15 minutes later. Enjoy your late breakfast of bacon and eggs, not to mention champagne and orange juice.

Contour Path: Kirstenbosch to Rhodes Memorial

21

Time: *3 hours (one way)*
Grade: *2A*
Water: *Available*

Like the first part of the Contour Path from Constantia Nek to Kirstenbosch, this section is also almost entirely in shade. It's a little more strenuous, though, as part of it belies its description of 'contour' path and zigzags up to a point about 150 m higher up the slopes of Fernwood Buttress before plummeting back down again.

The indigenous forest through which it meanders is quite remarkable for its diversity. The authorities have clearly labelled the main trees of the forest, and familiar names such as Yellowwood, Assegaai, Cape Saffron, Wild Almond, Ironwood and Rooiels are much in evidence. Start the walk at the car park next to the Kirstenbosch restaurant. (There is a small charge to take your car into the Botanical Gardens.) At the top left-hand corner of the parking area there is a sign indicating the way to Skeleton Gorge, Smuts' Track and the Contour Path. Follow the sign and subsequent ones along this gravel road and some 15 minutes later you reach some log steps leaving the gravel road. (This point is marked by a sign informing you that dogs should be on a leash.) Ten minutes up these well-built log steps brings you to the Contour Path.

At this point you'll want a rest. Sit on the same rock regularly used for a breather by former world statesman Field Marshal Jan Christiaan Smuts. A bronze plaque announces 'Smuts' Track' and it refers to the beginning of a long but fascinating trek to the highest point on Table Mountain which was followed regularly by the 'Oubaas' (see Chapter 18). Having taken in the peace and tranquillity of this resting place, so enjoyed by Smuts, take solace in the fact that your upward slog is temporarily over.

Follow the broad Contour Path in a northerly direction towards Cape Town. Fifty metres on, cross a stream (which can be a raging torrent after heavy rain). This is the stream which tumbles down Skeleton

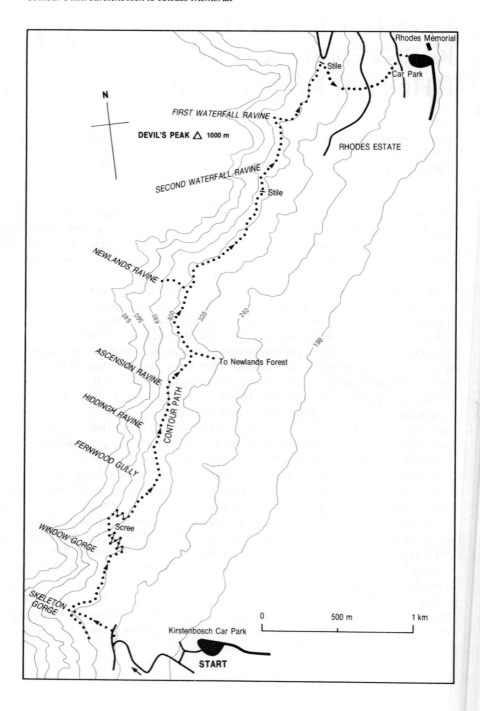

Contour Path: Rhodes Memorial to Kloof Nek

Time: *3½ hours one way. Add half an hour to explore Woodstock Cave.*
Grade: *2C*
Water: *Available*

This is a walk with a substantial cave to explore and a breathtaking view of Table Mountain which is thrust upon you all of a sudden. The only reason it's graded 'C' is because of one short stretch above the end of Tafelberg Road where the path is moderately exposed. Otherwise it's an 'A' all the way. You will need two cars if you don't wish to walk back.

Leave your first car 800 m up the road from Kloof Nek towards the Lower Cable Station. There is suitable off-road parking just below the second hairpin bend. From here to Rhodes Memorial is 12 km by road, but don't worry as you will only be walking about 8 km back. When leaving your car at the starting point, don't do as my wife did to us, and finish up with the wrong keys for the right cars!

Having parked your car in the Rhodes Memorial parking area, set off up the log steps at the top right-hand corner. Your immediate aim is the King's Blockhouse on the horizon above. It's going to take you about 40 minutes to get there, so put your head down and set to it.

From this angle Devil's Peak seems to have a twin. The right 'twin' is Minor Peak. Seen from afar, it is clearly a very much younger demon. On reaching a gravel road a few minutes up, turn left and follow the 'Contour Path' sign. Stick to the most well-used path, not losing sight of your destination. Eventually you will come to a turnstile and ladder over the fence marking the boundary of Rhodes Estate. Go through the turnstile and up the gravel road half left. About 100 m up, leave the road for a shortcut to the King's Blockhouse directly above.

On arrival at the King's Blockhouse you deserve a rest. This place is officially known on survey maps as the King's Battery and was built by the British during their first occupation of the Cape between 1795 and 1803. Its guns were never fired in anger, but at one time it was used to accommodate convict labour during afforestation of Devil's Peak in the

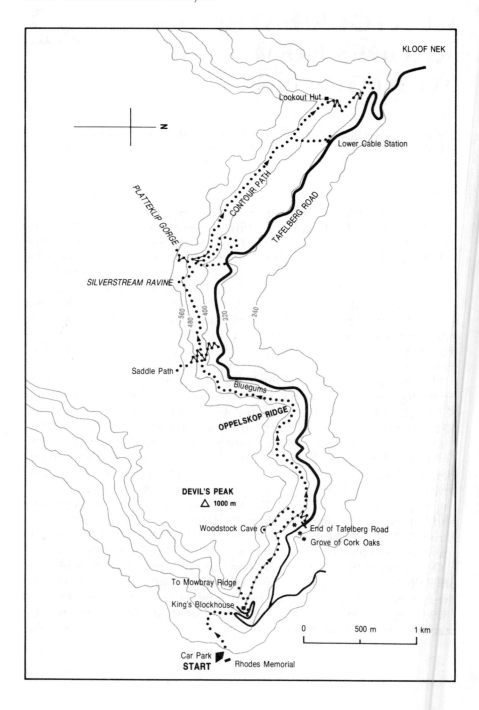

latter part of the 19th century. It is an excellent viewpoint, and one cannot help envying the forester who had a substantial house up here about a hundred years ago. The two oceans can be seen clearly, and also pick out the Liesbeek River, Groote Schuur Hospital, Newlands Rugby and Cricket Grounds and the University of Cape Town.

Find your way to behind the King's Blockhouse where you will see a small concrete reservoir: there is always water here. The steps going up past the reservoir lead to Mowbray Ridge and up Devil's Peak. However, you don't wish to be quite so ambitious on this walk, so keep on the level to the right of and just below the reservoir. This is the so-called Lower Contour Path. It is in fact a continuation of the Contour Path from Constantia Nek but assumes the 'lower' designation here on Devil's Peak as there are also Middle and Upper Contour Paths.

Ten minutes after leaving the King's Blockhouse, the path curves into a ravine. Look up and see Woodstock Cave (occasionally known as Devil's Peak Cave). It is a substantial rock overhang 50 m wide by 15 m deep and 3-4 m high at the mouth. It is well worth a visit, but you need to go well past it, then zigzag up and double back to get there.

Below you on the right is a parking area marking the end of Tafelberg Road. The point at which to turn up to get to Woodstock Cave is just beyond a fascinating grove of trees which have bark like cork trees and acorns like oak trees, but leaves unlike either. These apparent mongrels are in fact Cork Oaks. About 100 m beyond the Cork Oak grove, a path comes up sharply from the road below and crosses the Contour Path to continue zigzagging up the slope. Take this deviation up and back to reach Woodstock Cave. Count the number of zigzags, and after the seventh one, just as you are confronted with a steep log step and rock scramble, leave the main path and head back towards the King's Blockhouse along a clear path which leads you straight to Woodstock Cave. From the Contour Path to the cave will take you about 13 minutes up and 7 minutes down.

Once at the cave, see Table Bay framed by its narrow mouth, and the ruins of the Queen's Blockhouse just below and to the right of the parking area. Having recharged your batteries and enjoyed the view from Woodstock Cave, get back to the Contour Path and continue in the direction of town. Soon Lion's Head thrusts itself into view, and in no time the scenery changes dramatically.

After part of Table Mountain comes into view behind Oppelskop Ridge, the path descends slowly, and after passing a turn-off back down to the tarred road, starts ascending again. Look down onto a beautiful pool alongside the road way below you. If you have a fear of heights, this is where you're going to feel it. Continue your steady upward climb. When you draw level with the first of the three 'pepper pots' (circular high-rise apartment blocks) to the right, a path climbs up steeply to the left. Do not take this path, but rather carry on along the level. This steep branch to the left connects with the Middle Contour Path.

A few minutes later, as you round Oppelskop Ridge, Table Mountain suddenly appears in all its magnificence and splendour. What an awe-inspiring surprise! The sheer visual impact of walking around what seems to be just another corner is quite breathtaking. The first time I rounded this corner, I walked back and did it twice again! Mother Mountain just seems to tower over you.

Ten minutes later you pass through a bluegum plantation and then start to change from walking on the slopes of Devil's Peak to Table Mountain itself. Soon the Saddle Path crosses the Contour Path. Notice the yawning gap of Platteklip Gorge: this is the 'nick' in the table top as seen from afar.

Ten to fifteen minutes after crossing the Saddle Path you arrive at Silverstream Ravine, just 5 minutes before you reach Platteklip Gorge. Silverstream is identifiable as a deep and pretty ravine, rich with indigenous trees except for four intrusive pines standing guard on the far side. There is almost always water here, and rock overhangs provide a welcome resting place. On reaching Platteklip Gorge, you will see two parallel paths traversing the buttress on the other side: take the higher one. The lower alternative takes you back to the tarred road well before you want to be there. The Contour Path is true to its name for the rest of the way, staying just below the cliff face.

A few hundred metres before you pass under the cableway, look up to the skyline ahead of you and see the 'venster' (window) after which Venster Buttress is named (see Chapter 2). The cableway goes up India Ravine, so named because it forms the outline of a map of India when seen from the city. As you pass under the cables, a path goes down to the right. This leads to the Lower Cable Station. As your car is further on, however, you should continue along the Contour Path to its very end. It's only another 5 minutes before you come to a stone lookout hut which marks the termination of the Contour Path which began at Constantia Nek, but you simply *must* peep around the corner to see Camps Bay from on high. Just below the lookout hut are some stone steps which will take you down to your waiting car in about 15 minutes. Hopefully you have the right keys.

FURTHER READING

Branch, Bill, *Field Guide to the Snakes and other Reptiles of Southern Africa*, Struik, Cape Town, 1988.

Broadley, D.G., *FitzSimons' Snakes of Southern Africa*, Delta Books, Johannesburg, 1983.

Burman, Jose, *Latest Walks in the Cape Peninsula*, Human & Rousseau, Cape Town, 1979.

Frandsen, Joy, *Birds of the South Western Cape*, Sable, Cape Town, 1982.

Green, Laurence, *Tavern of the Seas*, Howard Timmins, Cape Town, 1975.

Kench, John, *Know Table Mountain*, Chameleon Press, Bergvliet, Cape Town, 1988.

Kidd, Mary Maytham, *Cape Peninsula Wild Flower Guide*, Botanical Society of South Africa, Cape Town, 1983.

Marais, Johan, *Snakes versus Man*, Macmillan, Johannesburg, 1985.

Mountain Club of South Africa, *Table Mountain Guide*, MCSA, Cape Town, 1983.

Muir, John, *Know Your Cape*, Howard Timmins, Cape Town, 1975.

Pellant, Chris, *Earthscope*, Timmins, Cape Town, 1985.

Visser, John and Chapman, David, *Snakes and Snake Bite*, Purnell, Cape Town, 1978.

HIKING CLUBS IN THE WESTERN CAPE

Apex Stap- en Buiteleweklub, PO Box 854, Brackenfell 7560
Bellville Hiking Club, PO Box 1089, Oakdale 7534
Berg-en-Dal Voetslaanklub, 16 Marthinus Street, George 6530
Cape Province Mountain Club, 15 Stanhope Road, Claremont 7700
Cumhike, c/o Cape Union Mart, 34 Barrack Street, Cape Town 8001
De Kuilen Voetslaanklub, 9 Mabille Road, Kuils River 7580
Disabled Adventures, 15 Kingfisher Walk, Pinelands 7405

Footloose Hiking Club, PO Box 4028, Cape Town 8000
Friends of the Hout Bay Museum, 4 Andrews Road, Hout Bay 7800
Gantouw Voetslaanklub, PO Box 316, Strand 7140
Happy Feet Hiking Club, PO Box 14661, Kenwyn 7780
Helderberg Avontuurklub, PO Box 16, Somerset West 7130
Hotfoot Hobblers, PO Box 6404, Roggebaai 8012
Hottentots Holland Hiking Club, PO Box 100, Somerset West 7130
Japtrappers, PO Box 713, Sanlamhof 7532
Kingsway Hikers, 14 Elberta Street, Grabouw 7160
Klein Karoo Voetslaanklub, PO Box 483, Oudtshoorn 6620
Kleinmond Hiking Club, PO Box 84, Kleinmond 7195
KWV-Voetslaanklub, PO Box 528, Suider-Paarl 7624
Langeberg Voetslaanklub, PO Box 354, Robertson 6705
Matzikama Voetslaanklub, PO Box 696, Vredendal 8160
Meridian Hiking Club, PO Box 18526, Wynberg 7824
*Mountain Club of South Africa, 97 Hatfield Street, Cape Town 8001
Oakdale Berg-'n-Toerklub, PO Box 615, Riversdale 6770
Old Mutual Hiking Club, PO Box 66, Cape Town 8000
Overberg Voetslaanklub, PO Box 35, Bredasdorp 7280
Paarl Voetslaanklub, PO Box 567, Suider-Paarl 7624
Paul Roos Gimnasium Voetslaanklub, Suidwal, Stellenbosch 7600
Peninsula Ramblers, PO Box 982, Cape Town 8000
Robertson Voetslaanklub, 3 Le Roux Street, Robertson 7530
Sanlam-Staptoerklub, PO Box 1, Sanlamhof 7532
Sapstap (SA Police Services), 32 15th Avenue, Bellville 7530
South African Speleological Association, PO Box 4812,
  Cape Town 8000
Stellenbosch Berg-en-Toerklub, c/o Studenteraadskantoor,
  Langenhoven Studentesentrum, Stellenbosch 7600
Swartland Voetslaanklub, 20 Rainier Street, Malmesbury 7300
Thilo Von Trota Stapgroep, PO Box 39, Gordon's Bay 7150
Tirmanmak Voetslaanklub, PO Box 556, Kuils River 7580
Trails Club of South Africa, PO Box 104, Diep River 7856
Trotters Hiking Club, PO Box 7329, Roggebaai 8012
Tuff Trax Hiking Club, PO Box 24511, Lansdowne 7780
Veldskoen Voetslaanklub, 5 Vuurdoring Street, Mossel Bay 6500
Viking Hiking Club, PO Box 162, Tafelsig 7785
Voetslaanklub Stellenbosch, Het Heerenhof 17, Oudebaan,
  Stellenbosch 7600

A CHOSEN NOVEL

WIND CATCHER

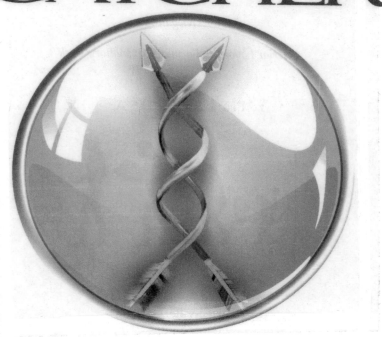

JEFF ALTABEF & ERYNN ALTABEF

FIRST EDITION SOFTCOVER

ISBN: 1622533143

ISBN-13: 9781622533145

Editor: Megan Harris

Interior Layout & Formatting: Mallory Rock

Printed in the U.S.A.

www.EvolvedPub.com
Evolved Publishing LLC
Cartersville, Georgia

Printed in Book Antiqua font.

Shatter Point

WINNER: Pinnacle Book Achievement Award, Fall 2014 – Best Book in the Category of THRILLER

What Others Are Saying about *Shatter Point*:

"An original gripping, saga. From genetic manipulation and twists of fate to cold-blooded murder, scenarios change with a snap but succeed in bringing readers along for what evolves into a wild ride of not just murder and mayhem, but social inspection."

- Donovan, eBook Reviewer, Midwest Book Review

"The book combines my favorite aspects of my favorite authors into one. James Patterson – the master of the psycho killer who kidnaps girls, Patricia Cornwell – scientific thriller, and Dean Koontz – really spooky plots."

– Kat Biggie, No Holding Back

"*Shatter Point* is an exciting novel of suspense, action, drama and even a little bit of horror…. It's definitely one of the best novels out there right now."

- Next Page Reviews

"When I reached the last 100 pages no one was going to be able to stop me reading until I knew the ending!"

- Olivia's Catastrophe

"An amazing read…. This is one of those books that no reader will be able to part with until they reach the end, I guarantee it."

"If you enjoy a great suspense novel, I would HIGHLY recommend this book. It will get your heart pumping and have you hoping the craziness will turn out for the good of everyone involved. You won't want to put this story down till the very end."

For my wife Karen, both my daughters, and for my mom who, through her love and talent as a storyteller, has sparked that passion in me.
— JA

For my wonderful family who has inspired me throughout the process of writing, and for my best friend Mary, who reminds me that anything is possible with a little faith.
— EA

PROLOGUE

Sicheii told me this story only once, which was odd because he always repeated his stories a half dozen times. Every time he told a story it changed—often in subtle ways. Other times, he switched around important events or characters. When young, I pointed out the inconsistencies as if he'd been caught cheating at cards, which he also did quite often. My grandfather never flustered. He patiently explained that his stories were living stories. That's what he called them—*living stories*. As such, they changed on their own from time to time. He never explained what he meant. Now I know.

Three years ago....

Sicheii opened my bedroom door and waved me inside. The taste of chocolate birthday cake swam in the back of my mouth and happily back flipped over my tongue where it swirled among my teeth. Mom stopped me after eating two pieces, but the rest of the cake was safely tucked into the freezer—a spoonful away.

Only the three of us celebrated my thirteenth birthday: Sicheii, Mom, and me. Other kids had big birthday parties, but for me, it was only ever us three. As usual, Mom was talking to her boss downstairs in her office so Sicheii and I were left alone.

He pulled me into my room, closed the door, and sat me on the bed. He rolled my desk chair over and bore his penetrating gray eyes into mine. That expression could mean only one thing. He liked to tell me stories when Mom wasn't listening. I know he told her the same ones when she was young, but this way, his stories were like secrets we shared together. Besides, Mom wasn't a fan of his tales. They weren't *modern* enough for her.

"Are you going to tell me another story?" I asked him.

He smiled and nodded. The lines of his deeply tanned face turned upward and his white hair shifted against his broad shoulders. "Yes, Juliet, but this is not just *any* story. This is the story of your birth."

"Mom's already told me all about how my life began."

He frowned. "This story is about your birth, not your beginning. The beginning of your story starts when the First World was new, as it does for all of our people."

"Troy says the same thing."

"He's right. Your friend enjoys a strong connection to the spirit world." Sicheii inched the chair closer to the bed, his eyes

2

intense and his voice stoic. His mood had turned dark as suddenly as an unexpected storm.

"Your arrival into this world was... difficult. Your mother had been admitted into the hospital the prior afternoon. She had already endured eighteen hours of labor when we all clustered about her bed. Sweat and strain clouded her face. My eyes never strayed far from the heart monitor, which measured both of your heartbeats. It was three twelve in the morning."

"Were you angry that Mom wanted to go to the hospital?" A small smile snuck across my face. I've always wanted to ask him about that. As the Tribe's medicine man, he helped dozens of other women deliver babies, so I imagined he was probably sore that Mom wanted to deliver in a hospital instead of under his care.

"Your mom is headstrong. She puts too much faith in *white medicine*. It's better to look deeper into the state of someone's spirit than treat symptoms, but that's not the intent of this story."

I pushed one of my pillows against my headboard and tried to get comfortable for the rest of the story. When I punched the pillow a few times to get the shape just right, he shot me a sharp look.

Once I was done fidgeting, he continued. "Tension filled the small room. At first, there were only four of us—your mom, the doctor, one nurse, and me. But more people started to squeeze into the small room and the activity buzzed like a beehive. Your mom pushed when the doctor told her to. Her entire body strained with effort. She screamed in pain. She had refused any painkillers. The intervals between your heartbeats lengthened. First, ten seconds, then fourteen, then twenty. I grabbed the arm of the nurse standing next to me.

3

"'There's something wrong. Something from inside,' I told him.

"He frowned. 'Everything's fine. She's just in active labor,'" Sicheii smirked. "The arrogant man thought he knew more about childbirth than me. My fingers dug into his thin arm, past muscle and tendon, until my nails pressed against bone. He had to pry them loose with considerable effort."

Sicheii's eyes burned white hot. Often, he used funny voices to enliven his stories, but his tone was flat, as if he wanted to tell these events exactly as they happened instead of how he wished they had.

My pulse quickened and butterflies swirled around the ice cream in my stomach.

"My eyes narrowed when your heartbeats stretched to thirty seconds. I locked eyes with the doctor. She was a friend of mine.

"She stared back at me, and at that moment, she suspected something was wrong also. Everyone looked at us.

"'Prepare the OR,' she ordered. 'We're doing a cesarean.' One nurse ran from the room. The nurse who had doubted me started to protest when a scream escaped your mom's lips. It sounded like a hawk's hunting call, loud and shrill. A chill raced up my spine.

His voice quickened. "Blood appeared where it should never have been. Doctors and nurses whirled around the room. IVs were injected into your mom's arm. The heart monitors were disconnected. New worried looking doctors appeared wearing operating gowns. An orderly wheeled your mom into the operating room. Stark white light burned my eyes, and I was left on the outside to pray." He took a deep breath.

"How come you didn't go inside?"

4

"That operating room was no place for me. What good could come of my presence? Praying was better. You know there are many spirits to call upon."

I nodded. Sometimes he made me recite all the spirits and what type of guidance I should seek from them.

"I called upon all of them, but focused on my favorite two— your grandmother and great grandfather. Time slowed as if the world spun more slowly than it had ever done before. I drifted between worlds and spent time in the shadow lands with my wife and grandfather. They told me much about you. They said you would be okay and sent me back. When my eyes opened, your mom's obstetrician stood before me, her face grim. Spider webs crept from her eyes and canyons burrowed into her forehead.

"She told me that you and your mother were out of danger. I waited for the bad news written in her sad eyes and downturned lips.

"'But?' I prodded her.

"She sighed. 'But your daughter's uterus ruptured. The damage was extensive. We've repaired the organ, but she won't be able to have any other children.' She leaned against a chair, exhausted from the delivery and operation.

"I nodded, and she retreated from the room."

I expected the story to end. Mom had told me most of this before, but Sicheii leaned closer to me. Only a few inches separated us. He smelled of incense—amber and cinnamon. His eyes were wide and sweat dotted his brow. My hands turned clammy. I'd never seen him worried before.

"After the doctor left, I thanked the spirits and slipped from the room. The nursery was on the same floor as the birthing room, but that wasn't my first stop.

"The time was early and the floor deserted. Unseen, I glided through the staircase door and found a plain tan backpack waiting for me with a blue hospital gown and an identification card hidden inside. One of my friends had left it for me."

"Who?"

Sicheii shook his head. To say he had many friends was the same as describing cotton candy as sweet. One of his friends always seemed nearby.

"Disguised as a nurse, I strolled to the nursery and avoided the gaze of the few sleepy doctors and nurses who lingered on the floor. One nurse was on duty—another friend. We shared a look, and she left. Three newly born babies slept in bassinets. All three were quiet. You were easy to spot. Even then you looked like your mother. I lifted you in my arms, kissed you on top of your newly born squished head, and unwrapped the white cotton blanket that bound you."

He touched my knee, and I held my breath. "I took a leather pouch from my pocket, removed an ancient needle blessed by the Great Wind Spirit, and found the sole of your right foot. I asked the Wind Spirit for strength before blessing your foot with the needle. You screeched, but your scream quickly died away when you stopped breathing. Your face turned blue and my heart raced, worry bubbling up inside of me. Time ticked past. I counted fifty seconds before I breathed life back into you.

"You began to breathe and cry again. Relief washed over me like a river over smooth stones. I wrapped you back in the blanket, returned you to the small basinet, turned, and left." Sicheii squeezed my knee and lifted his hand back. "We are the only ones who know this story. You need to remember it." Watery tears filled his eyes.

"Why would you do something like that? Were you crazy? Who does that?"

He stood without looking at me. The chair rolled away from the bed and bumped into the desk. He spun and strolled from the room, leaving me alone without answering any of my questions. I followed him downstairs, still peppering him with questions. *What was in the needle? Where did you get it?* He acted as if he didn't hear me and walked out the front door without saying goodbye to Mom.

When he left, I raced to the kitchen and asked Mom about his story. She bristled. Their relationship was best described as a seesaw, one end frosty and bitter, the other warm and loving. They argued often then, the seesaw tilting firmly in the frosty direction. She told me he had made up the story and for me not to worry about it. I wasn't sure what to believe.

That night, I took a flashlight and stared down at my right sole. I brushed fuzz from my sock away and found a small star-shaped scar.

CHAPTER

Everything about me is a lie.

My entire life is a leaning tower of lies that threatens to collapse at any moment and bury me so deep I may never climb out from under the rubble.

I slam the bathroom door and my hand trembles as the old-fashioned steel bolt slides into place.

Click.

The locked door offers no real safety. Locked doors can be broken, but it does give me a moment of privacy and a chance to breathe. So much has happened over the past few days. It's like I've become a totally different person, someone unrecognizable.

The adrenaline that had been pumping through my veins has completely melted away now as I lean against the wooden door. My breath comes fast and ragged. My body feels heavy and weary and my legs weaken. Gravity pulls me down. Too

8

tired to resist, I slide down the length of the door until the white marble floor rushes up to meet me.

I work hard to steady my breath and focus on taking in fresh air, expelling the old. It's a simple process, yet it takes all of my concentration. When air starts to flow, my eyes close. Time slows and drifts by erratically.

Images flash through my mind—an eclectic group of memories: childhood birthdays, second place in a spelling bee, hanging out with Troy, rock climbing with Sicheii. Most are happy, but they're all tainted now. The lies spoil them. They were never true. They were just part of a story, one that's changed forever.

My weary mind reaches for sleep, but I resist. Too much time would be wasted. There's too much for me to do. Too many loose ends need to be tied, so I open moist eyes and wipe away tears I don't recall crying.

When my vision clears, crimson-streaked fingers flutter near my face as if directed by someone else. I thought blood looked like ketchup, but it's darker and thicker than you would think. My hands spin in tight circles. Each finger is stained with thick, mud-colored smears.

Whose blood is on them?

A cold sweat coats my back and my chest tightens. This blood must be scrubbed away immediately. It starts to burn as if it's alive, as if possessed by dark spirits, spirits that want to harm me. It freaks me out. I have got to wash them clean now, this second, immediately, before....

I turn the faucet and hot water tumbles over my skin. I frantically rub my fingers together and hope friction and water alone will make the blood disappear. The water in the sink turns red and then pink, but traces of blood stubbornly stay behind. A bar of soap rests on the edge of the porcelain sink. Lather squishes between my fingers—twisting and turning, scrubbing and rinsing. My skin turns raw from the rubbing, and when the water has lost all its warmth, I turn the faucet off.

Hard to find specks of blood cling to my flesh, but I still see them and feel them.

Will they ever wipe clean? I don't think so.

A silent scream builds deep within me, which so desperately wants to be released it practically hurts, but no sound slips past my lips. I'm too tired to scream.

A square mirror hangs over the sink, but it's an enemy. I don't want to see who I've become, so my gaze stays fixed down toward the sink. Unfortunately, the blood-smeared faucet is shiny, stainless, and reflects back an image of myself anyway. I glare deep into my eyes, leaning close to the faucet to study them. They look familiar, but as I pierce them more deeply, a hollowness appears that has never been there before. It scares me.

People change. Sometimes they change over the course of a lifetime, and other times change happens swiftly because of a single momentous event. I'm not the same person I was just a few days ago. Too much has happened, too many lies revealed. Truths, solid and real, have crumbled away before me and left behind falsehoods, shadows, and a future as uncertain as a prisoner on death row waiting for a pardon.

The pendant Sicheii gave me flops out from underneath my shirt. It was supposed to protect me. I grip it until my knuckles turn white.

Knock! Knock! Knock!

"Juliet, we've got to talk, Love. We need to come up with a story for the police."

Just a few days ago, I was an average teenaged girl who looked forward to her sixteenth birthday, hoping for a little freedom and a chance to get a driver's license.

Being average is a joke. I will never be average. I was never average....

CHAPTER 2

A few days earlier...

Moms invented mornings to torture their daughters. It's the only thing that makes sense. Nothing worth doing needs to start at seven in the morning. Weekends are awesome mostly because I can sleep late and linger in bed until eleven or later. Most days, I'd like to sleep until afternoon, but Mom never lets me stay in bed past twelve. She thinks I'm wasting my life away. Still, this is a school day and sleeping late is not an option.

"Wake up, sweetheart."

The words drift toward me, alien at first until my sleepy brain puts them in the correct order and makes sense of them. Realization dawns on me. I stuff my head under my pillow and seek safety, hoping to shield myself from this awful affront.

Mom's voice turns stormy. "Wake up!" *Sweetheart* vanishes as she wraps razor-sharp barbed wire around her words.

I moan, roll over, and peek at the alarm clock. The fuzzy orange numbers read 5:30. She has to be kidding. It's inhumane to wake up this early.

Argh!

I jam my head back under the pillow and wish it were larger and soundproof.

When can I go back to sleep?

Light floods the room when Mom flips the switch. Suddenly, I remember why she's waking me up. She needs to catch an early flight for business, so she woke me earlier than usual to make sure I would be ready to take the bus.

"Don't make me take *extreme measures.*" Her voice is serious and rich with tension. It's her no-nonsense voice, the one she often uses for work calls.

I've missed more than my share of school busses over the years, so she's quick to ratchet up her terrorist-like tactics *to extreme measures*. Usually they start when she rips off my sheets and twice have escalated to ice cubes down my shirt. She's serious, so I groan something unintelligible, push my pillow to one side and crack open my eyes, which is practically heroic under the circumstances.

She's already dressed and hovers beside the bed in a plain white silk blouse, gray slacks and hands clutched to her hips. I promise to get up, but the words get tangled up with sleep and are practically unrecognizable. Still, it placates her enough that she stalks out of my room after tossing out a final warning about me falling back to sleep.

For a second, sleep pulls at me. I start to doze off when I remember the last ice incident. Not pleasant, and Mom's anxiety over her business trip will only make this one worse.

I open my eyes with an impressive amount of willpower,

stagger to my feet, bump into the bedpost, stub my toes hard against the doorframe, see stars, clutch my damaged foot, and hop into the bathroom. Luckily, there are no serious injuries — nothing but a red bruise — so I turn the water on in the shower.

Hair still wet, I search for my school uniform under a pile of clean clothes that never made it into the dresser. Despite my best intentions, they never do.

A light buzzing sound hums in my head as I yank out a fresh Bartens shirt. I do my best to ignore the noise. It just started one day. At first, it sounded like static, but since then it has grown louder and has begun to sound like voices. I think the voices want to tell me things, possibly important messages, but they make no sense.

It's annoying. No one else knows about them. Mom would definitely overreact if she found out. My plan is to ignore them. It might not be the best plan, but it's better than seeing Dr. Schmidt, our family physician, and being attacked by the Old Spice cloud that hovers around him. Hopefully, the voices will either tell me something important or go away on their own, so I shake my head and busy myself with getting dressed.

When I go downstairs, no one specific thing seems out of place, but the air is heavy, as if tension is spinning away from Mom in precise circles. She's headed out of town for two days to a convention in Scottsdale. She works as a lawyer who helps rich people avoid paying taxes. I'm sure there's much more to her job than that, but the details are a blur. She's great at what she does, but spends way too much time at work and should, in my opinion, have more fun and find a nice guy. I tried to set her up with a teacher from my old school two years ago, but that went nowhere.

She rests one hand on the black granite island in the kitchen with a mug of hot coffee perched in front of her. Her day never starts without two cups, always black. A crossword puzzle rests next to her mug. She never has problems with them, but this time she's only finished two thirds of it, and her letters look like they were carved into the paper with a chisel.

Her pretty oval face is tense with lines around the edges of her eyes and lips. She twirls her long black hair in tight circles, a sure sign she's worried about something. My internal alarm goes to yellow alert. This is the first time she's leaving me alone. I'm almost sixteen. *What could happen in a few days?*

"What do you want for breakfast?" Her eyes flicker to the time on the kitchen wall clock.

"I'll have some peanut butter and apples." I start to head for the refrigerator.

"Sit. I'll grab it for you." She swings the refrigerator door open and grabs an apple and a jar of peanut butter.

She hasn't made me breakfast in years. Yellow alert turns orange. I eye her suspiciously when she places the plate in front of me.

More hair twirling and another glance at the clock. Orange turns a light shade of red! "Mom, relax. Everything is going to be fine while you're away. Two days is not a long time. The house won't be destroyed."

She smiles thinly. "About that, *sweetheart.*" She pauses.

It might be early, but self-preservation kicks in. The return of *sweetheart* is ominous, and that pause means trouble. Something is wrong.

I narrow my eyes. "What did you do? You didn't hire a college kid like last time." I cross my arms over my chest. "That

15

was a disaster. She had friends over until two in the morning. They smoked and ate all the food."

"No, Juliet." She averts her eyes and stares down at her coffee mug as if she's found a miniature boat floating in her morning drink and it's the most interesting thing in the world.

My heart thumps. This is going to be bad. My alert turns deep red.

"Your grandfather is coming over to spend a few days while I'm gone. He'll be here by the time you return from school."

My stomach lurches. The buzzing in my head turns into a loud screech that makes me wince. "Not Sicheii! The college student would be better." I rise from my seat. I'm tall for my age, but she's still an inch taller. She glares down at me, ready for the fight, her eyes hot and her face flushed with color.

"I can't believe you're doing this to me!"

"Juliet Wildfire Stone, there's nothing wrong with your grandfather! You can spend a few days alone with him, and it won't be the end of the world. He loves you and that's final."

I cringe when she uses my full name. An out of control wildfire dominated the news the day after my birth, so "Wildfire" became my middle name. I shudder to think what would have happened if there was a garbage strike. Only a few people even know about it.

"Sicheii's weird. He's so...."

"Native American." She clutches her hands against her hips. "I don't understand how this happened. You were such good friends when you were younger. He taught you how to rock climb and swim. You used to spend so much time together."

"That was years ago. Before we moved here and you made me switch to Bartens."

"What does Bartens have to do with your grandfather?" She scrunches up her nose and squints her eyes. It's the same look she gets when she tries to help me with my algebra homework. Usually I feel sorry for her when she gets like that, but not now.

"Really, Mom?" I say through clenched teeth. *Can she be this clueless?* My trouble with Sicheii has *everything* to do with my new exclusive private school. I don't care if his beliefs are old fashioned. Old doesn't make them wrong. But they pull me in the opposite directions of Bartens. He doesn't care about Ivy League colleges, or fancy vacations, or high paying jobs. Not like they do at my new school. Sometimes I feel like a rubber band, pulled in two different directions. At some point, the band snaps.

I can't explain this to Mom now, especially because I'm pissed, so I take the easy way out. "I'm the only one with Native American blood in the whole place. It's impossible for me to fit in. Why did we have to move here in the first place and leave my old school? I hate Bartens. Home schooling would be better."

She rolls her eyes in that annoying dismissive way she does that drives me crazy. "We moved two years ago, and you're not the only one with Indian blood at Bartens. Besides, it's a much better school than your last one. There were too many *undesirables* at your last school."

Undesirables is her code word for my friends.

"You just need to become more involved. Why don't you play lacrosse? You're a terrific lacrosse player. The school team could certainly use you."

"You don't get it! I'd be the crazy half-blood Indian girl playing lacrosse. They'd never let me hear the end of it. You

17

don't understand how hard it is for me over there. Everybody is so... white and rich."

Mom's face softens. Her skin loses a little of its angry red hue, returning to her natural copper color and her brown eyes widen. Under normal circumstances, her eyes are large and beautiful, but when she gets all motherly and widens them, they take over her face until it is impossible not to become lost in the rich, coffee colored swirls. I'll never be as beautiful as she is. My nose is longish and pointy, and my eyes aren't nearly as wide as hers.

"How many Native American partners do you think there are at Dormit and Will?"

I turn my back on her. It's so annoying when she gets like this—all factual and logical and right.

She's trying to trap me, but I won't fall for it. I return to my best argument with my back still turned to her. "Why can't you trust me? I'm old enough to be on my own for two days. I don't need Sicheii doing his weird stuff around here." Panic strikes. I spin in a tight circle and lean against the table with both hands. "He's not going to pick me up at school, is he?" Air sticks in my throat.

"No, Jules, he'll just be at the house. None of your friends at school will even know he's here." She manages a weak smile.

I can breathe again. "I don't have any friends at Bartens except Katie." I look away, my head hung low.

"What about Tiffany and Ashley and what's her name?"

My jaw drops. Could it be that she hasn't listened to a word I've said over the past two years? "Do you mean *Morgan*?"

"Yes, that's her name. They seem nice."

She must be kidding. Bartens teams up each new student with a mentor. In my case, it was Morgan—the super popular,

Barbie look alike, head cheerleader with a giant trust fund who wants plastic surgery on her perfectly fine nose for her sixteenth birthday. She invited me to a party during my first month at school where she made it clear that I wasn't her *kind* of girl. To her, Native Americans had no place at Bartens.

No one spoke to me at that party except Katie, which put her on the outs with the *popular* crowd almost immediately. But that wasn't the worst part. The party had a Native American theme, including a viewing of *Pocahontas* in the giant-sized media room. *Pocahontas!* I hate that movie. It's the white man's version of the perfect hot Native American girl.

I stayed all night and even choked down some of the tepee shaped cake they wheeled in on a cart with "welcome" written across it. They weren't going to get the satisfaction of running me off, even if that was the longest night of my life.

"Mom, those girls are like a pack of super mean spoiled sharks. They're the last girls I'd be friends with." *How could she be so clueless?* Besides, it might sound lame, but I was looking forward to two days of freedom. I didn't have any particular plans except for catching up on a few television shows and maybe having Troy over.

Mom's lips purse in that way she does when she feels sorry for me, and then a horn honks from the driveway. "I'm sure there are other girls who would make better friends at the school. You just need to be more outgoing." She checks the clock on the wall. It's 6:15, and she sighs. "I've got to go. We'll come up with a strategy about Bartens when I come home."

She loves strategy sessions. They never work.

She bends down to kiss me, but I strategically step back out of reach. She scowls at me instead. "Do what your grandfather

19

says. Be respectful." She walks to the front door where her Tumi carry on bag waits.

"I'll call you later." She opens the door. "Love you."

She waits for me to say I love her back, but I'm still angry and won't do it. She shuts the door, strolls down the walkway, and slips into the silver sedan that waits for her without looking back. The sun is out, and the day promises to be steamy. As the car motors away, my anger increases in intensity.

I'm old enough to take care of myself! Sicheii will be a disaster. He doesn't need to watch after me.

The edge of my iPhone digs into my leg. I'm dressed in the Bartens uniform—blue slacks and a white collared shirt with the stupid logo on the chest. It makes me angrier. I reach into my pocket, remove my phone, and speed-dial Troy.

By the time the phone rings twice, I'm about to hang up when a sleepy voice answers, "Hey."

I hesitate, but there's no backing out now. "Want to cut today? It's too sunny to go to school."

"It's six in the morning."

"Pick me up in two hours. We can go to Slippery River and hang out."

Troy hates school so he'll be happy to spend the day at the river.

"Okay, I'll pick you up," he says, his voice still gravelly.

I hang up and stuff my phone back into my pocket. I've never cut school before and instantly regret my decision. Still, she should have trusted me. She forced me to do it. I stomp my right foot and pain stabs my heel.

It's a searing pain in the shape of a small star.

20

CHAPTER 3

Troy sees the world in black and white. Sometimes his certainty makes me jealous. My world seems filled with grays—some dark and others light, but rarely any certainty.

Both of his parents are Native American, and he looks the part with caramel skin and long, straight, raven-colored hair twisted in a braid that falls past his shoulder blades. He's never cut his hair. One time, I grabbed a pair of scissors and threatened to lop off his braid. He got angry. He believes long hair is a sign of power and spiritual strength. He'll never let anyone touch it.

Even though he knows the password to enter our gated community, the security guard calls to confirm he's a *wanted* guest. He'll be pissed. He takes slights like that worse than I do, so I wait for him on the edge of the driveway and worry our day will start off on a bad note.

I hear his bike, a 1980 Honda CX motorcycle painted in the original royal blue, before it rolls into view. He found it at a junkyard and worked on it for six months until he got it back on the road. Now the bike runs better than it did when new, but it's loud. He likes it that way.

He pulls the bike three quarters of the way up my driveway, and the tires stick to the hot pavement. He kicks down the kickstand, pulls off his helmet, and slides from the seat. Faded blue jeans cling to his legs and an extra-large, plain white t-shirt fits tightly against his chest and shoulders. Troy is big. He doesn't have a sculpted physique like you'd find on workout shows, but muscles grow on his body like powdered sugar accumulates on funnel cake.

"Outstanding security guard you've got. Does he treat all your guests the same way, or only the brown ones?" Fire blazes behind his eyes.

I smirk in hopes of dousing the flames. "Only the ugly ones with loud bikes." Troy is definitely not ugly, and he knows it. His chiseled jaw and deep set, almond colored eyes give him a pensive expression, as if he's really listening. Girls love him.

"Right." His tone is chilly, but the edges of his lips turn up and form the beginning of a smile so I know we're out of the woods.

My neighbor, Mrs. Jones, pulls back her living room curtains and stares at us through her front window. She's the neighborhood gossip and one nasty drunk. She's probably fifty years old, but looks like a hundred. Too many drinks and too much sun have sucked the joy and life from her. Rumor has it she was *Miss Arizona* twenty-eight years ago. It's hard to see her in the pictures on the web, but it's possible. I had hoped to sneak out without her knowing, but Troy's bike is too loud and she has a sixth sense for snooping.

She wasn't happy when we moved in—a single mother, and even worse, a single Native American mother and her teenaged daughter. But for the last two years, we've given her nothing to gossip about. Now a sharp guilt pang stabs me in the ribs. She'll tell everyone about her truant teenaged neighbor and her wild looking friend. She'll say she knew we were no good all along, that we were trouble, that our kind can't be trusted.

Why should I care what she does? But heat flushes my cheeks anyway.

Troy follows my eyes and glances over in Mrs. Jones's direction. Her stare deepens into a glare. She clutches a phone in her right hand and a glass that's probably filled with something a lot stronger than orange juice in the other.

He blows her a kiss, and she flips him the bird.

Troy smiles. "I like her. She's a nasty shriveled up person, but at least you know where you stand. There's no phony garbage with her."

"Great."

"So what gives? It's not like you to skip school."

I manage my best shrug with a backpack strapped on my shoulders. "My mom is out of town, so why not have some fun? Why waste such a great day by going to Bartens?"

"What's the rest of the story, Jules? You told me last week that your mom was going away for a few days. We could have made plans then and avoided the early morning wake-up call." He shoots me a knowing look. This is the problem with best friends. Even though we don't hang out as often as we used to, he still knows me better than anyone else. "What happened?"

I sigh. "Mom's got my grandfather staying with me for a few days. She should trust me." I hope to escape with a half-truth. He doesn't need to know about my problems at school. He'll take them poorly. He'll say I should be proud of my roots and tell the others to piss off. He might even stop by Bartens with some of our other Native American friends just to make a point. He could be like that sometimes — full of surprises, a little dangerous.

"Right," he says in a tone of voice that tells me he doesn't really believe me. "I don't understand what the problem is. Your grandfather is cool, way cooler than mine."

"Let's roll." I step past Troy and toward the bike. "Slippery River is calling us."

He tosses me his heavy all black behemoth of a helmet with a plastic face shield.

I catch it, but keep it at arm's length. "Where's the other helmet? I'll use that one." I wrinkle my nose at the odor. Troy's spare helmet is small and light and doesn't have a face guard or the sweaty smell.

"The chin strap snapped on that one." He smiles. "I need to fix it. This is all I've got."

"You wear it." I shove the monster in his direction. "You're the one who's driving."

He jumps on the bike and melts into the seat. "The way I see it, your grandfather will kill me if anything happens to you anyway. At least one of us will survive if we crash." He starts the bike with a kick. The engine roars as he revs it with a sly grin on his face and a glance at Mrs. Jones. "Put it on or we can hang out here all day with your neighbor gawking at us. It's your choice." He beams a smile at me.

A tickle climbs up my back. Sometimes his smile does that to me. I reluctantly strap on the helmet and hop on the back of the bike. Troy blows Mrs. Jones another kiss and glides us out of the driveway. We leave the gated community behind and travel in the opposite direction of Bartens. I love the rush that comes with riding Troy's bike, so my arms wrap around his waist and a smile slowly sneaks on my face.

Anything is possible on a day like this one.

CHAPTER

Freedom has a certain smell—sweet and fresh like dew on a spring day. It lingers in your nose and lungs and fuels your soul. I sniff a heavy dose as we reach Slippery River and the promise of a lazy afternoon. It chases away the guilt I feel over cutting school.

Twenty-five years ago, the Tribe owned Slippery River. The town took over the land to increase tourism and pays the Tribe only a third of what they make in admissions fees during a year. A bad deal, but the judge ruled in the town's favor. The weather is supposed to turn hot, so tourists flock to the park in disorderly groups of loud, sunburned, flip-flop wearing beer guzzlers.

Troy drives us through a little used side entrance to avoid the main gate and the fifteen-dollar entrance fee. He parks the bike off the pavement on the far end of the lot and secures it to a tree with a heavy chain. Dozens of tourists meander toward the middle of the park. A mild expression of disgust sprouts on my face. One twenty-something-year-old guy, wearing a ripped Black Sabbath t-shirt, huffs along while dragging a dented cooler I imagine is crammed full of beer for him and his two buddies. All three are pale like ghosts and will burn within the hour. As locals, we have the right to feel superior to tourists, so we shoot them one last disdainful smirk and flee northwest in the opposite direction, away from the marked trails and the main part of the park.

A mile upstream, Slippery River turns wide, deep, and lazy. As the river approaches the park, the water carves a path through a canyon, narrows, and picks up speed. It's called "Slippery River" because the moss-covered riverbed makes the footing slick. Most visitors start upriver and let the water pull them downriver like a natural amusement park ride, screeching the entire way.

Sicheii took me to the main part of the park a long time ago, but we came at night during a full moon when no one else was around. We never told Mom. She would have thought our sortie was too dangerous. Sicheii's definition of dangerous is different from hers.

My legs start to burn as we squeeze our way along a narrow game trail, and I scrape my elbow on a rock jutting into the path. When we reach a particularly steep stretch, Troy pulls me up effortlessly with one strong hand. Fifteen minutes later, we find our favorite spot underneath a soapberry tree with just enough leaves to shade us from the worst part of the morning sun.

From the lofty perch, we stare down at the river far below. I glance at Troy and let him decide if he wants to keep going since I dragged him out of bed this morning. We can continue to the top of the cliff, but the rest of the climb is steep and it's not worth it.

"Why don't we stop here? There's plenty of room to stretch out under the tree."

I nod, toss down the backpack, and settle under the soapberry's branches. "What's the latest between Ella and Marlon?"

"They're still in *love*." He shakes his head and his braid flops from side to side on his back. "They're the most unlikely couple in the universe of unlikely couples. Ella is still on track to be valedictorian and Marlon's majoring in shop. And *majoring* is being generous."

I smile and time slows. Since we don't see each other in school every day, I miss these conversations. "What's the latest about the casino? Are they paying bonuses this year?"

"My dad says the casino is packed every night, but you know the management company." He rolls his eyes. "Somehow they always just barely break even, so they never have to pay bonuses. We should have listened to your grandfather. He said they'd steal from us. They're supposed to give the Tribe part of the profit, but we haven't seen a dime in five years." He unzips the backpack and takes out a bag of Doritos and a tin of chocolate chip cookies.

I grab a handful of chips before he munches through them all and look out across the canyon. Devil's Peak spirals dangerously high in the near distance on the other side of the river. No one's ever climbed the soaring collection of red rocks. My mouth drops a little as it always does when I gaze at it. It's beautiful and dangerous at the same time. I point to the crest of the formation. "It looks like Satan is watching us today."

As a young girl, Sicheii showed me how the rock formation changes with the light. We had climbed to the top of the cliff opposite Devil's Peak. When we reached the edge, he pointed out the profile of the Devil's face carved into the rock, complete with horns at the peak. Then he made me close my eyes and told me a long winding tale of how the Great Wind Spirit defeated the Devil when time began. At the end of the story, he let me open my eyes and pointed to the rock formation with a sly smile on his face. The Devil's face was gone and replaced by ordinary rocks. "The Great Wind Spirit was victorious again," he pronounced with a wry smile.

Troy huffs. "I don't know why we call it Devil's Peak. The face looks like Coyote to me."

"What's the difference, Coyote or Devil? Either way, it's a dark spirit."

"They're different. Coyote is *our* dark spirit. The Devil has nothing to do with us." His voice has an edge to it. He grabs another handful of Doritos and glares out into the distance.

Troy is right. Coyote is different from the Devil. He's a dark spirit who tricks people into bad behavior, but he's not all bad. Sometimes he protects animals and Mother Earth from humans, but it seems like he's fallen down on the job lately. Either way, I'm not going to challenge him on dark spirits. They're all the same to me.

I pull a sketchpad from my backpack and notice a handful of fishermen by the base of the rock formation. Among the fisherman, a father is teaching his young son how to cast a rod. I start drawing them both while Troy closes his eyes and listens to his iPod, which is really my old iPod. Mom bought me a new iPhone for Christmas.

Time stretches on quietly while I sketch. A smile sticks to my face as a warm sensation fills my body like the inside of a jelly donut. "What has Ms. Combs been up to?"

"She's been promoted to the principle of the middle school."

My sketchpad drops in my lap. "No, it can't be. She was a horrible teacher! She never liked me."

"She didn't like me any better. At least she won't be dividing kids into reading groups and sorting some in the D group like she did for us. What did Matt Flynn tell you again?"

I chuckle and answer even though he knows exactly what he said. "He said *D* was for dummies, so I told him *K* was for kick, right before I kicked him in the nuts."

Troy laughs a full body laugh. I can't help but join. His laugh is contagious.

"He was twice as big as you. If I didn't jump on him, he might have sat on you and squashed you."

"Yes, you were my hero." I playfully bat my eyes at him.

"That's not the only time I've saved you from fights." He starts ticking off names with his fingers and chuckles as he goes. "Joyce Janice, Michael Rivers, Michele Mason, Jason Hill—"

"You had better stop right now, or we're going to have a problem. It's not my fault they pissed me off."

He lifts his fists in a play-fighting stance. "I'm ready for you." We both burst into combustible laughter. It feels good to laugh with him, like I'm wearing my most comfortable sweatshirt. I can just *be* when we're together. *Why is it so hard for me to be that way with other people?*

I turn back to my drawing before the fishermen leave, add some finishing touches, and close my eyes to enjoy the warm sun on my face. The heat overpowers me as I slip into a daydream.

I'm in a cave, standing close to a small fire. Flickering firelight swirls along the cave walls. Jagged rock configurations appear and disappear with the fire's dance. White wisps of smoke spiral upward and vanish into an opening in the craggy ceiling. Next to the fire sits an old man, cross-legged, a stoic expression on his lined face. Sweat coats his face and bare chest. He wears only a leather wrap connected at his waist, and his long gray hair is tied behind his neck. His back is straight and stiff, but his eyes dance around the cave nervously. Still, strength lives in him, in his sharp jaw, bright eyes, and broad shoulders. I sense movement and know we are not alone, but I can't turn.

The old man speaks, his voice strong and clear. The language is old and weathered, like something Sicheii might say during a ceremonial feast, but I've never learned the old language, so the words drift toward me, meaningless syllables in the flickering light.

A long metal brand emerges from the fire, glowing angrily. The unseen guest must be holding it. Smoke swirls around the end of the marker, masking its shape. The old man tenses but does not budge. The brand inches toward his chest. Violet colored eyes, intense and demanding, reflect off the long metal rod. The brand scorches the old man in the chest. It sizzles when the marker kisses his skin, but he doesn't cry out. Tears flow from his eyes, but they don't look sorrowful. The stench of burned flesh fills my nose. It smells rank, like death and responsibility. I jolt awake, body trembling, breath rapid.

I glance around, relieved to find the soapberry tree and Troy and Slippery River, all as they should be. People say you can't smell while you sleep, but I don't believe them. Smells often linger after my daydreams, like they do with this one.

I push the last vestiges of the daydream from my mind with a mental shove. Luckily, they fade quickly from my consciousness. One time, Sicheii suggested I study them to understand my ancestors' messages, but I'd rather push them from my mind. Who wants messages from their ancestors like texts from the grave? Life should be lived in the present and the future, which, as far as I can tell, has little to do with my heritage or my ancestors.

An empty bag of Doritos rubs against Troy's sneaker. His head rests against the backpack, eyes closed as he listens to his music. The light bounces off his hair, which has grown longer from the last time we were together almost two weeks ago. I miss seeing him every day and knowing the important things going on in his life that we never text or talk about—whether his father is hassling him, or which girls have crushes on him.

For a moment I imagine him with short hair and in a Bartens uniform. The fuzzy image refuses to focus in my mind mostly because he would never cut his hair or wear the stupid uniform. I shake my head and frown. I'm being selfish. He'd be miserable without the Tribe or the rush of wind on his bike that ruffles his hair or his mysterious camping trips.

I yank one of his ear buds from his ears. He's not listening to music, but an audio book instead.

"Hey!" Troy swivels his head toward me.

I frown, and he pulls off the other ear bud.

"Still having a difficult time with the dyslexia?" Even with the reading disorder, Troy is incredibly smart. He can perfectly recall everything he hears, but his teachers give him a hard time about his reading, so he constantly struggles in school. If his family was rich and he went to Bartens, the school would find a way to get around his learning disability and he'd be an *A* student.

He shrugs. "If I listen to the books, at least I'll pass English."

"You need to work on those exercises the school counselor gave you." I shoot him my most disappointed scowl. He can be so pigheaded. He spent three months finding the exact original color paint to fix his bike, but he refuses to work on his dyslexia. "You're not going to make it through college by listening to books on your iPod."

"I'm not going to college, Jules." He glances farther up the rock canyon away from me. "We both realize it. I'll work as a mechanic in town with my uncle. There's not a car that's ever been made that I can't fix."

"You're too smart to give up on school. If you do the exercises, you can overcome the dyslexia. Other people get past it." We've had this argument in one fashion or another dozens of times over the past five years. He deserves a future brighter than anything this small town could offer him. *We* deserve something better, and I can't imagine my future without him in it.

"I've tried, but the letters mix up. There's nothing I can do about it." He balls his hands into fists and pounds his right hand into his thigh.

I'm about to start round two of our fight when a high-pitched shriek startles me. A red shouldered hawk circles through the air currents high above us. This type of hawk is Sicheii's animal guide. He believes hawks warn him about pending trouble, so I always pay close attention to them. Something about the call strikes me as odd. A bush sways awkwardly in the ridge above us, but there's no wind. A biting chill runs through me.

No one else can see us from our remote location, and no one knows we're at Slippery River. Suddenly, I feel vulnerable, like we've strayed too far from the herd. "Let's get out of here."

Troy squints at the sun, which has traveled well past midday. "Sure, it's getting late. I've got to help my uncle in the garage later anyway." He rises and stretches with a soft groan.

The hair on the back of my neck stands on end as I stuff our trash into the backpack. Faint noises that sound like footsteps come from the ledge above us. I swing the backpack on my shoulders and walk to the edge of the cliff. We need to get to the river fast, and the trek down will take too long. "Lets dive." I smile at him. It's forced, but luckily he doesn't notice.

He peers over the cliff and shrugs. A deep river pocket is right below us where we can safely land. "We'll have to dive over seventy feet to the river."

I know the jump is good with him. He's a great cliff diver, but the shrug leaves the window open for me to back out.

Another high-pitched hawk call shrieks from above. Something or someone is closing in on us. It might sound ridiculous, but Sicheii taught me to trust my instincts. He believes they come from spirits we cannot see.

"Are you chicken?" A shadow appears on the ledge just above us. There's only one way to ensure that he'll dive, so I cram my iPhone in a waterproof pocket in my backpack, take a few steps back, and run for it. I kick up stones and leap with a screech. I'm suspended in air for a second, and then plummet to the river. Wind whips through my hair as my long legs knife into the water and the cool river embraces me. Two kicks and I break the surface with a smile on my face.

34

Troy follows with a loud splash. He clears the water smoothly and chops water at me with both of his hands. I laugh and forget what compelled me to jump in the first place and counterattack with a two-handed splash of my own.

All is good until the hawk calls one last time. I glance up as the bird flies north and get that same unsettling feeling as before.

CHAPTER 5

We splash the river at each other for a few more minutes, but the water is frigid, so we swim to the bank. Without a towel, the sun will have to dry us. Luckily, it's still hot as we follow a trail toward the parking lot.

When we near Troy's Honda, we turn a corner in the game trail and hear beer cans crunch, rock music blare, and something that sounds like water flowing from a hose—all signs drunk college students are hanging out by his bike.

We share a look, and he says, "Crap" right before he sprints ahead. I race a step behind. Drunken college kids are worse than nasty raccoons, and our town collects them like a cactus does needles.

Three students have surrounded Troy's bike. Crushed beer cans have been tossed about and a small, gross looking puddle sits right by his back tire. The student closest to the puddle fumbles with his fly.

"Hey, move away from my bike," Troy shouts as he slows into the clearing.

All three guys appear sloshed with flushed faces and unsteady gaits. Two stand off to the right and one farther from the rest to the left nearest to the bike. They all have "State" t-shirts on with different designs. Of the three, the middle one looks the most dangerous. He seems the steadiest with beady, calculating eyes.

The guy farthest to the right is the largest, his thick arms bulging with muscles. The extra extra large white and red t-shirt he's wearing says "Rugby" on it and barely fits over his barrel-chested frame. "Cool bike," he mutters with a smirk. He must weigh fifty pounds more than Troy.

The beady-eyed fella sweeps his vision over Troy and sneers. "I want to take it for a ride. Tell me the combo for the lock."

Troy tenses, the vein in his neck pulses, and his body coils. He looks explosive. "No one needs to get hurt." He lifts both of his hands above his head. "Just step away, and we'll take off."

The student on the left wobbles toward me. His greasy hair hangs down to his shoulders. Sunburns blotches his face and arms and he grins stupidly. He's thin, about my height, and reeks of beer and stale cigarettes.

"You're cute. Why don't you come with me and leave the *chief* with them?" He stumbles a half step toward me.

His two friends snicker.

I turn to face the greasy haired idiot. He's only a little wider and heavier than me. His eyes are dilated and glassy and he smirks like a spoiled child in an ice cream shop. I smile at him and wave him closer. "Boy, you're a real prize, aren't you?"

The dope doesn't hear my sarcastic tone and continues to stagger unsteadily toward me. Beer in the form of sweat pours down the sides of his face. He stops five feet away and flashes me crooked, yellowish teeth. He's only one step away.

I glance at Troy and say, "K."

He shrugs. "Is for kick."

I turn back to the drunk and boot him right in the balls with all my weight behind the kick. He seizes up into a fetal position and collapses on the dirt. One hand grabs his privates while the other pounds the ground. He mutters something. It's hard to make out, but it sounds like he wants his mother.

When I turn, Troy has already grabbed Rugby Shirt by the arm and twisted hard. When he squeals, Troy drives his elbow into his arm. The bone breaks, but Beady Eyes lands a right hook against Troy's jaw when he isn't looking. The punch sends him spinning.

I don't like Beady Eyes's confident swagger as he stalks after Troy. My chest tightens. I move toward him ready to jump on his back when my foot kicks the ridiculously large and slightly smelly helmet.

Troy straightens himself and darts at Beady Eyes, clenching his arms around his waist. I grab the helmet and step toward them. Beady Eyes hits Troy with another right, this time in the side, and Troy grimaces.

My eyes narrow. The helmet feels heavy in my hand. I focus on the back of Beady Eyes's head and swing it down hard, bashing it into his skull. He goes limp and tumbles to the ground.

I turn to face Rugby Guy who's holding his right arm gently with his left. He's sweating profusely and fear fills the white portion of his wild looking eyes. He speaks fast and groans a little at the end. "We're just messing around. We didn't mean *nothing*. I think my arm's broken, man."

Troy moves next to me. "Step away from my bike."

"No problem. Just keep away from me." Rugby Guy joins his greasy haired friend who's still groaning and squirming on the ground off to the side.

Troy works the lock to the chain while I watch over the two drunks. In a minute, he starts the bike and spins the back tire, spraying loose stones at Beady Eyes, who starts to moan and throws up.

Did my earlier unease have anything to do with the college kids?

As I leap on the back, the creepy feeling returns and settles in my bones. No, something else is wrong.

CHAPTER

Troy navigates the bike along the narrow side road that leads out of the park. Tension knots his back.

"I wish we could ban drunk college kids from our town," I yell in his ear. "Now I've paid you back for Matt Flynn."

He chuckles and the rigidity is gone. "That still leaves Janice Joyce, and—"

I punch him on the shoulder. "What did I say about that on the cliff?"

We both laugh as he turns left on Route 100. He opens the throttle, and the wind embraces me and distracts me from the horrible things I'm sure Mom will do once she learns that I skipped school. My distraction is short lived because sirens wail behind us and I jump.

Troy glances in the side mirror and grumbles under his breath. "What now? I hope my dad hasn't done anything else."

Troy's relationship with the sheriff's department is sketchy. Nothing seriously bad, but his dad gets into bar fights, so they like to know what he's up to. Small towns suck that way. I want to live somewhere big like New York or Paris or London, a city where no one knows my family tree or his, and we can be free to be ourselves without the past getting in the way.

When he slows the bike, the two police cars scream past us with a *whoosh*, sirens blaring. "I wonder what that's about?" I shout, trying to compete with the wind. "When was the last time two police cars raced in the same direction?"

"Let's find out. That's Sheriff Daniels's car." He twists the accelerator, and the Honda spurs forward. The wind roars and I'm flying. I tighten my arms around his waist and my body bends toward his. I can feel his heartbeat through his t-shirt. He smells like summer.

Within a few miles, the police cars turn right onto Canyon Avenue. "They're headed into the Reservation," Troy says. His body stiffens, and the knot returns. He lives in the Reservation.

The Reservation isn't technically a *real* reservation. It's paradise when compared to the real Rez, which is 50 miles away in the middle of nowhere. Many families on the Rez don't even have electricity, and only half the kids graduate from high school. Broken down cars and trucks litter the yards like weeds. There are no chain stores or malls or Starbucks. Only a few mom and pop stores are permitted on the Rez. It seems like a third world country stuck in the middle of Arizona.

Sicheii goes there often, bringing supplies and help when he can. I used to go with him, but that was a while ago. Last year, Mom and I only went during the harvest celebration to see the tribal dancers.

This Reservation is actually a run down neighborhood where most of the residents are poor and have some Native American blood. Troy swings the bike on Canyon Avenue and follows as far behind the flashing lights as he can while still keeping an eye on them.

We pass dozens of ranch-style houses clustered close together with peeling paint, slanted walls, and weed infested, rock-filled yards. The difference between this neighborhood and my gated community is stark. They might as well be on different planets, which brings a guilty lump to my throat. We have so much and they have so little. As we move farther from Route 100, the houses become more dilapidated. Some are missing windows, and one has its front door leaning against the porch.

Troy slows the bike as the police cars turn left on River Road. "This is a dead end," he says. We crawl along the winding street, turn a corner and find three police cars their lights spinning parked in front of the last house.

He swerves to the curb a few hundred feet from the cruisers and turns off the bike.

I squint at the home in front of us. "That's Old Man Roundtree's house. Why would three cruisers stop at his place? How much trouble could Roundtree get into? He's as old as dirt."

"Maybe one of his potions backfired. Jack bought a sickness curse from him last week and cast it on Mr. Stevens our chemistry teacher. He was out for a week with strep throat."

"Rumor has it you've been buying love potions again." I poke him in the ribs with my elbow.

"He's been making potions and casting spells for a long time, Jules. Science can't explain everything." Troy jumps off his bike. "Come on, let's take a closer look."

I groan. "Do we really need to snoop around?" I'm in plenty of hot water for skipping school already, but he ignores me and jogs toward Roundtree's house. Why look for trouble? But what choice do I have? So I slink after him, trying to stay in his shadow.

Roundtree's house is set back fifty yards from the road. It's older than the other houses on the street, a small clay ranch-style home with a red-tiled roof. At least the walls are sturdy and all the windows and doors are intact.

A wooden sign by the front door proudly proclaims *Medicine Men Make the Best Lovers*. A small smile spreads across my face. Sicheii would not be happy.

Troy scoots toward the right side of the house, bent at the waist, stopping behind an ash tree. I run behind him, doing my best to keep up. Roundtree's property stretches all the way to Fishkill River. An old chicken coop leans precariously behind his house and directly in front of us. A few bushes, four trees, and a discarded lawnmower separate us from the coop. Patches of green dot the yard, although there's little grass. At least not the type you'd find in my neighborhood.

I tug on Troy's shirt. "Let's turn back. We'll find out what happened soon enough through the rumor mill."

He shoots me a mischievous look. "Come on. We can run along that line of trees and hide behind the coop." He points to three trees, which make an uneven line toward the coop. "If the coop doesn't collapse on us, we should be able to see what's going on in the backyard. No one's going to catch us."

He races out from behind the ash tree before I have a chance to protest. He knows I want to go back, but once he starts, he also knows I'll follow him. Best friends can really be a pain in the ass sometimes.

We run from tree to tree, trying to be as quiet as we can, but the rocks crunch under our sneakers. When we reach the coop, we're breathing hard. Sweat soaks my shirt and my heart pounds. Luckily, no chickens are home.

A surreal quality fills the air as if I'm standing in the middle of a photograph. It's hard to explain. Something just seems weird, as if the world is not quite right, and I should be able to figure out what's wrong, but nothing jumps out at me. We hear Sheriff Daniels's muffled voice, but other than that, it's quieter than it should be. The air is crisper, the colors brighter.

When we shuffle to the back of the coop, we edge along the rotten wood until we see Sheriff Daniels and the rest of the backyard. Three goats graze together along the river's edge. They watch Daniels and the other officers who stand in a loose circle around the base of a wide maple tree.

I strain my eyes to check out what they're looking at, and then Deputy Johnson moves. I wish he hadn't. Roundtree is tied around the trunk of the maple by his arms, his bare chest smeared with blood, his body slumped lifeless against the rope. We are too far away to see him in detail, but the blood pooled at the base of the tree tells the story well enough.

I want to pull my eyes away, but they're stuck. I've never seen a dead body before. Sure, there are tons of television shows where dead bodies are as common as sunrises, but it seems a lot different in person. I'm struck by the complete lack of motion as Roundtree's body pulls against the ropes. Even when you sneak up on someone who's sleeping, his or her chest still moves up and down. Here, there's nothing.

Troy flattens his body against the back of the coop, which leans with his weight and creaks a little until it steadies back in place. "Who could have done that?" He looks at me and all I can do is shake my head.

"We'd better sneak out of here. They're not going to be happy with us snooping around a murder scene," he whispers.

Finally, we agree, but a sharp pain knifes through my skull and a waterfall of noise cascades in my head. I bend over at the waist. My head's dizzy and I gasp for breath. My lungs explode. The coop sways against my back. Images flash in my mind — close-ups of Roundtree's body: cuts ripped into his chest, a jagged gash down his face, purple bruises mar his neck, his open eyes lifeless, blood everywhere.

I squeeze my eyes shut tight, but the visions only intensify. He has a tattoo on his chest of two arrows twisted together with a circle around them. Both arrows have different arrowheads and feathers. I know this tattoo. My grandfather has the same one.

I gasp for air, chest tight. Short bursts of oxygen spurt into my lungs. The ground sways under my feet. My mind turns fuzzy and my head's on fire. My stomach churns and bile fills my mouth. The ground rushes up to meet me when Troy grabs my shoulders and steadies me.

"Argh." I clasp my head because it feels like it'll shatter if I don't hold it together.

The images linger for another heartbeat and then vanish. I lean against Troy and breathe deeply. Air fills my lungs, and my legs feel stronger. I open my eyes and concentrate on Troy's face. It looks fuzzy and then focuses.

"Are you okay?" His eyes are wide and his lips are turned down softly.

"I'm fine." I shake my head to clear it. *Fine* is definitely not the right word to describe how I feel. I've never experienced pain like

45

that before, but at least I didn't toss my lunch. My hands tremble as air begins to flow more smoothly into my lungs.

Movement catches my eye. Deputy Johnson wanders in our direction. He hasn't seen us yet, but if we move he'll spot us for sure. "We've got to wait," I whisper. We push flat against the coop. A pointy piece of wood stabs me in the back, and I shift away from the jagged edge.

Only a few yards away, Deputy Johnson's steps are slow and cautionary. He hesitates and stares at something on the ground. My skin crawls. He's sure to catch us. He squats low and picks up a broken piece of stone in the dirt. Holding it close to his face, he turns to face Sheriff Daniels. "This is the tip from some type of ceremonial carving knife. It has blood on it. This could be from the murder weapon."

When Johnson stands up, he scans the area, looking for other clues. He glances toward the coop and looks right past us. Just when it seems that he'll definitely spot us, one of the goats darts toward him, grunting with its head down, brandishing its horns.

"Make sure that goat doesn't come near the body!" Daniels shouts.

Johnson curses as he dodges the goat's charge and races after the angry animal to keep it away from Roundtree.

With Johnson chasing the goat, I tug on Troy's t-shirt. "We'd better go." He follows me to the side of the coop, and we sprint back to the bike, no longer worried about staying behind the trees.

When we reach the Honda, his face is screwed together angrily and his eyes burn. "Do you think someone used a ceremonial knife to kill Roundtree?"

"Beats me, but why would it matter?"

"It matters to me." He starts the bike with a hard kick.

CHAPTER 7

People judge others by their appearances—what clothes they wear, the color of their skin, whether they have tattoos. It makes no sense, but it happens all the time. When most people see me, they only see a Native American teenaged girl, and with that come a slew of judgments and prejudices having nothing to do with me. The baggage for Troy is heavier, and sometimes he gets tired carrying the weight.

Joe, the security guard, smiles at me from the little hut at the entrance to my neighborhood, but scowls at Troy distastefully. It's obvious what he's thinking. Troy's too wild looking for him. He doesn't *fit* in our gated community. He could be a *troublemaker* and deserves careful scrutiny. Joe's attitude makes me angry, but I'm not going to say anything now. Roundtree was murdered. Bigger worries occupy my mind.

The same must be true for Troy because he grins back at Joe. Without a word, Joe presses a red button and the metal bar rises out of our path. Troy winks at him and continues on, pulling the Honda to a stop in front of Mrs. Jones's house. This is our second stop after leaving Roundtree's house. First, we visited the Dairy Freeze on the way home where I changed into my school uniform just in case Sicheii arrived home before I did.

I hop from the bike.

"Are you okay, Jules? Has your headache gone away?"

I had a hard time describing what happened to me by the chicken coop. I've never felt anything as intense as that before. The headache was real enough and simple, so that's all I told Troy. Why talk about visions, which were probably just another product of my overactive imagination anyway? The blood pooling by Roundtree's feet must have caused my imagination to fly into hyper-drive fueled by my NCIS addiction.

I yank off the helmet. "I'm feeling better now that this thing is off my head. It makes a better club than a hat." I manage a weak grin. At least the noise in my head has quieted down to a manageable level. "I still can't believe someone killed Roundtree. Who would do that?"

Troy rubs his face with his hands and takes the helmet from me. "Beats me, but he must have really pissed someone off. I'll call you later. Maybe I'll find some clues when I dig around the Reservation." He dons his helmet, starts the Honda, waves, and motors away with a squeak of the tires.

I trudge up our driveway toward the front door. The door opens, but it moves only a few inches and jolts to a stop as the shiny metal chain bars entry. Sicheii is home. Why would he use the chain? We never use it.

"I'm home, Sicheii. Let me in." Thirty seconds pass. My foot starts tapping against the stoop and there's no answer. The day is still hot and sweat starts to coat my forehead and back. What weirdness is he up to now?

I drop my backpack with a thud, amble over to the three-car garage and peek into the windows. Next to Mom's Volvo is Sicheii's mint condition, burgundy, 1973 Porsche 911. The license plate reads, "MED MAN." Wherever he goes, everyone recognizes the sports car as my grandfather's, which is only one reason I hate driving in the thing. It's also loud, has no cup holders, gets only AM stations, and smells like oil. Still, Sicheii loves the car. It's old, but he drives it fast.

I sigh — he's here somewhere.

Just then, Mrs. Jones pulls up in her silver Mercedes and screeches to a stop. She manages to keep two wheels on the pavement. The other two leave a skid mark on her grass. Stumbling out of the car, she slams the door shut, and weaves her way over to me.

Great! Could my day get any worse?

"Hey you! Janice. How was school?" A wicked grin flickers across her face. "I see you've put on your uniform." At least that's what it sounds like she's saying. It's hard to make out all the words because she slurs them.

I groan and walk toward her. "My name's Juliet."

She stops only a foot from me, which is good because for a second it seems like she's about to crash into me. Her breath stinks of Scotch. "Right, Jane. I know education isn't high on your people's list of priorities, but listen to me — "

"My Mom's a partner at Dormit and Will! She's way more educated than you!"

She grabs my arm. "No need to shout, Jackie. You people are always so loud with the drums and... whatever. I'm just saying, tramping around isn't going to get you far. Once your... looks goes, you'll have nothing without an... education."

Heat flushes my face and I yank my arm free from her talons. "Thanks. At least I have you as a role model."

Her mouth drops open far enough that a fly zips in. She doesn't notice. "You little—"

"*What?*"

She must see the fire in my eyes because the color drains from her face and she mumbles, "Nothing," before she turns and staggers away.

I watch her make the entire trek into her house before my breathing goes back to normal.

Now, where's Sicheii?

There's no place to walk to in my neighborhood, so that means he must be in the backyard. I plod my way to our gate, push it open and find him holding a shovel, plunging it into the grass, a mad grin across his face.

Argh! What's he doing?

Grass is rare and expensive in our town. Mom pays landscapers a fortune to keep it green, just so our lawn can have the same color as our neighbors' lawns.

When I swing the gate closed with a thud, Sicheii stops digging and glances up toward me. His white linen shirt is unbuttoned. Dirt splashes his Lucky jeans, and his soft leather moccasins are neatly placed off to the side near the stone patio.

"Welcome home, Little Bird." I'm not sure why he calls me *Little Bird*. I hate it, but at least he doesn't call me Wildfire in public anymore.

My jaw drops once I get a better view of the hole he's dug in Mom's lawn. It's already five feet across. "What're you doing? You're destroying Mom's grass!"

He smiles. His bright, white, perfectly straight teeth contrast with his deeply tanned skin. "I'm making a barbecue pit." He proudly points to a pile of rocks and a flat slab of stone to the side of his newly created hole. "I caught fresh fish for us."

He speaks casually, like it's absolutely normal for him to dig up Mom's yard. I have to suppress a grin. "We own a perfectly good barbecue right there." My outstretched finger points at our rarely used gas Weber grill. Everyone in the neighborhood owns an identical one.

He scowls at the grill as if it's an alien device. "I don't know what that is, but I'm not using it. That's not how *the people* barbecue. The fish were good enough to sacrifice their lives for us. I'm not cooking them on such a thing."

Sicheii refers to Native Americans as "the people." I shrug. This isn't my problem. Mom decided Sicheii should stay, so she'll have to deal with the new pit in the lawn. "You'll have to explain the hole to Mom. Maybe you'll dig up some gold nuggets? You'll need them."

He shoots me a disapproving glower with his slate gray eyes. Gray eyes are unusual among our people, and Sicheii's are bright. "How was school?" He locks his eyes onto mine.

Big red warning lights flash in front of me. I panic and do the only thing I can think to do—lie. "School was... fine." My voice wanes like a balloon losing its last bit of air. I glance down at my feet and scratch the back of my neck. The sun burns hot against my face. My feet seem to fidget on their own. What can I say? I'm a bad liar.

"Really, Little Bird?" Sicheii leans against his shovel. He wears leather deerskin gloves to protect his manicured hands.

I double down. "I had a test in English, but I'm sure it went okay." My hands shift through my hair, straightening it.

He frowns. The lines on his face all move at once, conveying generations of disappointment at me. "Why don't you tell me the truth?" He tosses the shovel on the grass.

My face tints red. "I skipped school today." I feel better now that the truth is out. In only that short moment, I've started to feel nauseous.

"I know. You went to Slippery Rock with Troy Buckhorn, didn't you?"

I take a half-step back. "How'd you know?"

He smiles and flashes his pearly whites at me. "The wind told me."

I plant my hands on my hips. "Now who's lying?"

Sicheii's eyes narrow, but he isn't angry, only amused. The twinkle that brightens his eyes betrays him. "I heard Troy's bike from the street and can smell the river on you in the breeze. Besides, your school left a message. They were wondering where you were."

Of course Bartens would call. I'm an idiot.

"I'm sorry. Cutting school was stupid. But that place gets to me, and the weather was perfect." I twirl the ends of my long straight hair. "And I haven't seen Troy in weeks." He likes Troy, so I grab onto him like a life raft.

He pauses for a moment and rests his gaze on my face with a half smile on his. I give him my best, most remorseful frown, widen my eyes as much as possible, and bat my eyelashes at him. None of my antics will change his mind, but I try anyway.

He shoots me a sly smirk. "The rainbow trout is in the refrigerator. Clean the fish for dinner the way I taught you."

I dash toward the backslider when he calls after me.

"Don't forget to thank the fish for their sacrifice. I'll heat up the stones."

He gave me a break. I'm still worried Mom will find out about my skipping school, but there's still a chance she won't. Hope is a good thing.

I slide the backdoor open and try to remember how to thank a dead fish for jumping on my grandfather's hook.

CHAPTER

Sicheii's life is free from structure. He doesn't care about what the *right* time of day is to do things. For him, dinner isn't a particular time, but a desire to consume the largest meal of the day. He'll eat dinner whenever he decides he's hungry —often in the middle of the day, sometimes for breakfast, other times late into the evening. He calls it "Indian Time." It must be great to live that way—free from rules and other people's expectations. He bends life to his will instead of the other way around. Only the art gallery tethers him to conventional time and even then he'll close the store to do more *important* things.

The sun still lightens the sky, but the trout smells delicious as the fish sizzles on the thin, flat slab of blue stone, and my stomach growls. All I ate for lunch was a few handfuls of Doritos I snatched before Troy scarfed them all down.

We go inside to the dining table where he places a platter of fish and grilled squash between us. He doesn't like to use separate dishes. He thinks the proximity brings us closer together when we share food off the same plate. It's just more of his weirdness.

Before launching into dinner, fork primed in my hand, he says grace. "We thank the fish and the squash for their sacrifices for our nourishment. Their spirits will unite with ours, and we will forever be joined as one."

When he finishes, he closes his eyes, hums softly, and starts meditating. He expects me to follow along also, so I close my eyes and hum. I'm not sure what he wants me to meditate on: everything I'm thankful for, or the connection between our food and myself, or perhaps the sacrifice the fish and vegetables made for me. Instead, visions of Roundtree creep into my mind. They're still vivid enough to make me wince. *What did he do to deserve that?*

I'm not sure how long I hum with my eyes closed, but he has stopped first. He's staring at me and looks through me as if he suspects something is wrong. He doesn't say a word about it —he respects my privacy with the spirit world.

I nod, and we begin eating. I'm not sure if I thanked the fish properly, but I shovel in heaping forkfuls and thank them now. There's nothing as tasty as freshly caught fish.

Sicheii is still watching me with a raised eyebrow and a weird twinkle in his eyes, so I start a conversation about something far removed from Roundtree and those visions. "How are things at the art gallery?" He owns a successful gallery in Old Town where he sells Native American art and antiquities. He lives in a modern, luxurious loft above the store. "Shouldn't you be at the gallery selling to the tourists?"

"Lisa is running the store for me. She is more than capable."

I roll my eyes. Neither Mom nor I like Lisa. She's young and beautiful and as phony as a politician on Election Day. We both suspect she's a moneygrubber, and we don't have any idea how they met. One day, two years ago, we entered the gallery and Lisa was working there. That wasn't surprising. He hires college-aged kids all the time, but we both noticed the ease in which she touched him on the shoulder and the friendly glances they shared. Six months later, she moved into his apartment.

He ignores my reaction and smiles. "So how are you doing at that school of yours?" He hates Bartens almost as much as I do. He never mentions it by name. At least we share that in common. He had epics fights with Mom when she decided to make me transfer schools. He wanted me to stay connected with the Tribe and be around a more *diverse* population. He argued that life shouldn't revolve around Ivy League schools and trust funds and materialistic things. Mom wants the best for me, and her definition of best is different from his, so I transferred to Bartens.

I shake my head. "Everyone is so perfect there. They all like horseback riding, and look the same, like they're clones. There isn't much color among the students. I mostly stick to myself." I shove a forkful of fish in my mouth.

He scrutinizes me, fork frozen in the air. "You're stronger than that, Little Bird." He places his fork on the table. "They will see your worth if you let them."

"They don't care about *my* worth. All they care about is what car they drive or whether they're spending the summer in the French Rivera or the Caribbean." I swallow. "I'm better off without them."

"Either you are a river or a rock."

"What?" I instantly regret asking, having unwittingly opened the door to another Sicheii lesson.

I can almost hear the door creak on invisible mental hinges as a grin sneaks on his face. "Both rivers and rocks existed on the First World when time began. Rivers change with the conditions. Water will always find the least resistant path. Build a dam and the flow stops, or construct a canal and the river will flood the new easier path."

He pauses and I nod, so he continues. "The great rock formations are unchanging. They're unbending and have strength and value in their unique beauty and construction." He smiles knowingly as if he's made sense. "You don't have to choose between that school and your heritage. You're either a rock or a river."

I shake my head. He's definitely a rock. If only my life was as simple as his.

The doorbell rings.

"Are you expecting anyone, Little Bird?"

"Nope." I jump to my feet. No matter who's at the door, it must be better than another lecture from Sicheii.

Daniels and Deputy Johnson stand on the front stoop and look through the small window in the center of the front door. I'm totally wrong. My heart leaps unevenly. *Do they know Troy and I were at the crime scene? Did the college kids file a complaint? How much trouble are we in?*

Sicheii appears behind me. I undo the chain lock and open the door. Sheriff Daniel's face is pinched tight, and his lips are turned down in a deep frown. Sweat rolls down the side of his face where he has a thin scar near his right ear. *Is he going to cuff me right now in front of my grandfather?* I'm so certain he's going to arrest me, I almost lift my wrists together and thrust them at him to make the entire process easier.

"Good evening, Juliet," he says as he looks beyond me and stares at Sicheii. "We need a moment alone with Jake." Daniels is tall and stocky with wide shoulders, but Sicheii's shoulders are wider.

"Of course, Sheriff," Sicheii answers. His legal name is Jake Clearwater Stone. I've always called him Sicheii, which is a Native American word for maternal grandfather. "Come right in." He casually waves Daniels and Johnson into the house as if he's expecting them.

Both men take off their hats and stiffly enter the foyer. They look nervous as they twirl their Stetsons. Daniels glances at me. "If you don't mind, Juliet, we'd like to talk to Jake alone for a minute." He looks sullen and speaks softly, which I don't like. In my experience, the softer the voice, the worse the trouble. I stand up straighter and am about to tell him that I'm not going anywhere when Sicheii answers.

"Why don't we go into the living room, Sheriff?" Sicheii glances at me. "You should go back to the dining room and finish dinner before the meal gets cold. I'm sure this will be a brief visit."

Daniels shuffles forward with Johnson a step behind. They've never been inside our house before and their steps are uncertain.

Left with no real choice, I trudge to the dining room, but the expression on the Sheriff's face worries me. I swing the door mostly closed but keep it open a crack. The living room is on the other side of the house, so I really shouldn't be able to hear them, but what the heck? It's worth a try.

At first, only muffled sounds reach me, but when I concentrate harder, the voices become clearer and grow louder.

Their husky quality tells me they're speaking in hushed tones, but they sound as clear as if they're standing next to me.

"I have some bad news, Jake," Daniels begins. "Charles Roundtree was murdered earlier today."

After a short pause, he continues. "Where were you earlier?"

"At the art gallery. Why?"

There's another pause, and then Daniels says, "One of Roundtree's neighbors said they observed you arguing with him yesterday."

"He said it got heated," Johnson adds in his gruff voice.

Sicheii sighs. "We've been fighting for forty years in the same way day battles night. You both know that, but I respected him and we had an understanding. He lived in balance with the world in his way. His way was different from mine, but I had nothing to do with his death."

A plastic bag ruffles. "Do you know what this is?" Sheriff Daniels asks.

"It looks like the tip of a ceremonial carving hatchet. I've never seen this one before."

"Can you identify anyone who could've harmed Roundtree or anyone selling Native American antiques like this one?"

The question is pregnant with suspicion. Of course — Sicheii is the most successful dealer in Native American antiquities in town, and everyone knows it.

"I don't have any idea who harmed Roundtree." Sicheii's voice sounds final and hard like stone. Heavy footsteps lead to the front foyer, so I push the dining room door open another inch to hear better.

"If I think of something, I'll call you." The front door opens and closes with a soft thud.

I scoot to the dining table and attempt to wrap myself around what they had just said. *Why did Sicheii lie about where he was earlier today?* He went fishing. He wasn't at his gallery. Roundtree's house abuts Fishkill River. We've gone fishing for trout from those waters before, but there are other rivers to fish also. He could have caught dinner at one of the other ones.

When Sicheii returns, his body is stiff. Tension bunches in his shoulders, and shows in the rigidity in which he walks, and the lines in his clenched jaw. "Roundtree was killed earlier today. You wouldn't know anything about that, would you?"

I try to display as much shock in my face as possible without overdoing it and shake my head.

He must have been fooled because he asks me, "Have you been feeling well lately, Little Bird?"

"Fine." It isn't the whole truth, but I'm not going to tell him about my recent headaches and those noises in my head. I can't predict what he'd do if he knew the whole story, but he certainly wouldn't like it, and I can't take the chance that he'll do something really weird.

He steps close to me, looming over me in my chair. A trace of his musky cologne mixed with the smoke from barbecuing the fish hangs in the air between us. He seems to gaze right through me. "Have you been experiencing any weird headaches?"

"Not me." I turn away and fiddle with my fork. Sweat beads on my forehead. Who would believe me? I am such a bad liar.

His face softens as if he feels sorry for me. The lines in his jaw disappear and the canyons in his forehead smooth. "The time is coming when we must stop lying to each other. Events are going to move quickly. Soon, we won't be able to control the spirits. You must open your heart. You can't run from who you are." He lightly grazes my cheek with his fingertips. "I've got to go. I'll be home late. Don't wait up for me. Keep the door locked."

He spins and strides out of the house. The Porsche starts up moments later and speeds away.

I'm left sitting in the kitchen feeling hollow, full of questions but no answers.

CHAPTER 9

I call Troy within five seconds after Sicheii leaves. "Sheriff Daniels and Deputy Johnson just stopped over. They questioned my grandfather about Roundtree."

He pauses for a second. "I'm sure they're talking to all the people who knew Roundtree. Jake has to be at the top of their list. How many other medicine men are there?"

"Yes, but they said someone saw Sicheii arguing with Roundtree yesterday. They showed him the tip of a ceremonial hatchet that was used to murder Roundtree. It's probably the same one Deputy Johnson found while we were at the house. They sounded suspicious."

"There's a long list of people who have argued with Roundtree. Don't worry about it, Jules. People here think his murder is connected to some type of drug deal gone bad. Maybe Roundtree stumbled onto a combination of roots or herbs he made into a new designer drug. You hear about them all the time on the news. He was known to dabble in things he shouldn't have messed with."

"I have a bad feeling about this, Troy. After the Sheriff left, Sicheii acted weirder than usual. He seemed to know about my headache from earlier in the day."

"You looked pale when I dropped you off. Did he ask you how you were feeling, and you said you were fine?"

"Yes, but he asked me specifically about headaches before he took off, like he knew I had been having some lately."

"We both know you're a terrible liar." He chuckles but it sounds forced to me. "And Jake has been a medicine man for a long time. He's like a natural lie detector. I'd never try to fool him."

Troy's not making me feel better, so I squeeze the phone harder. "He also said some weird stuff about spirits."

Ten seconds pass before he speaks. "What... did he say?"

"Something about running out of time." I try to remember what he said exactly, but the precise words don't come to mind. "That the spirits are going to take over soon or something odd like that. He took off in a hurry after the Sheriff left. He never explained what the heck he was talking about. But then again, he never does." I don't tell him Sicheii lied about where he spent the day. I'm not sure why, but it doesn't sound good when rummaging around in my head.

Troy hesitates again, which is unlike him. "It's probably nothing, Jules. Your grandfather lives a complicated life and believes spirits influence everything. He probably needs to... check in at the art gallery, or maybe he wants to break the news to someone close to Roundtree."

Both reasonable possibilities but they don't feel right. Sicheii didn't leave to deliver bad news and he wasn't worried about the gallery. He looked nervous and concerned about the *future*. I'm lost in a maze of possibilities, so I forget that Troy's on the phone until he says, "Juliet. Are you still there?"

"Yes. Why did you become so upset when Deputy Johnson found that ceremonial knife? Why does it matter what Roundtree was killed with?" That question had been bothering me since we left Roundtree's house.

"I know you don't believe in this stuff...."

"But..."

"But, the spirits didn't just die when Steve Jobs invented Apple. They still exist today, working their magic on us. We know *how* things work, but not the *why* so much. I think the spirits cause us to take action sometimes, whether good or bad."

"And the knife?"

"Ceremonial knives are dipped into the spirit world. They make the separation between worlds thin."

He wants me to agree with him or, at least, open my mind to the possibility that he's right, but I can't wrap my arms around spirits and spirit worlds. I won't lie to him, so I don't know what to say.

After a long pause that feels like two lifetimes, he says, "I've got to go, Jules. I have a math test tomorrow and I'm pretty sure the spirits aren't going to help me. Just chill out about your grandfather. I'm sure he's fine." Trace amounts of disappointment in his voice magically travel through cyberspace and brush against my ear.

"Sure. Good luck on your test." I hang up and go online to discover what torture, disguised as homework, my teachers expect me to complete. Bartens uses an online blackboard where teachers post assignments. I throw my pillow when the two-page Global History assignment pops on the screen.

Mom calls halfway through my homework. She sounds tired. "How was your day?"

"My day was fine." I'm determined to limit my lying, and let's face it *fine* could mean anything.

"Are you minding your grandfather? He didn't pick you up at school or embarrass you or do anything else you'll need therapy for, did he?"

"No, *Mom.*" *Mom* stretches out in a kind of whine I'm not proud of. "Everything is good. How goes the conference?" I change the subject to avoid questions I don't want to answer.

"Great but exhausting." She perks up. "I moderated an outstanding panel on...." Her voice drones on. I'm not really paying attention, until she says, "Can you put your grandfather on?"

"He went... out to find a new... ice cream flavor from the Dairy Freeze. Something about... natural Indian corn." How lame is that? Especially since a wide assortment of ice cream takes up space in the freezer, but Sicheii is generally weird, so Mom has no problem believing he wants me to try a new "natural" flavor from the Dairy Freeze.

"Okay, Jules." She yawns. "I'm going to sleep. It's been a long day. We'll make up a strategy about Bartens when I come home. Love you, sweetie."

"I love you too," I say before hanging up and almost feel her relief through the phone that I'm no longer angry with her.

The rest of my homework takes me past midnight to finish. The orange numbers on my clock say it's 12:25, and Sicheii is still out. My thoughts are troubled, but my pillow is soft. Sleep finds me.

My eyes open, but I'm stuck in another dream. I'm outside on a clear night under a black canvas specked with dazzling points of light. The stars are brighter than usual, which means that no man-made lights from buildings or houses dim their brilliance. Sicheii would call it a new sky.

Four men are sitting around a campfire in a loose circle. Sharp peaks of red rocks jut up around them, creating a bowl effect as if they're in the middle of a crater. The campfire dances off of gemstones and crystals that litter the ground and reminds me of the old legend about Devil's Peak. The crown of the Devil's head is supposed to be covered with precious stones, but no one has ever climbed the peak, so no one really knows.

The men have long obsidian hair and wear leather shirts that are uneven on the bottom. Tan breechcloths hang from their waists. Even though the campfire is small, the gems glow red and purple around their feet, amplifying the light. One face is familiar—the man from yesterday's daydream. He sits cross-legged with four objects placed neatly in front of him. He's speaking the old language again. Even though I don't understand what he's saying, he's clearly in charge and has the full attention of those around him.

The other faces around the campfire are all different looking, with various ages and features, but they share the same expression. They look enraptured as if they're being told secrets that change everything. The leader lifts a small leather book and hands it to one of the men, who eagerly takes it from him. The process is repeated two other times with another journal and a small leather pouch.

My eyes strain to see the last item in front of the leader. It's hard to make out because it lies flat on the ground. The wind

66

puffs. The campfire flickers brighter for a moment and reveals the item's outline. It's a crystal, sharp and beautiful, but it's still cloaked in shadows. A turquoise pendant dangles around the leader's neck. It looks familiar.

I've seen one just like it before, but where?

This meeting affects me somehow. I don't know how, but the feeling burrows deep into my mind. There's a connection between these four men and me.

What is it?

A hawk circles the meeting and squawks angrily, which only grows louder until I realize my alarm has gone off. I try to smack the off button, but I miss and knock the clock off the bedside table and onto the floor. The buzzing stops when I pull the plug from the wall socket. I usually go through a couple of alarm clocks each year.

I stumble into the bathroom and start my day, brushing off the dream as just another byproduct from my active imagination. What could an ancient meeting among Native Americans have to do with *me*?

My shower is hot, and after a few minutes, the fog clears from my head. Memories of Roundtree, Sheriff Daniels, and Sicheii's hasty departure flash through my mind. I rush through my morning routine quicker than usual and scoot downstairs, wondering whether I'll find my grandfather.

Pueblo music, with its steady drumbeats and complicated vocals, wafts from the kitchen. Incense is burning—jasmine and cedar wood. Sicheii has definitely returned. I open the kitchen door and find him standing by the island wearing a plush white cotton bathrobe tied around his wide frame. Steam spirals above a fresh mug of tea in his hand.

He flashes a full-faced grin at me as if it's a normal

morning, as if the Sheriff never questioned him and he didn't race off in a hurry only to return this morning. "Good morning, Little Bird. What time does your bus arrive?"

I check the clock. "7:30." There's plenty of time. "When did you come home last night?"

He looks at me quizzically; both eyebrows arch upward. "Did you have any problems?"

"No, nothing happened." My face flushes with color. It's not my place to question him. *Besides, do I really want to know what he was doing?* So I drop it. He seems relaxed and unworried, which puts me at ease.

He claps his hands together. "Good, now let's enjoy our morning meal." He sweeps his hands at the kitchen table. A bowl of yogurt, fresh strawberries and blueberries, granola, and two glasses of orange juice await us.

I have no intention of sharing that meal with him, so I walk into the pantry, grab a box of Kellogg's cornflakes, find a bowl, pour, and go to the refrigerator for some milk. When I return to the kitchen table, he's already sitting with a spoon in his hand. He shoots me an annoyed look, then closes his eyes and starts humming and meditating. I follow along and force my mind to go blank. I don't want a repeat of yesterday. I don't want to see Roundtree again. When he stops humming, I open my eyes.

I dive into my cereal with feigned enthusiasm and peek at him across the table. He starts singing along with the music, his mug held steady in front of him. His singing voice is rich and strong, but he can only reach two notes. It works when he performs ceremonies, but he'll never make it on American Idol. I told him this once, and he told me true music comes from the heart, not the voice.

I smile at him, but after a few minutes, his singing grates. "How is the art gallery? Was there an emergency last night?" I'm not sure why I start down this road, but once the words start coming out of my mouth, they keep tumbling out as if it's a jailbreak.

Sicheii glances at me, his expression blank. "The gallery is fine. All is as it should be." He deliberately places his mug on the table without taking his eyes from me. "Why don't you ask me about what is really on your mind, Little Bird?"

My chest tightens. "I was just thinking about Roundtree. Who could have killed him?"

"Roundtree was a complex person. He lived life in accordance with his own rules and the spirits he sought guidance from." Sicheii slides his mug away from himself. "He made many enemies. It's hard to say who could have wanted to eliminate his spirit. I'm sure the Sheriff will figure out who's responsible for his murder."

Normally, that explanation would be enough for me, but I am still anxious and want more. "Sheriff Daniels seemed eager to talk to you." I gulped down half my glass of orange juice. "What did he want?"

"You have excellent hearing, Little Bird." He chuckles. "I'm sure you heard exactly what he wanted." He tosses a few blueberries in his mouth. "Why did your mother think I went out to buy ice cream?"

Of course she would try his cell phone. Sometimes, I can be so stupid. "She called and I didn't know what to say. She wanted to talk to you."

"The truth is usually best." A sly expression twists his lips and brightens his eyes. "She might be stuck in Scottsdale for a few extra days. She's meeting with a new client."

My heart sinks. Sicheii glances at the kitchen clock. "You'd better catch the bus, or I'll have to drive you."

I leap to my feet. Sicheii driving me to school would be a major disaster. My head aches as I snatch my backpack from the floor and march out the front door. The smell of incense lingers in my nose as the morning sun temporarily blinds me.

This day is going to be a bad one. Sometimes you just know.

CHAPTER

Bartens uses the same beaten down yellow buses as my old school. It's the only similarity between the two places. Sure, they teach some of the same subjects, but that's in name only. Bartens specializes in AP or college level courses we'll never receive college credit for anyway. It seems like they want to skip high school altogether and make believe they're something they're not, a college. It's all smoke and mirrors—the illusion of harder class work to slip as many students as possible into the Ivies. The more Bartens students that go to Harvard, the more they can charge in tuition. You don't need to be a genius to figure that out.

I trudge my way on the bus, and tap George, the bus driver, on the shoulder. A storm cloud hovers over him, and I see the score of the Suns game in my mind's eye. The Suns lost big. I get the feeling he bet a bunch on the game.

"Tough game last night?"

"Tell me about it." George closes the doors with a hard yank.

I glance down the length of the bus and a pit grows inside me. I'm used to the feeling by now. The same pit grows every time I step on the bus, *every* school day for the past two years. Only three other students take the ride. Each sits alone, and each looks as miserable as I feel. The bus could hold fifty students, yet the most it ever takes is five. No one wants to take the *Loser Limo* as the other kids call it. It smells — part sweat and part rotten food, as if old sandwiches are stuck in the seats. Katie sits toward the back. At least she'll share the trip with me. I sigh and plop down on the bench behind her.

"Hey, are you feeling better?" Concern is scribbled onto her round face in small lines that ring her eyes and mouth. "I texted you last night, but you never got back to me."

Guilt jabs me, and I smile weakly. "It must have been a twenty-four hour thing. My stomach feels much better." Katie is a straight arrow and would never have approved of my cutting class yesterday, so I fib to avoid the topic.

When the bus bounces along our way, she flops next to me, filling up her seat and overflowing into my space a little. She's slightly overweight. Nothing extreme, but in the perfect world of Bartens, she stands out, and no one wants to stand out. I've threatened more than one person about calling her names, like *Katie the Cow* or *Weighty Katie*. Luckily I haven't had to hit anyone yet, but I've come close.

Dark circles smudge underneath her bloodshot eyes, new tear tracks mark her cheeks, and she sniffles. This is bad. "What's up? Are you okay?"

She whispers even though no one can hear us anyway. "Channel Seven News did a special on my dad." She bites her nails—her nervous habit. They look like stubs. "The trial hasn't even started yet and they've all but convicted my dad of these terrible crimes. They say he ran the largest Ponzi scheme ever." New tears brim her eyes.

I wrap my arm around her shoulders as fresh tears start dribbling down her face. "You shouldn't watch those shows. They're idiots. They'll say anything to trick people to tune in."

As the bus turns left through the arched brick entranceway into Bartens, Katie pulls out a tissue from her backpack. Going into school with watery eyes would be like spilling blood in shark-infested waters. The other kids are already vicious toward her. Some of their families lost a bunch in funds her father managed.

The bus lumbers toward the back of the main building past a half dozen different brick structures with tall windows, white wood trim, and even a round glass English conservatory where we eat lunch. The design might work for our sister school in England, but the Arizona heat makes it totally ridiculous.

We pull to a stop on the south side of campus, away from our lockers. A gust of hot air smacks us in the face when we hop off the bus. I check her face—all evidence she had been crying is gone, so we amble our way to first period, Global History.

Ms. Arnold stands in front of the classroom waiting for her students to arrive. She started teaching this year and bubbles with energy. Apparently no one has told her yet that she's supposed to hate the students like the other teachers. She's the assistant tennis coach, has curly blonde hair that bounces to her shoulders, and is in great shape. All the boys have a crush on her—it's easy to understand why.

As I walk past, she asks, "Are you feeling better, Juliet?"

I sniffle, slump my shoulders, and frown slightly. "I'm feeling better." I add a slight cough for effect. "Yesterday was a little rough."

Small class sizes suck. There's no place to hide. Teachers always know who's absent, who didn't finish the homework, or who's distracted by some crisis or another. I hate it. I want to blend in the back of the room, be anonymous, but how can I disappear when the class only has three rows of seats?

She smiles and nods, but her eyes linger on me. She studied Native American culture at Arizona State, which explains why she stayed behind in our little town. A few months ago, she stopped in my grandfather's shop when I was there and talked to him about some of the antique tools. She stood in the back of the shop and pointed to a case with some arrowheads, a knife, and two hatchets.

I freeze and my throat tightens. *There were two hatchets.*

One of the kids on the football team bumps into me on the way to his seat, so I remember to keep moving as the rest of the students file into the room and class begins. Ms. Arnold wanders around the class, asking questions, prying open ideas and comments from students who'd rather keep them hidden. Global is my favorite class even if she gives a horrendous amount of homework.

The bell rings and she grabs my arm as I leave. "If you're still not feeling well, you should go to the nurse's office. I'm off next period and can take you."

I shake my arm free. "I'm feeling much better."

Katie and I leave the social studies wing, withstand another heat gust, march through the double doors, and enter the main classroom building to find our lockers. I pause for a second in the doorway, something is wrong. A vision of Tiffany's face with a sly grin flashes in my mind and it makes me cringe. She's not visible yet, but she's up to no good. I can feel the bad vibes float toward me like a gust of wind.

I clear the doorway and find a larger than normal crowd loitering in the hallway, which looks like a clogged artery. Four clusters of *cool* kids create an obstacle course down the tight corridor. Between classes usually only a few people hang out near the lockers. Something is definitely up. A nervous energy fills the small space, so my antenna goes all the way up, and I eye them suspiciously as we weave around them toward our lockers.

Tiffany, Morgan, and Ashley gather in a small circle across from our lockers, standing close together with smug expressions on their faces and smartphones in their hands. I hesitate for a second as a weird déjà vu feeling creeps up my back. Tiffany looks *exactly* as I imagined her only a moment ago. The Bartens uniform doesn't leave much room for improvisation, and Tiffany generally looks the same, her hair always perfect, as if a cosmic stroke of good luck blows her hair in the ideal place every day, but this similarity is uncanny. She *never* wears the same earrings twice. She must have a vault with them stacked inside. I doubt I've ever seen her wear these golden starbursts before, but I just imagined her wearing the same ones. Weird.

I shake off the eerie feeling and focus on her and her shark pals. When they see us, Tiffany nods, and they snicker. She is the undisputed great white shark of Bartens, and it looks like she's ready to attack. My eyes narrow. A piece of paper is stuck on Katie's locker, which is two down from mine.

Katie hasn't noticed the note yet. A distant look has settled in her eyes, so, I grab her arm, pull her to a stop, and whisper in her ear, "Is that Tyler back by the door? I think he called your name." Tyler smiled at her last week, and that was enough for her imagination to weave stories of love, wedlock, a house, and a picket fence. He's one of the few nice kids, but I don't see any possible romance between the two. He's the star of the basketball team and smiles at everyone. *Still, why dampen Katie's imagination?* It's better for her to think about Tyler than her dad.

She squints and sorts through the thicket of students, which buys me just enough time. While she bites her nails, an explosive energy builds in my body and I bolt past her, dart forward and zip by the four groups of students in a blur. It seems like I reach the locker in one giant step, as though I'm fired from a gun.

A newspaper cartoon stuck to Katie's locker depicts a jail cell with her father's hands clutching the bars. A giant, bald, beefy looking inmate lurks behind him. The muscle-bound criminal blows him a kiss. She would have been devastated if she had seen it.

By the time she turns back toward her locker, I've ripped down the paper, crumpled it in my fist, and jammed it into my backpack. I turn to face the great white shark. I'm not going to let them hurt her. They can say what they want about me, but Katie just can't take the ridicule right now. Blood pounds in my head.

Tiffany's face twists into a scowl, her nostrils flaring out angrily. It transforms her perfectly symmetrical face into something misshapen, something mean. I sneer back at her when a sudden bolt of pain jolts through my head. She calls me *Indian Trash.*

I'm not going to let anyone call me that, especially not Tiffany, so red clouds my vision, and I make a run at her—

straight through the pack of sharks in a blink. Before she reacts, I grab her shoulders and ram her into the almond-colored lockers.

Clunk!

She crashes hard against the metal and grunts, but she manages to grab two fistfuls of my hair, and yanks me to her side. Pain shoots through my scalp. It feels like she's ripping out my hair, so I go for her throat and clasp my hands around her perfectly tanned neck. I squeeze and slam her head against the bank of lockers. *Clunk!* I let go after she collides with the metal. Hard.

She releases my hair, but before I can grab her again, the hallway bursts with teachers and commotion. Ms. Arnold appears behind me, grabs my arms and pulls me away from Tiffany while the shark bends over at the waist, grabbing the back of her head and wincing. I make one last lunge at her, but Mr. Davies, my math teacher, stands between us and pushes me to the side, and Ms. Arnold increases her grip around my arms.

The entire pack of sharks point in my direction and shout. They scream out different things, but the brunt of their message is clear; I started the fight. Katie is ash-white. Tiffany smiles. Her face becomes even uglier than it was with the scowl.

I sigh and let my arms drop to my side. This is going to be bad.

CHAPTER 11

I sit in the Headmaster's office in a small chair as far away from his mahogany desk as possible, my head hung low in my hands, pondering my fate. How much trouble am I in? How long will Mom ground me? The longest was two weeks when I got into a fight in ninth grade. I get the miserable feeling this time might stretch until my eighteenth birthday.

To distract myself from my impending doom, I study the office. This is my first time here. Cherry wood paneling stretches halfway up the stuffy walls. A tightly woven burgundy carpet covers the floor, and numerous portraits of unknown, disapproving, pasty-white men stare into the room with annoyed expressions as if they had somewhere better to go and are totally uninterested in what's going on around them. Twenty-two faces in total stare back at me. Who are these people, and why are they at my school?

The office smells old and dusty and a bit acidic, like

corroded batteries. I'm not sure why. Maybe the smell comes with the paintings?

Forty minutes have passed since they dragged me here. Sicheii is supposed to retrieve me, but the time stretches on and seems like a dozen lifetimes.

The office door swings open and the Headmaster, Alistair Cordingly, strides into the room, followed by my grandfather. Cordingly matches the office, smells old and is imported from England.

He could not look more different from my grandfather, and for a moment I forget about my problems and smile. Cordingly's light complexion, thinning straw-colored hair, and general stuffiness are all England with no trace of Arizona. He wears a navy blue pinstripe suit with a gold tie and gold handkerchief as if he had just stepped out of a *Brooks Brothers* catalogue. No one likes him or understands what he does. All the students believe he has an expiration date stamped on his palm when he'll be called back to England or curdle like sour milk.

Sicheii rolls into the office a step behind him. His sky colored linen shirt billows around him and over faded blue jeans. His favorite straw, wide-brimmed hat with a lone hawk feather stuck into the band sits on top of his white hair. Confident and self-assured, he knows exactly who he is and why he's here. Neither Cordingly nor Bartens intimidates him in the least.

Cordingly uses short, brisk steps to retreat to the safety of his desk while Sicheii strolls behind him with easy loping strides. Safely behind his desk, Cordingly smooths his tie and settles into his leather chair, his smile fake, his small black reptilian eyes skittering around the office.

Sicheii makes him anxious. Instead of sitting in the chair opposite him, as I'm sure he expects, Sicheii saunters along the edges of the office while studying the portraits with a grim expression on his face. He's not interested in the paintings. He's sending Cordingly a message that he cannot be dismissed lightly. I sit up straighter. He's done the same thing to me many times. When I'm in a hurry and want an answer to some critically important question, he delays just long enough for me to realize he's in charge and will answer on his terms.

I smile now that Cordingly learns the same message. Time languishes for a few more uncomfortable minutes. Finally, Sicheii pivots on his moccasins and turns his attention to the Headmaster, who has been staring at him quietly, fidgeting in his chair and tapping his fingers on his desk.

"I believe the art someone surrounds himself with reveals much about his character." From his expression, it's clear Sicheii is unimpressed with the portraits.

"Yes, well, these are portraits of significant alumni from our sister school in England." Cordingly points to the largest portrait behind his desk. "That is Sir Godfrey. He served as Chancellor for England's High Court. He graduated from our very first class almost one hundred and twenty years ago. Some legal historians still write about his greatest verdicts today."

Sicheii regards the painting with his arms crossed against his chest. "I'm sure he was an impressive man in person." Switching his eyes to Cordingly, he bores them into him as if they were daggers. "I understand there is a misunderstanding involving Juliet."

Cordingly settles his gaze on me. He keeps if fixed on me

probably because he's more comfortable looking at me than my grandfather. "Juliet instigated a physical altercation with another female student this morning." He frowns and taps on the desk. "I do not need to tell you how seriously we take this violation of our conduct code."

Sicheii's focus unwaveringly falls on Cordingly. He doesn't even blink. "In my experience, disagreements are two-way rivers. The currents often travel up and down river. Perhaps the best way to fully understand the nature of this dispute is to ask both students what happened."

"In this case, all the witnesses report that Juliet attacked this other girl without provocation. This is not acceptable behavior at Bartens." Cordingly flattens his hands together, brings the tips to his lips, and glances at Sicheii. "I know she has a history of fighting in her other school. However, this is her first offense at Bartens. Is there some issue at home? Students often act out when matters are unsettled at home."

Mom is probably the only single mother at Bartens. For the first time, I'm happy she is out of town and Sicheii is here instead. She would have already buckled under the pressure and blamed everything on me.

"Who is the other student?"

"Tiffany Johnson, but I must repeat that all our witnesses confirm Juliet as the provocateur." Sweat sprouts on the Headmaster's forehead like weeds. He picks up an expensive fountain pen and twists the writing instrument in his hands. The Johnson family is an elite member of the privileged class in our town.

Sicheii flashes his sparkling white teeth. "According to your rules, both students involved in a physical altercation are supposed to be suspended for a week with a full hearing where the dispute can be heard."

When did he read the school's rulebook?

Cordingly sputters words so fast they bump into each other on the way out of his mouth. "Y-yes, those are the s-stated rules, but in this case I do not believe we need to follow the rules precisely. As I said earlier, this is Juliet's first offense and luckily it was a brief one. Today is Thursday. I suggest Juliet stay home tomorrow and ponder her actions. She can write an apology to Tiffany and return to classes on Monday." He glowers at me and slows his pace so the words come out measured. "Of course, we would have to take more severe actions if this behavior happens again. Perhaps even ex-pul-sion."

The last word takes forever from start to finish and sends a shudder down my back. I'd happily return to my old school, but expulsion would be bad—the type of offense that would stay on my permanent record and prevent me from going to a good college. If I don't go to a good college, I'll never get into a top graduate school. Without a top graduate school, there's no chance I'll land a high paying job and live in a big city in an apartment with river views and expensive clothes and Apple products and cars and vacations and all the other luxuries I'm supposed to want. At least that's what Bartens tells me, yet Mom makes a lot of money and I can't help but think she'd be happier with more free time and less stress.

"I'm sure there will be no more incidents like this one." Sicheii turns and saunters from the office without another word. He doesn't even glance at me. I jump from the chair and race after him.

The Porsche is parked out front. Before I can buckle the safety belt, Sicheii pulls away from the curb with a squeak of the tires. His disapproval drapes over me like a wet blanket.

"What happened?" He speeds from school, working his way around slow moving cars.

"Tiffany stuck a nasty cartoon about Katie's father on her locker. I yanked it off before she could see it. When I turned, Tiffany called me Indian trash."

He keeps his eyes on the road as he works the manual stick shift. "Do you think you were doing your friend a favor?"

"Katie would have been devastated if she saw that cartoon. She was already upset over a news show from the night before that said her dad was guilty and going to jail."

He glances at me for the first time. "How is she going to feel when a new cartoon gets stuck on her locker tomorrow? Especially when you won't be around?"

"I didn't think about that." Heat flushes my face.

"A good friend helps those she cares about face their challenges, not hide from them. We must embrace our destinies. Did anyone else hear Tiffany call you Indian trash?" He turns down a side street, swerves the car to the side of the road, and stops so suddenly the seatbelt jabs into my chest.

"I heard her. It sounded like she yelled it to me, but no one else said they heard her say anything."

"Even Katie?"

I shake my head. "But I'm *sure* she said it."

Sicheii's white eyebrows arch for a moment and then turn downward as if they tired from the effort. "I thought we raised you stronger than this. You are special. Your blood is special, more special than you realize. How others view you is the least of your concerns. A rock doesn't care if others think it is a diamond or piece of clay. The rock is strong because of its nature." He frowns. He appears sad, and something in his eyes that's hard to identify seems melancholy. "You are special because of your nature. You must accept this. You must be the rock, not the river."

"I know they shouldn't bother me, but sometimes it's hard." Oddly, I think we're talking about two different things. With Sicheii, it's hard to know for sure *what* he's talking about.

Sicheii swings the car back on the road. "The spirits are not entities that existed a long time ago and have since died. The Wind Spirit is as strong today as she was in our ancestors' times. She touches all of us, you in particular." He glances at me as if he is telling me a secret only meant for us to share. "I need you to think on this. I have errands to run today. I'm not sure when I will return."

Didn't Troy tell me the same thing last night?

CHAPTER 12

With nothing to do, I wander to my room, dive on my unmade bed, and pound my pillow a dozen times, making believe it's Tiffany's smug face. When feathers start flying about, I toss the Tiffany Face Pillow at my mirror, flip open my laptop, and surf the web. Googling Roundtree produces a number of hits that pop on the screen. The first three all relate to his death.

The Sentinel has the longest article with the headline "Mystic Slain at Home. " I skim the piece, looking for details, looking really for anything that would mean my grandfather wasn't involved in Roundtree's murder. I don't find what I want. The reporter quoted Sheriff Daniels as saying that he has no suspects in custody, but he's following up on a number of promising leads. The reporter raises the specter that the killing had something to do with the occult. He writes that Roundtree had long been suspected of participating in satanic rituals.

Satanic rituals?

Roundtree was certainly weird, even stranger than Sicheii, but I can't imagine him involved in satanic rituals. The reporter probably made that up.

The last line of the article catches my eye. "Sheriff Daniels believes an arrest is imminent." *An arrest is imminent?* Did Daniels speak to the reporter before or *after* he came by last night? He didn't sound like he was close to arresting anyone then, unless that someone was my grandfather. But if he had any solid evidence against him, he would have taken him in for questioning. At least, that's what they do on the television shows.

Nothing else of interest appears in the current articles. All three local newspapers describe Roundtree as a secretive medicine man who had no family and lived an odd life. None hint at who might have committed the crime, or why, and nothing exonerates Sicheii. Only *The Sentinel* mentions anything about satanic rituals, which I dismiss as nonsense.

I glance at the rest of the search results and find some that go back over decades. There are dozens of them. Outspoken, he frequently criticized the town government and led a protest against the casino, claiming it was going to be built on a culturally significant site. The original location for the resort was planned near Devil's Peak, but he forced a compromise. They moved the project to the other edge of town.

The protest made him unpopular with the developers and business owners in town who all supported the casino. A small blurb about him being arrested for disturbing the peace around the same time appears in a local paper. I'm sure the protests against the casino are what got him thrown in jail. Still, that was a long time ago and the casino *was* eventually built. Now, it's the largest employer in town. Too much time has passed to connect his protest of the casino to his murder fifteen years later.

Since my news searches into Roundtree's life hit a dead end, I check the web for images of the medicine man. Most were snapped at one of our Native American festivals with him wearing traditional clothing. I hover over one image taken during a Changing Woman Festival, which marks thirteen-year-old girls as women. It's one of the most important Tribal ceremonies. It takes four days to complete and is full of dancing and singing. We went to one when I was thirteen. We've never lived on the Rez and have always been outside of the official Tribal structure, but I couldn't help but feel like I was part of the ceremony. Roundtree and Sicheii were there, though they deferred to the medicine men who lived on the Rez for the official duties.

A few other photos pulled up by my search were taken years earlier when he was protesting the casino. One shows an angry Roundtree in handcuffs, long hair blowing in the wind, a twisted sneer plastered on his face. He isn't alone in the picture. He's in the center of a group surrounded mostly by Native Americans, but the other faces are blurry.

I scan further down the search results and notice a picture dated twenty-six years ago. It's a blurry photograph of a group of men around a campfire. I click on the photo and it enlarges. A caption underneath reads—Secret Native American Society Among the Shadows by John Dent, July 25, 1986.

Six men appear in the photo. Four are familiar: Sicheii, Roundtree, Samuel Brooks, and Joseph Hunter. Brooks's shirt is unbuttoned and reveals a tattoo on his chest. I zoom in on the ink, but the image becomes increasingly grainy. It could be the same two twisted arrows my grandfather and Roundtree have on their chests. Or, it could also be something totally different.

It's silly, but the photo reminds me of my dream this morning of the campfire and the ancient Native Americans. I can't put my finger on it, but when I study the expressions on the men's faces, I realize the connection. They share the same raptured look, as if they've been told an important secret. A chill creeps down my spine.

I search for the article, which should be connected to the photo, but nothing shows up on the web. *Secret Native American Society?* I type the phrase into Google, but nothing related comes up. I try Bing and then every other search engine I can think of, but nothing connected to Roundtree or our town comes up. I'm just about out of ideas when I Google John Dent's name. He wrote three articles, mostly about local events. None of the other articles were dated after July 25, 1986—strange. Only one J. Dent lives nearby, and he lives in Old Town, not far from my grandfather's art gallery.

It's already past two when my phone pings. Katie has left me seven text messages, three emails, and one voice mail. I ignore them. She should have backed me up with Cordingly, so I toss my last pillow from my bed and go downstairs to the kitchen.

I gobble down a peanut butter sandwich and try to come up with a plan. I could ask Sicheii about this secret society, but without knowing any more facts, he'll likely just tell me something odd that makes no sense at all. Without more to go on, asking him will be a dead end.

Another incoming call on my cell phone interrupts my

anemic plan making activities. I glance at the number, worried it might be my mother, and find Troy's smiling face.

"What's up, Troy?"

"You're never going to guess what happened." He sounds edgy.

"I'm not guessing." He always wants me to guess at the latest news. It's annoying. "What happened?"

"There's been another murder in the Reservation."

An acidic taste grows in the back of my throat. Two murders in two days can't be a coincidence. We might not live in the safest town, but two dead guys constitute a murder spree for us.

"You won't believe who they found dead this afternoon."

This time I take the bait. "Samuel Brooks." He lives in the same neighborhood as Troy and is in the photograph with Roundtree and Sicheii. It's a silly guess, but the silence on the other end of the phone is deafening.

"How... did you know?"

I grip the iPhone hard. My hand turns red. "Something weird is going on. I'm worried Sicheii is involved in it." Now that I've said the words out loud, I realize they're true and they frighten me.

"Stay put. I'll be right over."

CHAPTER 13

Troy arrives first on his bike, but Ella's beat-up white Ford Fusion pulls up right behind him. A fresh dent marks the front bumper where it looks like she hit a tree, and duct tape wraps around the side mirror, which dangles precariously from the door. That's not the only duct tape on the car — the right taillight and rear bumper both benefit from patches of tape to hold them together. I open the front door, and Troy leads Ella and Marlon into the house. It's good to see my old high school friends again. I hadn't noticed how isolated I had become. It must be a couple of months since we last hung out together and that's too long. The fault is likely mine.

I march them toward the kitchen, grinning and shaking my head.

"What's the problem," Ella asks, a bite in her voice.

"I can't get used to you two together," I say. "You're barely half his size." She's just short of five feet and resembles a pixie with short brown hair, cream-colored skin, freckles that bunch around her cheeks, and wide, chestnut eyes. Marlon is quiet and big. He's slightly taller and wider than Troy, dark skinned, and round in a natural, puffy way like a human cheese doodle.

Ella shrugs. "You know what they say, opposites attract. Besides, I like my guys big."

"And we all know Ella's way tougher than Marlon," Troy adds. More than a trace of amusement sparkles behind his eyes.

Ella chuckles. "Just don't call me—"

"Tinker." Troy and I complete the sentence for her.

We all laugh and it feels good. I feel a little more like the person I was before switching schools.

"Billy Trout will never be the same," Marlon says. We all smile and think back to eighth grade. A few of the older boys started calling Ella *Tinker*. She marched toward Billy, the largest of the bullies, kicked him hard in the shin, and pounced. Marlon and Troy pulled her off him, but not before she left the boy with a bloody nose, two black eyes, and one cracked tooth. No one dared call her Tinker again.

"He deserved it. Besides, he left me with no choice. No way I'm going through high school called Tinker. I'd rather cover myself with sugar and kick a beehive." Ella speaks in one quick burst.

When we reach the kitchen, Troy asks, "So how did you know Sam Brooks was murdered? You couldn't have just guessed. What's going on?"

"I didn't know for *sure*." I lean against the center island.

"How did you guess, Juliet?" Troy rubs his hands together. His eyes are suspicious, narrow slits.

"I was surfing Roundtree's name to find some clues why he was killed and came across an old photograph." After a few keystrokes on my laptop, the old picture pops up and I hand the computer to him. He holds it low so Ella and Marlon can see.

"Secret Society?" Marlon rumbles, his voice as deep as a desert well.

"I don't know what that's about, but my grandfather's in the photo, plus Brooks, Roundtree, and Joe Hunter. I don't recognize the other two guys."

"That one is Edward Taylor," Ella says. "I recognize him from old pictures at school. He died five years ago. I think he had cancer. He was also a medicine man."

"Another medicine man. What are the odds of that?" A nervous fluttering twists my stomach. We have a puzzle and the first pieces are fitting together, but a little voice in my head tells me it's going to be complicated, and I'm not sure I'll like the picture when all of the pieces fit together.

"This doesn't prove anything," Troy says. "It's probably just a coincidence."

"Did you find anything else about this secret society on the internet?" Ella asks.

I shake my head. "Nothing. Even when I Googled John Dent's name, only some old articles and an address for him in Old Town came up."

She takes the laptop from Troy. "Did you look through *The Sentinel's* archives?"

My blank expression tells her everything she needs to know.

"My uncle works at the newspaper. For their 50th anniversary last year, they placed all of the old editions on their website under archives so people can go back and look at them." She glances up from the computer. "It was in all the papers. They'll probably go totally electronic soon anyway. The cost of paper keeps going up, and they make most of their money on e-advertising. I'd be surprised if anyone prints a paper ten years from now."

Troy shrugs, and Marlon eyes the refrigerator. He's always grazing.

"Are you guys hungry?" I ask. "We have leftovers in the fridge."

Marlon swings his wide frame toward the fridge. "No need to trouble yourself." He opens the door. "I'll help myself."

Ella has *The Sentinel's* website up on the laptop and clicks the Archives tab. "Do you remember the date of the photograph?"

Marlon carries a plate of fried chicken in one hand and a drumstick in the other. "Did you know there are more chickens than people in the world?"

"Where'd you get that from?" Troy asks.

"Snapple cap. And the date on the photograph was July 25th 1986." The words compete for space with chicken. I shoot him a look and he shrugs. "I have a good memory."

"Like an elephant," Troy jokes.

"You're just jealous," Ella says.

My world goes fuzzy. One moment Ella is typing on the laptop and the next, my mind swims, my legs buckle and a splitting pain cracks open my skull. A jumble of voices all mutter at the same time. They don't make any sense. I squeeze my ears shut and shake my head from side to side. Worried I might fall, I lean heavily against the counter and luckily, the pain and noise vanish as quickly as they came.

Troy grabs my waist. I didn't even notice him move toward me. "Are you okay, Jules?"

All three faces stare at me nervously. I don't like their expressions, especially Troy's, so I shake him off and lie. "I'm fine. I haven't eaten anything in a while. I got a little dizzy." Apparently, the new me lies constantly.

Marlon thrusts the plate of fried chicken toward me. The last thing I want is to eat something, but what choice do I have? I grab the smallest drumstick and bite into the chicken with fake gusto.

"You're sure you don't want to lie down or anything?" Troy asks.

"I'm good." To prove it, I finish the chicken leg in three bites and hope to keep it down.

Ella types in the date for the article and flashing red words appear - *Improper Date.* "That's odd." She tries the day before. The newspaper appears on the screen. "Hmm," she says, and tries the date after. Another newspaper pops on the screen.

"Someone's deleted the July 25th issue from the archives," she explains. "I wonder why. The issue before and after are both available online. Every issue *The Sentinel* has ever published is supposed to be on the archives. That's what they said."

"It's obvious," Marlon rumbles.

We all stare at him. This time, he holds a chicken wing in his hand.

"Someone doesn't want us to read what's in that paper."

I have a sick feeling he's right.

"We can ask your grandfather," Troy suggests. "I'm sure he would remember an article written about secret Native American societies with his picture attached to it. There's probably an easy explanation for all this."

"No way. We need to know more before I ask Sicheii. I have a feeling this is more complicated than a newspaper article. Too many coincidences are lining up, and I don't like the way my grandfather is in the middle of them."

I retrieve the laptop from Ella and type in a search for Dent. The address for J. Dent in Old Town flashes onto the screen. "We're going to have to visit Mr. Dent and ask him."

"Let's go for a drive," Ella says.

Marlon places the now empty plate into the sink. "I'm in." He takes Ella's hand and marches toward the front door.

I know it isn't right, but a twinge of jealousy stabs me in the side. I've never had a real boyfriend. I sneak a furtive glance at Troy, who follows the happy couple a step behind. He's always been around, but our relationship has never been more than just friends. I'm not sure why, or if I want it to be more. He's had many girlfriends over the last couple of years, but we have an unspoken agreement. I never ask about them, and he never tells me.

How stupid is that?

CHAPTER 14

Ella zips through traffic on her way to Old Town, revving the engine hard, swerving around a slow moving station wagon and plowing across a light she claims had just turned orange. She drives the way she thinks: fast and on the edge of chaos. I try not to look out the window as we screech to a stop inches away from a truck stopped at a red light.

Troy sits in the backseat with me and we share a look. Driving with Ella is a little like riding a roller coaster without the safety features.

"How did you guys find out about Brooks?" I ask no one in particular, hoping to distract myself from the swerving and screeching of tires.

"Marlon lives a few blocks from his house. He saw police cars and his brother at the scene," Troy says.

"His brother?"

"Yeah. He started working for the sheriff's department a

few weeks ago," Troy says.

"Good for him," I say.

"If he doesn't screw up, I'm hoping he'll get me a job after high school," Marlon says.

"With your brother, that's a big *if*," Ella shoots me a look in the rearview mirror. "He was late for his first day. He forgot to set the alarm."

"Could happen to anyone," I say. "Some of us aren't morning people. How did Brooks die? Was he tortured like Roundtree?"

"My bro didn't give me the details, but he looked white and his face puckered up like he was about to lose his lunch. I could tell from his expression Brooks was murdered. I don't know about torture."

"The two killings have to be connected." I sigh. A sick feeling tells me these murders are tied to the photograph and my grandfather. I just need to figure out how the pieces fit together before Sheriff Daniels or the killer.

Ella swings the car into a parking lot on the East end of Old Town and screeches to a stop between two white SUVs with out-of-town plates. Old Town consists of a collection of narrow winding cobblestone streets, which are too tight for cars. Locals rarely come to Old Town except to work. As a young girl, I used to go with Sicheii to his art gallery during the weekends when Mom went to her office. We spent many hours in the ice cream shop next to his gallery. I always got chocolate and rummaged through the red rock souvenirs they sold from large plastic boxes.

As we pile out of the car, I ask, "Do you guys know if Brooks had a funky tattoo on his chest?"

They all shake their heads.

"Why?" Ella asks.

"Roundtree had weird ink on his chest. I saw it in one of the pictures. Maybe it's a clue." I don't mention my grandfather's tattoo. I feel bad about withholding information from my friends, but I don't want to make my grandfather seem more like a deranged killer than he already does. After all, he's still my grandfather. There must be some explanation for these murders that doesn't involve him wielding an antique hatchet.

The streets are mostly empty, it being that lazy time after lunch and before dinner. The address for Dent lists him on 3rd Street. While Old Town attracts mostly tourists, many of the old brick buildings still have apartments above the storefronts.

My legs grow heavy as we approach Sicheii's gallery on the way to Dent's place. We pass two restaurants and one t-shirt shop. I slow to a creep when we cross the street and onto the block with his gallery. I stop at the ice cream shop next door and feel a little foolish. My relationship with Sicheii has always been complicated. He's not like a normal grandfather who sits in a rocking chair, reads books, and goes to school plays. He has an edge, a wild side he's always shared with me in glimpses. It probably has to do with his medicine man training. He just sees life differently from most. I worry that edge has led him into real trouble this time.

"Are you sure you don't want to just ask Jake about all of this?" Troy asks as we stand on the edge of his building, just before the windows. "I'm sure he'll give us a simple explanation."

I snort. "When has my grandfather ever given a simple explanation? I need to understand what's going on before we talk to him." I inch forward as we reach the corner of his store and peek through the window.

"Who's talking to Lisa?" Ella asks. "They seem to be having quite an argument."

Lisa is waving her arms around, her face squeezed tightly together. She leans forward aggressively. Ms. Arnold crosses her arms against her chest, her face flush.

"She's one of my teachers from Bartens. I didn't realize they knew each other, but they both went to Arizona State." I start to feel a little dizzy. I'm sure they're arguing over my grandfather, and the argument has something to do with these murders. I have no idea how or why, but I had better find out soon.

"Well, whatever they're fighting about, they certainly seem angry," Ella says. "I don't see any sign of your grandfather."

"He's probably upstairs," Troy says.

Ella checks the windows above the gallery. No light sneaks past the drawn curtains. "It looks like he's out to me."

I don't like waiting around on the street by the gallery. I keep expecting Sicheii to jump out from behind me like he's done a hundred times before. I bite my lip to gain control over my imagination. The pain helps.

I'm about to suggest we move along when a wet, sticky, tongue licks my fingers. I look down and find a chocolate cockapoo staring up at me. My attention was so fixed on studying the gallery I didn't notice the dog sneak up on me. He's knee high, has beautiful chestnut eyes, curly fur, and a cute little soul patch of gray fur on his chin. He cocks his head to one side as if he's asking me to rub the fur on his head, so I oblige, and swear he smiles at me.

A middle-aged woman jogs toward us. "Come back, Charlie!" she shouts as she crosses the street.

"Don't worry, the Dog Whisperer has him," Ella tells the red-faced woman.

"I'm so sorry. He never runs like that. I don't know what got into him." She picks up the end of his black leash.

Charlie sits at attention and stares at me. He drags a smile from me because he could be the cutest dog I've ever seen. "I just have this effect on dogs." I shrug. "They seem to like me." Dogs have always acted weirdly around me. I don't know why. Troy used to joke that I smell like a milk bone, but he stopped when I stomped hard on his foot and elbowed him in the gut the last time he said that two years ago.

Ella rolls her eyes. "I'll never go to a dog park with her again. One time, three dogs jumped on top of each other just so she could pet them. She's the Dog Whisperer."

"Do you have one of your own?" the woman asks.

"No, Mom's allergic."

The woman shoots me a sidewise glance and says, "Thanks" to me, and, "Come on," to Charlie. I watch as she leads the dog away. He keeps looking back at me, but she tugs him along.

"You could always walk dogs for a living," Marlon says.

"Really?"

"What? Dog walkers make good money."

"Let's keep going." I tug on Troy's arm.

We scoot past the gallery toward 3rd Street. We take a right onto Dent's road and stop at number 125, right next to Aunt Maye's Big and Tall Western Outfitter. A blue neon sign makes it clear where we are.

"This store is perfect for you, Marlon," I tease him.

He wrinkles his face. "I doubt they have my style."

I grin at his oversized t-shirt and loose fitting shorts.

"Marlon likes casual chic." Ella chuckles as she loops her arm around Marlon's. I chuckle along with her, but a new pang of jealously stabs at me. They seem so close. *Do they know how lucky they are?*

A glass door stands to the left of the storefront. I check the names on the directory. J. Dent lives in apartment 302. The walkup uses a buzzer system.

"How are we going to get in?" Marlon asks.

"Should we buzz Dent?" Ella suggests. "Or maybe we should buzz everyone else and hope someone lets us in. Of course, there's a third option."

All eyes turn to me. This is my show. "I vote for the third option. We should surprise him." I glance at Troy. "Can you pick the lock?"

He frowns, leans forward, and examines the lock. It's an old pin and tumbler, something that hasn't been updated for decades. By the time he looks up, Ella has already grabbed a bobby pin from her hair. Troy grins, takes the pin, and removes his keychain from his pocket, which has an assortment of small tools stuck in it. He slides out an Allen Wrench and goes to work on the lock.

This is not the first lock he's picked. My old high school uses the same type. We've gone exploring a few times after school hours. Nothing bad, just bored kids looking for something to do.

Troy twists the wrench, the latch clicks, and the door opens. "After you," he says as he holds the door open.

I lead us up the wooden staircase, and in a minute we're facing apartment 302. Only three apartments are on the floor. 302 faces the street and has a simple red wooden door with brass numbers toward the top. My pulse accelerates. Some of the puzzle pieces are behind this door. I rap on it three times, wondering if Dent is home, wondering what we'll learn.

We wait. Time slows. Marlon breathes heavily behind me. Anxiety surrounds us like moisture in a rain cloud. Just when I think no one is home, a rustling sound comes from inside the apartment.

As the noise gets closer, a high-pitched voice cries out, "It's about time. The toilet won't flush since this morning. I'm too old to wait all day!" The door opens and a thin, gray-haired woman stands on the other side. Her severe, gaunt face twists into a question. "Who are you? Where's Carlos, the Super?"

I'm in front, so I manufacture my sweetest smile. "We're looking for John Dent."

A sad shadow drifts across her face. The expression is fleeting, as if she's had much practice chasing it away.

"There is no John Dent living here. You have the wrong place. I'm Jane Dent." She starts to swing the door closed, but she moves slowly, so I walk into the apartment before she gets the chance. I don't know where this confidence comes from, but there's more to the story, and I need some answers. My friends reluctantly follow me.

"I didn't invite you in," the old woman protests, but she moves to the side as we walk past her. The apartment is nicer than I expect—exposed brick walls, hardwood floors, and tall windows with a view of Old Town.

She shuts the door behind us. "So why are you looking for my John?" Her voice lilts, fading at the end. Her eyes pierce mine and sparkle like emeralds .

"John Dent wrote a newspaper article we're interested in," I say. "We thought we could ask him a few questions. It's for a school project."

The old woman leans against a dark blue couch. Behind her is a fireplace with a plain brick mantel with family pictures placed on the ledge. The largest picture shows a middle-aged woman with her arm around a young man's shoulders. They have the same green eyes, her eyes. Other pictures flank that one - pictures of grandchildren and two women who also resemble her. They're probably her daughters.

"John wrote a few newspaper articles, but that was a long time ago." She crosses her arms against her chest. The sleeves of her thin yellow blouse droop from her wrists. "I can't help you with any of them."

"Do you know where he is?" I study her closely, trying to read her. "We need to talk to him."

"My John died some time ago. You need to leave, or I'm calling the police." She bites her lip.

I hesitate. There's more that she's not telling me. I can feel it. Troy has already started for the door, but I stay solidly in place. "When did he die?"

The old woman's eyes flutter to the floor. "Four years ago. Now please go. I'm sure Carlos will be coming any minute."

I nod, and we leave. When we reach the street, we bunch together in a huddle.

"That seems like a dead end," Troy says.

"Really, Troy?" Ella says. "She was hiding something. It was obvious from her body language. Something happened to her son that she didn't want to tell us."

"She only had one picture of him on the mantel, and he looked like he was in his twenties," I say. "I wonder when he really died."

"There's only one way to find out," Ella snaps. "We'll go to the cemetery."

"Let's stop at Tito's Tacos first." Marlon licks his lips.

"I can't believe you," Troy jostles him with an elbow.

"What? I'm hungry."

CHAPTER 15

Packed as usual, a line stretches beyond the Tito's Tacos food truck at least ten customers long, and when one leaves, another takes his place. Mostly day laborers that quit work early wait patiently for their turn, but a few others with collared shirts and khakis who might work in Old Town blend in, too. No one from Bartens is here. I'm not surprised.

Do I belong, or is it too late for me? Have my two years at Bartens changed me so much that Tito's is no longer a place for me?

I grind my teeth. I feel comfortable with my friends but we're not close like we were before Bartens. A distance has grown between us since I changed schools. It's not any one thing, but the ease we used to have between us is not the same. I'm always one step behind, trying to catch-up and figure out the latest, like what's up with Marlon's brother. I should have known that he got that job with the Sheriff's Department, but now these things, small but important events, slip by without me knowing.

Which world do I belong in?

It can't be both. Sometimes I feel isolated, like I'll never belong anywhere. Troy and Katie are really my only two links to both worlds. They're the only two I can count on, but some days that's not enough. There's ice beneath my feet and it's cracking. I'm afraid if I fall in, no one will be around to help me out. Sicheii wants me to be a rock, but if I'm a rock is it possible to be comfortable in both places like he says or neither?

What if I'm just not strong enough?

I take a deep breath and my lungs fill with a greasy, spicy scent that makes my mouth water. I imagine that odor lingering well after Tito's Tacos is gone. It probably lives in the trees, the soil, the rocks....

The smell helps cleanse my thoughts and brings me back to my immediate worries. We sit on a picnic bench as far away from the food truck as possible. Marlon has already eaten three tacos and launched himself into his fourth without any loss of enthusiasm. He is a taco-eating machine.

"So what do we know?" Ella asks. "Someone killed Roundtree and Brooks. They both died violently, within a day of each other, so both murders are probably connected."

"Brooks, Roundtree, Hunter, Taylor, your grandfather, and one other person were in the photograph," Marlon adds between bites. "And that article was removed from the newspaper's website."

"Yes, and John Dent died, and his mom lied to us about when. I have a strange feeling his death is connected to these two new murders," I add.

"We don't know that she lied," Troy objects as he purses his lips. He looks frustrated and rubs his hands over his face, which is unlike him. "There may be no connection between the killings and the photograph. The picture was taken over twenty-seven years ago. That's a long time. Brooks and Roundtree were both old and knew each other. There could be many other explanations for the murders."

"True, but you have to admit it's strange that the only edition of *The Sentinel* not online is the one with the photo. Marlon is right." I frown at Troy. "Somebody doesn't want us to see the article."

Marlon beams a smile at me as he shovels the last bite of taco in his mouth. "Guess what's my favorite day of the year?" he asks. A small river of pepper sauce leaks down the side of his face and splashes onto his t-shirt.

Ella hands him a napkin.

"Christmas?"

"Nope. October 4th."

"Why?" Troy asks.

"October 4th is National Taco Day."

"Great." I smile and shake my head. "Let's find John Dent's gravestone so we can discover when he died. I'm sure his mother lied about that, and if she did, something else must be going on."

"What about John Dent's Secret Society article?" Ella asks as she rises from the bench and stretches. "What could Dent have been writing about?"

Troy shrugs his wide shoulders. "Outsiders have always believed rumors of secret societies involving magic or pagan rituals among the tribes. He probably wrote some nonsense along those lines. I doubt there's much to it. If a secret society exists, they're sure doing a good job of keeping it quiet."

"That would be the point, Troy." Ella rolls her eyes.

"Your attitude is starting to bug me." I jab my finger at him.

"Why? Because I have a hard time believing there's a secret society filled with people we know that's been meeting for over thirty years. And this secret society has dangerous information that someone's willing to murder to discover?" He uses air quotes when he says secret society, and I want to deck him. I know it sounds far-fetched, but the pieces are starting to fit together. There's more to this mystery that I need to find out.

"Actually, Troy, there have been many secret societies that have gone on way longer than thirty years." Ella starts ticking them off with her fingers. "There's the Skull and Bones, the Freemasons, the Templars, the Illuminati—"

"Don't forget about Area 51," Marlon interrupts. "We all know the government has an alien corpse hidden in Area 51."

Troy shakes his head and lifts his arms up in mock surrender. "I give up. Let's go find the gravestone and discover when John Dent died. Maybe he was abducted by aliens."

I walk briskly toward Ella's Ford. Moving feels good. We need to find more puzzle pieces. Time is running out. The cemetery is huge, and the sun has started sinking. We don't have much light left.

Ella pilots the Ford into the cemetery's massive parking lot. The place is quiet—no more than ten cars are parked toward the entrance. All the locals use this cemetery, including the town's five founding families. I don't even know if there's another cemetery around here.

As we walk through the gate, we hear the bubbling sound of the meandering creek that splits the burial grounds roughly in half. Narrow green bands dotted with grass and a few short conifer trees create a thin line on both sides of the stream. When the graves spread away from the water, clay, red rocky soil and the random cactus replace the grass.

"Let's split up in two groups," Ella suggests. "Marlon and I will cross the bridge and check the West side of the cemetery, and you two can stay on this side and check out the East side."

Troy and I walk methodically down the rows of the dead. I spot a palm-sized piece of petrified wood and start tossing it and catching it as we go.

"I don't understand why anyone would want to be buried in a box," Troy says as he marches, head swinging from side to side. "I want to be cremated and returned to the earth, so my death will benefit other living things."

"You sound like Sicheii."

"That's not a bad thing. There's value in the old ways. You can't ignore them."

"The world has changed a lot since the old ways." I trudge up and down the rows and keep my head down while I study the names. I call out the unusual ones to pass the time. Most of the gravestones are simple rectangles half buried in the ground. "To advance, we need to evolve. No one hunts buffalo with bows and arrows anymore, Troy."

"You used to care more about our traditions before you went to that school." Troy kicks some loose stones.

He's right. I was closer to Sicheii back then and would spend lazy afternoons with Troy talking about Sicheii's stories and the different spirits. We don't do that anymore.

Troy romanticizes our past and believes the old ways are more than superstitions primitive people needed to get by. Technology replaces all those superstitions for me. Who needs the Wind Spirit to praise or Coyote to fear when we have Apple and the Internet and science and the super-mean spoiled sharks at Bartens to contend with?

We wander into the oldest part of the cemetery, and I find something odd on an old tombstone and hesitate. It looks like a circle is carved into the stone. Dirt has crusted over it, so I wipe off the brown bits of earth and stare at the marker for a moment and wonder if my eyes are playing tricks on me, but they aren't. A Steven Holden died in 1845. Next to his name is a carving of two twisted arrows in a circle. The carving looks the same as Roundtree and Sicheii's tattoo—exactly the same.

My chest tightens and goose bumps run up my arms. I squeeze the stone in my hand hard as I stare at the symbol and wonder what it means. Steven Holder doesn't sound like a Native American name, but there was a time when young Native Americans were taken to "American" schools to change them into "Americans," including changing their names. Maybe he was one of those people.

"Did you find something?"

"No," I answer, reluctant to share the symbol with Troy or anyone else. The twisted arrows worry me. It's connected to Sicheii and the more often it shows up, the more likely he's in the middle of a storm. "This part of the cemetery is too old. We should head farther north."

I glance down at my hand. I've reduced the petrified piece of wood to dust. *Weird.* They're usually as hard as stone, but this one must have been defective. My phone pings.

Troy stops and stares.

"It's from Ella."

He slides over. "Let's see what she found."

I click on the text. It contains a photograph of a tombstone. I enlarge the photo. The writing is clearly visible: "John Dent, Born April 15, 1961 – Died July 26, 1986."

My heart races. "John Dent died the day after his article was published."

But that's not the worst part. Next to his name is a carving of two twisted arrows in a circle.

CHAPTER 16

We regroup in the parking lot near Ella's Ford. Troy and I have been arguing the entire trip back to the car. He's being stubborn. "There has to be a connection between John Dent's death and the article. It can't be a coincidence that he died the day after he published the story, Troy," I say.

He just stares ahead, a blank expression on his face. I've seen that look dozens of times. He's lost in thought. The gears spinning in his head are almost visible. Usually he'd have no problem believing in a conspiracy, but since this one involves Native Americans, he's struggling with it. He doesn't *want* it to be true, but I don't *want* my grandfather involved in this mystery and the evidence is starting to stack up. Sometimes things happen you can't control.

"I think you're right," Ella says, "and did you see that weird symbol after John Dent's name on his gravestone? I've seen it before, but I can't place it."

My heart skips. I was hoping to keep the twisted arrows a secret, but if Ella has already noticed it, I don't have a choice. She deserves to know everything. I swallow the lump in my throat and say, "Roundtree had the same symbol tattooed on his chest, and I saw the same thing on another tombstone in the cemetery, an old one."

"That's why you asked us if Brooks had a tat," Marlon says, "to see if he had the same one?"

"But why didn't you tell us about the symbol right away?" Ella's eyes sharpen and her hands fly to her hips.

I sigh. "My grandfather has the same tattoo on his chest. I don't know what it means, but I'm sure he's mixed up in this mess somehow."

"The symbol was probably just a popular design thirty years ago. I've never seen it before," Troy says.

"Perhaps it has something to do with this secret society Dent wrote about." Ella purses her lips. "We need to visit Joe Hunter. He's in the photograph. He should know something."

Hunter owns a general store near the Reservation that makes the best flavored ices. He used to work in the store all the time, but now his nephew is usually behind the counter, which only makes the store more popular among teenagers because his nephew will sell beer to almost anyone.

"Hunter lives in Red Rock Commons," Marlon says.

We all shoot him a look.

"*What?* My grandmother's dating him."

"Your grandmother's a hundred years old," Troy jokes, which is more like his usual self.

Marlon shrugs one of his beefy shoulders. "You know what

they say. One hundred is really the new seventy-five." Marlon leads us to the car.

Troy lingers a step behind so I playfully shove him. "Come on. Maybe we'll interrupt Marlon's grandmother and Hunter on a hot date."

Troy moans as we file into Ella's car. "Great. That's a picture I don't want to see."

Ella floors it and swerves the car onto Route 100, barely sneaking in front of a blue BMW. Red Rock Commons is a senior community made up of townhouses not far from the cemetery. It takes less than ten minutes for us to enter the complex.

"Hunter's unit is number 127," Marlon says.

I point out the sign for Unit 125, which means we're close, so Ella swings the Ford into a parking space on the right side of the street next to a plain white van. After we pile out of the car, we plod our way to 127.

"What are you going to say to Hunter?" Troy says.

"Beats me. I guess I'll have to wing it." When we turn a corner, we see Unit 127 and a gray sedan in the driveway. As we reach the curb, the front door to the townhouse opens. Joe Hunter steps through and slams it shut. He's wearing khakis, a blue cotton shirt, and clutches a green and red-checked Samsonite in his right hand.

He sees us and speeds his pace toward the car, limping noticeably. I move to intercept him, and we reach his car at the same time. Hunter's eyes touch on us, but mostly they dance down both sides of the street.

"I'm in a rush, kids," he says as he presses a button on his key, and the trunk pops open. Sweat runs down both sides of his face, and his shirt sticks to his body. The day is still hot, but not *that* hot.

I jump right in. "Does your trip have anything to do with Roundtree and Brook's murders?"

Hunter hoists his bag with a grunt. His arms shake against the weight as he drops the Samsonite in the trunk. He doesn't look at me as he talks. "I knew them both. They were good men." He leans his hands on the trunk lid and slams it down hard with a thud.

I step between him and the driver's-side door. Marlon and Ella flank me and we create a sort of human wall between him and the car. "Tell us about this secret society you're all part of."

He frowns when we block his path, but his attention is still elsewhere. His head swivels from side to side. Fear drips off him as if he's just taken a dip in a pool.

He speaks fast, too fast. "I don't know what you're talking about. I need to go."

When he moves toward us, I stand my ground. "Do these murders have anything to do with the two twisted arrows in a circle?"

Hunter freezes, his hand darts to the collar of his shirt, and he stares at me wide-eyed. "Juliet Stone, you of all people should not be asking these questions. These are dangerous times."

"I don't understand what's happening. Is my grandfather mixed up in all this?" My heart is thumping.

He smiles at me with moist eyes, grabs my hand, and kisses the back of it. "You are a remarkable young woman. For the answers you seek, you'll need to ask Jake. I wish I could be there when he tells you what you need to know, but I must go.

It's for everyone's protection." He sweeps his eyes across all of us, but they linger on Troy. "You shouldn't be here. You need to be careful."

"Careful about what?" Ella asks. Her hands are on her hips again.

He pulls me close to him and whispers in my ear. "You're special, Juliet. You've been chosen."

"Holy cow! That was creepy," Ella says as she turns to watch Hunter drive away. "He sure seemed scared."

I can still feel his lips pressed against my skin as his car zips out of sight, so I wipe the back of my hand on my jeans. "Let's go." I start walking toward Ella's car.

"What did he tell you? Why did he whisper something in your ear? Was it some type of secret? Why couldn't he tell *all* of us? Did it have anything to do with your grandfather?" Ella asks all five questions in one quick burst as if they're all just one question.

"He said I was special." I shrug one shoulder.

"We already know you're *special*," chuckles Troy, which causes both Marlon and Ella to laugh. I glare at him. He's smiling, but his eyes look nervous.

When we cram in the Ford, Ella says, "Things are getting weird super fast. There must be some connection between Dent's article, the twisted arrows, and these murders."

Marlon adds his opinion from the front seat. "I'm sorry Jules, but it seems as if Jake is in the middle of this. I mean, Hunter said to ask *him* about it. He wouldn't mention Jake if he wasn't connected."

Everyone stares at me. I sense their thoughts and don't like it. "If Sicheii's involved in these murders, then why would Hunter tell me to talk to him? He should have warned me to stay away or go to the police."

"And he said he wished he could be there when you speak to Jake, which is odd, too. He wouldn't say that if he suspected him of murder," Ella adds as she starts the car.

"Maybe we should just ask Jake what's going on," Troy suggests for the millionth time. "He could be in danger and we can help."

"Not yet. I need more to wrestle a straight answer out of him." If my grandfather is in trouble or mixed up in these murders, then I need to help him. The only way I can do that is to force real answers from him. Stories about spirits or rocks and rivers won't do me any good, and that's what he'll tell me if I haven't put the puzzle together before confronting him.

The air conditioning kicks in and the overworked blowers rattle in protest. The car is oven-hot even though the sun melts into the horizon.

"We need to find out what Dent wrote," Ella says. "We need to read that article."

An idea buzzes into my mind like a bee on a flower. "I'll call Katie. She's a first-class hacker. If there's something on the web, she'll find it." Hacking is Katie's release from her strict rule-following world. Masked by an alias, the computer gives her freedom, freedom she uses to uncover other people's secrets.

"Can we trust her? I mean, if Jake is somehow involved, we need to be careful who knows what. At least until we know what's going on and what we should do about it." Troy fires me a look, his eyes cutting.

"She *is* part of that Bartens crowd," Ella adds. "Her dad used to be one of the biggest fish until he got caught stealing from everyone."

I feel the Bartens wedge between us. "I trust Katie as much as anyone else, even you guys." My voice is abrupt and defensive. As far as I'm concerned, the matter is settled, so I hit Katie's speed dial number. She answers on the first ring.

Katie sputters words in one long, breathless burst. "Are you okay? Why haven't you returned any of my messages? Are you mad at me?"

Heat flashes across my face. I had almost forgotten my fight with Tiffany, but now that I am talking to Katie, the whole incident comes rushing back to me — the anger and Katie's betrayal. "Why didn't you tell them what Tiffany called me?"

"I don't know what you're talking about! Tiffany didn't say anything. You ripped down something from your locker and raced at her. It all happened so fast. I didn't hear anything."

Her answer comes in a speedy *whoosh*. I take a deep breath. She sounds truthful; her voice cracks at the end, close to tears. At least she didn't realize Tiffany had hung the cartoon on *her* locker or that the cartoon was really of her dad. Sicheii is right about that — I should tell her the truth, but I'm not ready to deal with that now and definitely not over the phone. I'll need to be face to face with her for that conversation, or I'll mess it up and only hurt her.

"I'm sorry, Katie. Tiffany called me Indian trash. I thought she shouted it, but you were farther away. I guess you didn't hear her."

My anger deflates like air leaking from a balloon. I feel bad accusing Katie. Besides, two people are dead, my grandfather could be next, and this strange symbol keeps popping up everywhere. A little name calling from Tiffany can't compare to all that.

"Did you get suspended? What did she put on your locker? Did—"

I feel like a prisoner facing a firing squad, so I interrupt her before she fires more questions at me. "Katie, can you do me a favor?"

"Sure...."

"Don't worry. The favor has nothing to do with school or Tiffany. I found a photograph online from *The Sentinel*. It's part of an article written by John Dent on July 25, 1986. Can you retrieve it?"

I hear Katie typing on her laptop as her fingers fly over her keyboard. In less than a minute, she has the photo on her screen. "I've got the photograph up. It's not much of a picture."

"I can't find the article connected to the photograph. Do you think you can find the piece?"

"All *The Sentinel's* old issues are online in an archives section on their website."

I guess everyone else knows that but me. She types in staccato fashion.

"Strange, this issue is missing. The issues before and after are online."

"Exactly. Can you find it?"

Katie pauses for a second. "Why do you want it?"

I'm not ready to explain everything to her. She's trustworthy, but I don't want to spook her, and I'm not sure what we're looking for anyway. "I'll tell you everything later," which is probably true. "You'll just have to trust me for now."

She sighs. "I can try to access *The Sentinel*'s server. If the newspaper was originally put on the system and then deleted, the old paper should leave a shadow. If I find the shadow, I can download the article. It might take a while."

"Thanks, Katie. Just do your best. I'll talk to you later."

"I'm not sure what we do next," Ella says as she swerves around a bus. "We could go back and talk to Jane Dent. Maybe we can find out why she lied to us."

"Maybe we should wait and see if Katie can find the article," Troy says. "It might prove to be nothing."

"I think Troy's right," I say. "I'd like to question Jane Dent after we read what her son wrote. Something tells me she won't be happy to see us again. We'll be lucky to have one more crack at her."

"I wonder why Hunter kissed your hand and whispered to you," Ella says as she drives back toward my house.

I'm thinking the same thing. I know Hunter like all the other kids in the area, but we've never been close. I doubt I've had more than a two-minute conversation with him, and every one of those conversations ended with me paying for a flavored ice.

As we pass the Diary Freeze, fear pricks the back of my neck, so I glance out the back window. A plain white van drives a few car lengths behind us. It looks like the same van we parked next to by Hunter's townhouse. The driver has black, slicked backed hair and broad shoulders. I don't like the look of him — something in his eyes seems dangerous.

Ella slows, turns right, and stops at the security gate. The white van speeds past while the driver focuses solely on the road ahead.

I'm being silly, seeing bogeymen who aren't there.

CHAPTER

My mind spins when Troy and I step out of Ella's Ford. Is Sicheii's life in danger, or is he involved in these murders in a more sinister way?

He's closer to me than the average grandfather. He's played a big role in raising me, almost like a father. Even though I didn't want him to stay over, that was more about me than him. He's always been the same, always been a rock for Mom and me—a weird rock with lots of dents and cracks, but still a rock. I can't believe he'd kill anyone, but a whisper of doubt tickles my mind and that makes me feel like a traitor. He did lie to the Sheriff yesterday about where he spent the day. He went fishing. He didn't spend the day at the gallery, and he had two antique hatchets at his store.

I hesitate as we reach the garage, nervous Sicheii might be home. I glimpse through the window before starting for the door—the Porsche is gone. I take a deep breath and some anxiety drains from me. I still need more puzzle pieces before confronting him. I only have edge pieces that form the beginning of the picture. Like any puzzle, the most challenging parts are yet to come.

I turn the key, the lock clicks, and the front door opens. My head throbs as I make my way to the kitchen and drop down in a chair next to the table. Troy's face is lined with concern—his eyebrows pressed together, his deep brown eyes wide and sparkling. The expression changes his handsome face into something more, something better, but I would never tell him that. That would open up too many doors I don't want open right now. Besides, he's all too aware of his good looks.

"Are you okay?" His voice is soft like velvet. "Your face looks flushed like you have a fever." He touches me on my shoulder, and I sense his warmth through the fabric.

"It's just hot. Why is everyone always asking how I'm feeling? Ask me again, and I'll knock your block off!" I even shift in my seat to lunge at him if need be.

He removes his hand from my shoulder and frowns. He knows me well enough to realize I'm serious. He shrugs and swings open the refrigerator door, finds a pitcher of lemonade and grabs two glasses. A moment later, he sits across from me and we both gulp down full glasses and feel better as our bodies absorb the cold liquid. The air conditioning in Ella's Ford was almost useless.

My mind sticks on the twisted arrows symbol and grinds like gears in need of oil. What do the twisted arrows mean, and why is the symbol popping up everywhere? How come I never noticed it before?

My phone rings. Mom is calling. I stuff the phone in my pocket and glance at Troy sheepishly.

"Aren't you going to answer your phone?"

"No way!" I drain the last of the lemonade from my glass. "Mom is the last person I want to talk to now. She'll suspect something is wrong just by the sound of my voice and catch the next flight back. I'll never figure out what's going on with her watching me."

"Maybe she can remember something about John Dent." He refills my glass. "She might recall his article. She would've been a teenager back in 1986."

Troy is right, but I have a difficult time imagining Mom as a teenager. The Mom I know has always been a responsible lawyer and mother. It's hard to think of her as anything else. The only blemish on her perfect record is her brief relationship with my father, and that topic is off limits. I doubt she had even met my father by 1986.

My father.

Once my mind turns to him, it tumbles down a waterfall. I've fallen down this slide so many times before. Questions, anger, and guilt churn in the water after the free fall. Still....

"What's going on, Jules? You look like you're a million miles away."

I grip my glass harder. "I was thinking about my father. He was released from prison four months ago." He was convicted of manslaughter not long after I was born. I search his name on the first day of each month since I got my own computer. It's my ritual. I'm not sure why. Maybe a part of me wonders what he's up to, whether there's any news to report about him.

"Did he call?"

I shake my head. "Nothing. He's never called or written or sent me an email or text." I've never met him and have only seen his face once, in an old photograph with Mom at Slippery

River that was hidden in her room. I needed to borrow some socks and found it stuffed under a dozen pairs in her dresser drawer. I never asked her about it. What would be the point? He obviously wants nothing to do with me or us. Why she's kept that picture this entire time totally confuses me. I would have ripped it up long ago.

Troy narrows his eyes. We've talked about my biological father more than a few times and he's made his feeling clear. "You understand it isn't personal, right? The jerk has never even met you?"

"It sure feels personal." I chug the rest of the lemonade. *Could I be so bad, such a disappointment, he doesn't even want to meet me?*

I glance at Troy. He so wants to make this better for me. I see it in his eyes and the lines that drip from both ends of his lips. When he got his license, he offered to take me to see my father in prison, so I could meet him, tell him what an ass he is in person. When I said no, he suggested he go alone, but I forbid it. He'd find him for me if I asked him. He would do anything for me.

Heat flushes my face, my throat burns, and tears well in my eyes. I glance away so he won't notice.

I look at the clock on the wall and change the subject before the specter of my absentee father swallows us whole. "Do you really think my mom could help us?"

Troy swirls the lemonade in his glass. "Anything is possible."

The doorbell rings. I jump and knock my glass over on the table. Luckily, it doesn't break, but a new thin line spreads around its base as if it is about to shatter at any moment.

Troy chuckles, so I manufacture a fierce scowl, but I'm not really angry with him. I'm more interested in who rang the bell.

He strolls cautiously toward the door, and I follow in his wake, feeling better and safer that he is here. Dusk has already settled in as the sun drifts below the horizon.

Sheriff Daniel presses his face against the glass. He isn't alone. Deputies Johnson and Jackson are with him. I swerve around Troy and open the door.

Daniels seems edgy. His eyes shift beyond me toward the rest of the house. "Good evening, Juliet," he says as he tips his cowboy hat. "Is your grandpa home? We're looking for Jake."

I glance at Troy, whose expression is stoic. Returning to face Daniels, I say, "No, Sheriff, he's out. Is something wrong?"

Daniels steps inside the doorway. "You don't mind if we come in and check, do you?" His voice is tight. He doesn't give me a chance to object. He and the two deputies are already inside the house before I can say anything.

"It will only take a second, Juliet. We just want to ask him some questions." As if he gave a silent command, the two deputies leave the foyer and start to search the house, calling out "Jake" as they go. Deputy Jackson brushes his hand against his revolver, and my legs go weak. I remembered the words from the newspaper article— *Sheriff Daniels expects an arrest to be made imminently.*

Daniels smiles thinly. "I'd sure like a glass of water. It's been a hot one today."

"Of course," I say, and Troy leads us toward the kitchen. I grab a glass from the cabinet and fill it with cold water from a water cooler. My hand trembles as I hand the glass to the Sheriff.

He tries to sound casual, but a seriousness underlies his voice. "When was the last time you saw Jake?"

"This morning. He picked me up from school."

"Around what time was that?" He questions me in a tone that makes it sound like he's just making conversation, but his eyes are locked on mine, and I can tell he wants the information for other reasons.

"Around 9:30 or so." Daniels's eyebrows lift, so I add, "I wasn't feeling well, so he picked me up early." Another lie. This one flows easily.

"I'm sorry to hear that, Juliet." Both deputies return to the kitchen, and Deputy Johnson frowns and shakes his head.

"Where is your mother?"

"She's at work."

He glances at Troy suspiciously, as if he shouldn't be with me unattended, but he lets it pass. "Tell her to call me when she gets home, and if you hear from Jake, tell him to contact me right away." Daniels's tone of voice is deadly serious and his eyes bear down on me to make a point.

I nod, and then my heart skips a beat. An origami swan sits perched on a white plate next to the sink on the kitchen counter. How did *that* get there?

Sicheii used to make them for me. He wrote messages on the paper meant only for me. It was our secret code. Two years have passed since he last left me one.

My jaw must have dropped because the Sheriff asks if I am all right and glances in the direction of the sink. I bite my lip. "I'm... fine. I'm just... under the weather."

The Sheriff gently places his glass on the kitchen table, tips his hat, and shoots me another piercing gaze. "Juliet, it's important Jake call me. It'll be better for him if he does. Let me know if you hear from him. You too, Troy Buckhorn." He glares at Troy for a second, but Troy stays mute, and the Sheriff

127

saunters out of the house. His shoulders sway from side to side while both deputies follow a step behind.

Troy shuts the door after them. When the two police cruisers leave the driveway, I march back to the kitchen.

"They looked serious," Troy says.

"Did you see the way Deputy Jackson touched his gun? They must suspect Sicheii has something to do with these murders."

He rubs his hands over his face. "That's just crazy."

I walk to the sink and stare down at the paper swan in the porcelain dish. Coiled around the bird is the pendant and necklace Sicheii gave me when I turned seven. The pendant is made from turquoise and shaped as a slanted rectangle on its side, with a smaller silver rectangle etched inside the larger one. The slanted rectangle is my tribe's symbol for the Wind Spirit. Sicheii called the pendant a Wind Catcher. When I wore it, the Wind Spirit would help me, protect me, guide me.

I lift the necklace by the buffalo skinned strap. I used to wear it every day until I started school at Bartens. The leather strap chafed against the collar of my uniform, so I left it behind. At least that's what I told myself.

"Read the inscription on the back and tell me what you find." I hand the necklace to Troy.

"'You are Chosen. Love, Sicheii.' There's a circle and two twisted arrows after his name. The symbol looks the same as the one after Dent's name on his tombstone."

I had forgotten about the inscription and the symbol, having not looked at it in years. I take the Wind Catcher from Troy and loop it over my head. I'm not sure why. It just seems like the right thing to do.

The paper swan beckons me, so I lift it with shaky fingers and unfold the paper to find the message Sicheii has left for me in his flamboyant cursive.

Little Bird:

Events are moving fast. We are running out of time. I can't come home tonight without putting you in danger. Meet me at Slippery River on the South End where you and Troy enter the park tomorrow at noon. I'll explain everything then. Keep Troy close. It's time for you to become the swan you are meant to be.

Love,
Sicheii

After his name, he draws a circle with what looks like two twisted vines in the center. He always adds the circle next to his name when he writes messages for me. I had forgotten about it. I assumed the symbol was some weird Native American thing and never asked him what it meant. Now I look at the circle more closely. It *could* be a simple version of the two twisted arrows. I hand the note to Troy.

While he reads it, I remove my iPhone from my pocket and stare at it.

"Who're you calling?"

"I've got to call Mom. If Sicheii's in danger, she's got to know. And from the look on the Sheriff's face, he might need a lawyer soon." I press the speed dial button and wait. Worries swirl through my mind. Am I betraying Sicheii? For some reason I'm holding my breath. By calling Mom, everything seems to become real, like clay turning into brick in the hot Arizona sun.

Could he really be swept up in these murders? If so, how?

Mom's phone turns to voicemail. I groan and leave her a message to call me.

"I guess we wait until tomorrow," Troy says, his face long as worry clouds his eyes. His phone rings and he hesitates to answer it.

"You better get that." I shoot him a look. "Maybe Ella's found a new clue."

Troy retrieves his phone from his front pocket and glances at the screen. My eyes beat him to it. A full screen picture of a blonde-haired girl from school named Candy smiles at him. Candy has a certain unsavory reputation for boy hopping. He shuts off the phone and stuffs it back into his pocket.

"Aren't you going to answer that?" All of a sudden, my arms are crossed against my chest and my foot starts tapping. "Candy is probably wondering where you are. You must have a hot date planned tonight."

"Candy is just a friend."

"Right, just another one of your *friends*. You have so many of them." I'm not sure where this comes from, but it gushes right out of me. I see red, and all I can think of is Candy and Troy alone — his lips on hers, her hands in his hair. "I bet she's a lot of fun to hang out with."

Troy's left eye twitches, his brow furrows, and his face turns red. He starts to say something but stops. I wish he would just say whatever he really feels. There are some things you just can't change. I don't have blonde hair and don't look like a model. With my pointy nose and eyes that are not quite wide enough, I'll never be able to compete with the blonde-haired Candys of the world.

Instead, he waits a few seconds and mutters, "I'll call her later," through a clenched jaw.

I open a closet and toss two jackets on the floor until I grab the light one I'm looking for. I've got to find more puzzle pieces before tomorrow. I don't want to stay here in this house or this kitchen knowing Troy should be on a date with Candy. I need to move.

"What're you doing?" Troy's hands are up. "Aren't we going to hang out here?"

"You can go on your hot date with Candy if you want. You don't *need* to stay with me. I'm sure you wouldn't want to disappoint her. I want some more answers before I meet with my grandfather."

I turn toward the door.

My answers are out there.

CHAPTER

Troy blocks my path like a boulder. I think about steamrolling him but hesitate and take a deep breath instead. Candy's perfect cheerleader face flashes in my mind. She's the *last* person he should be with, but that's *his* mistake.

Why should I care anyway?

I take in more oxygen. He's free to date anyone he wants, just as I am.

I breathe again. It's just that I *choose* not to date anyone.

Another breath, and steam releases from me like a teakettle.

He must have noticed because he asks me, "What do you have in mind?"

"I want to go back to Roundtree's house and check it out." His eyebrows bunch together, and he looks at me as if I have two heads. "Maybe he hid something in his house that'll give us a clue about what's going on. Roundtree has to be the key. He had the twisted arrows tattoo, he was the first in the secret society to be killed, and he stood at the center of that photo."

"What would we look for?"

I'm not sure why, but I feel a little better when he says *we*, so my voice slows and the jagged edge in my tone smooths out. "The twisted arrows must be important. I know it sounds strange, but everything with my grandfather is weird. Maybe we can find the symbol in Roundtree's house somewhere and it'll lead to a clue that might tell us what's going on."

"But whoever killed Roundtree probably searched his house. They'd have found anything worth finding."

I pull open the drawer underneath the toaster and retrieve a flashlight. "Maybe, but maybe they didn't know about the twisted arrows. Perhaps Roundtree has a hiding spot with that symbol on it. He was tortured before he died. He might not have given away his secrets." I shrug. "It's worth a try. It's better than sitting here and doing nothing all night. I need to move, do something productive. Otherwise, I'll go crazy."

I step toward the door, but he grabs my arm and stops me cold in the foyer. He slides inches from me, and we breathe the same air. A bolt of electricity flows through me and I forget all about Candy and her blonde hair and small nose and floozy reputation. Well, not completely, but I shove those thoughts to the back of my mind when his face is so close to mine.

"I'll go," he whispers, his words feathery soft and eyes wide, bright, and caring. "You stay here. It might be dangerous. Whoever killed Roundtree and Brooks is still out there. I'm sure he won't want us to search for secret messages. I'll tell you if I find anything."

I can't let him go without me, even if a small cowardly part of me does. Sicheii is caught in the middle of this mystery, which means it's my mystery to solve. "This isn't a movie. Killers don't always go back to the scene of the crime." I pull my arm free from his grasp. "I'm going with you or without you." I add as much determination in my voice as I can manage even though it's all bluster. Without him, I'd lose my nerve. Whenever I shut my eyes, images of Roundtree's bloodied body still float in my mind, and every time they appear, I shudder. He doesn't need to know that, so I act bold, bolder than I am.

"How are you going to get to Roundtree's house without me?" He smiles.

"I'll hitch. I've done it before."

He smirks. "Okay, we both go."

He peeks through the glass at the front door. "I don't see anyone, but if the Sheriff thinks Jake is involved in these murders, he'll probably have someone watching us. We're not going to be able to cruise to Roundtree's house without a deputy tagging along."

"I don't see anyone." Darkness has fallen outside. "I bet they have a deputy stationed by the security gate at the main entrance, but everyone forgets about the service road. If we take the bike through the dirt road, we can escape unseen."

Troy groans. "I hate the service entrance. That road is nothing more than a dirt trail. We'll kick up rocks that'll wreck the bike's paint job."

I open the front door. "Don't worry about scratching the paint. I'll help you fix the bike." I'm pretty sure the paint job is going to be the least of our problems.

I take the smelly helmet without complaint. He starts the bike with a roar, and we drive to the service road. A metal gate blocks the path with a chain secured by a padlock. The gate is meant for cars, not bikes, so we find an opening in the side and pass around it, working our way onto the dirt road behind the gate. When we reach the trail, he opens up the throttle, and in no time we leave the dirt road behind and find ourselves back on Route 100, headed to Roundtree's house. An uneasy sensation settles over me, so I tighten my grip around Troy's waist to chase it away.

The quiet Reservation unsettles me as Troy stops the bike where we parked yesterday. Yellow police tape stretches across the front door and a yellow sign in front of the house reads, "Police Crime Scene - No Unauthorized Admittance."

We jump from the bike. "Are you sure you want to go in?" he asks, his eyes jumpy as he scans the empty street.

"You're not afraid of ghosts, are you?" I tease him with feigned confidence and stroll toward the side of the house. "We'll have better luck going in the back way." Today, it's my turn to tug him along with an invisible chain forged by our friendship.

Troy lopes behind me. An eerie quiet blankets us. We move swiftly, guided by the slippery light thrown off by the moon and the stars. When we scoot to the back of the house, soft river sounds fill the night air as water splashes against the riverbank. Random thoughts occupy my mind and crowd out the dread I feel when returning to the crime scene. The goats are gone. Did they leave on their own now that Roundtree is dead or did someone from the town take them away? Where would they have taken them?

I flip on the flashlight and sweep the light across the back of Roundtree's house. The beams catch more yellow tape around the maple tree where he was murdered. The cool night air turns frosty when the light from the flashlight sweeps over crimson streaks in the dirt at the tree's base.

Troy points toward an old glass door with an antique brass lock and studies it for a second, unsure what to do. He hands me a small screwdriver as he twists the tiny Allen Wrench free from his keychain. Before he goes to work, I grab the doorknob, twist, and push. The door opens without much resistance, so I pocket the screwdriver, smile at him, and shrug one shoulder as we step into the house. Sometimes you just have to try.

The floor creaks under my feet and my breath catches in my throat. The place is a mess—upturned furniture, books and papers strewn around, bits of wood and stone artifacts, broken pieces of Roundtree's life tossed about haphazardly. It takes the wind out of me. I feel the violence and rage of the attacker, as if a two year old had thrown a temper tantrum, only this tantrum lasted hours and was way more intense than anything a two year old could muster.

Troy whistles and scratches his head as he steps over smashed objects. "Someone certainly trashed the place."

"Either that or Roundtree could have used a housekeeper." I smirk, trying unsuccessfully to lighten the mood. "Let's check out the living room. That's the oldest room in the house." Sicheii had brought me here once to show Roundtree a new artifact he had purchased for the gallery.

I step carefully around debris, trying not to smash anymore of Roundtree's stuff. The living room is more of the same. We don't live in tornado alley, but this is what I imagine his house would look like after one hit.

One item sticks out from the rest and I pick it up. "This *is* weird."

"What is it?" Troy asks.

"Well, this is the only thing that's burned. You can only see the edges, but I remember it. Sicheii gave it to Roundtree a few years ago. It's an ancient piece of buffalo hide with an odd painting on it of a white ghost with purple eyes. It looked like rays were shooting from the ghost's eyes. I once asked Sicheii about it and he told me it had something to do with Coyote, but I've never seen Coyote drawn that way. Why do you think they burned it?"

Troy shrugs and looks away. "Who knows? I guess it wasn't that important or they would have taken it with them. Where do we start looking?"

I drop the hide and run my hands through my hair. "Let's take a look along the walls. Maybe there's a safe." Dark wood paneling covers the walls. We start at the nearest one and swipe the light from the flashlight against the wall in a slow arc. Troy follows the path brightened by the beams and brushes his hand against the wood in places. He disturbs dust as he searches for the smallest sign of a safe or a hiding spot, or the twisted arrows symbol. We work quietly, but his breathing speeds up. Mine starts to match his.

We inch our way along the wall when a lightning bolt threatens to split my head in two. I bend at the waist. A vision of a white van, the same one from earlier in the day, flashes in my head. It's pulling up to Roundtree's house.

My hand trembles, and the light from the flashlight dances unsteadily around the room. "We have to go, Troy. Someone's here.... They've pulled up in a van."

He glances at me oddly. I can't blame him, but he has to start moving, so I grab his t-shirt to push him toward the back door. But before we go back the way we came in, the front door crashes open.

Bang! Wood splinters.

Troy shoves me toward the back door. "Run," he whispers.

I'm not going to leave him. We're in this together. I shut off the flashlight and hope the darkness might hide us.

I should have known better.

CHAPTER

Events slow. Air freezes in my throat. A silhouette appears at the doorway, sweeping a beam from a flashlight across the room before it lands on us. The intruder's slicked black hair glistens in the darkness. A dark golf shirt stretches taut against a well-muscled chest and arms, and he moves with the athletic grace of a dancer or a martial arts expert.

A sinister smile twists his lips. "Gotcha!" he says.

"Run!" Troy shouts as he leaps toward Slicked Back Hair. I try to grab his arm to stop him. This is no drunken college student, but I'm a second too late and he darts ahead before I can hold him back.

Slicked Back Hair sidesteps him and swings the heavy flashlight forward in a short chop. It crashes hard into Troy's face. He goes down in a thud. Blood spurts from his nose and bone breaks.

My chest squeezes and my vision tunnels around Slicked Back Hair. I tense to take a run at him, but strong hands grab my hair from behind. A second intruder must have snuck in through the back door. He swings me in a painful circle and flings me to the hardwood floor. The flashlight tumbles from my grasp, switching on as it leaves my fingers.

My forehead collides with the floor. I rise to my knees when the beam from the flashlight catches my attention. The light finds a speck of silver on the wall. A silver twisted arrows symbol is carved into the corner of the room. It's so small we would probably have missed it.

I stand on shaky legs.

Troy struggles to get up when Slicked Back Hair plays soccer with his head.

Thud!

His neck snaps back. He crumples and lies still on the floor.

I'm so angry my whole body shakes. My hands ball up into fists when Slicked Back Hair pulls a revolver from the small of his back and aims the gun at Troy's prone figure. "Make another move and I plug your boyfriend." He speaks calmly and measured and is more terrifying because of the control in his voice. "We're supposed to take you alive. Him," he nods toward Troy, "we don't need."

My hands shoot up. I take him at his word. From the look on his face, I figure he'll enjoy killing Troy if given an excuse. The second guy who grabbed my hair glides in front of me and stops no more than three feet from my face. He smells like peppermint. He's shorter than Slicked Back Hair, wider in the chest, and clumsier looking.

He smiles at me and reveals a gold front tooth. "She's the one we're looking for mate," he says with a slight English accent. "She's the medicine man's granddaughter."

What has Sicheii gotten us into?

140

I stare at Troy and my heart tightens as if a tourniquet twists it. He's breathing, but he's still out cold, blood splashed on his face. *How badly is he hurt?*

"Don't worry about him, love," Gold Tooth says. "We won't kill him *if* you come with us peacefully."

"Try to run for it, and I'll gladly put a bullet in his skull." The sneer on Slicked Back Hair's face ominous and unmistakable.

Gold Tooth shoves me toward the front door. "We're going for a ride. If your grandfather behaves, you'll be fine."

When was the last time Sicheii behaved?

Panic swells inside me. I fight the urge to check on Troy. I need him to be safe. This is my fault.

"Come on now. We don't have all night." Slicked Back Hair points the revolver back at Troy.

I have to go. The faster I leave with them, the safer he'll be. If I give Slicked Back Hair an excuse, he'll shoot him for sure, so I go quietly with them, shuffling my feet in short quick steps, just short of a run. I need to leave Troy behind to get Slicked Back Hair and his gun away from him.

I exhale when we leave the house. I didn't realize I was holding my breath, but at least they've left without shooting Troy. Maybe he'll be safe. I cling to that thought like a life preserver.

Slicked Back Hair grabs my arm and pulls me toward the back of the van. His fingers dig in my flesh. Gold Tooth opens the double doors and removes steel handcuffs from a hook, while grinning at me. It is a wicked grin, a sadistic grin, a scary grin. His eyes are alive with dark possibilities.

I stare at the handcuffs fearfully as moonlight reflects off the shiny surface. I don't want them circling my wrists. I don't want to go in the back of the van. "There must be some mistake. I haven't done anything. I'm sure my grandfather will tell you whatever you want to know, if we just call him."

Gold Tooth grabs me from behind and wraps his thick hands around my shoulders. I struggle, but he's bear strong and I can't budge. Slicked Back Hair clasps the cuffs tight on my wrists, takes my iPhone from my back pocket, and tosses me into the back of the van. He connects a two-foot chain to the cuffs and locks it into an iron ring in the floor with a heavy padlock. The ring looks worn.

How many other people have they captured this way?

A new level of fear ripples through me. Panic trickles down my spine. I want to cry, but I stuff the tears down my throat. I yank on the chains with both hands and they hold.

"My, she is a feisty one. Usually they start begging by now." Gold Tooth laughs at me. "Pulling on those chains won't help you. Be good and we'll try not to hurt you."

"What about the boy?" Slicked Back Hair asks. A certain amount of eagerness animates his voice. He's a predator and senses an easy kill. My heart sinks and my hands turn clammy. In my mind I shout, *No! Don't kill Troy! Please. Anything but that!* But no words slip past my lips. I can't breathe.

Gold Tooth glances back at the house. "Piss off. The Seeker wants as little mess as possible, mate. Let's deliver the girl first. We can always kill him later if he wants. He won't be hard to find."

The doors slam shut, plunging my world into darkness. I can breathe again. At least Troy is safe for now. I try to survey the inside of the van, but it takes a full minute for my eyes to adjust to the darkness. Cardboard covers the back windows. Only a slight trace of light escapes from the small, round window separating the back of the van from the front.

The van starts with a healthy rumble, and we lurch away from the curb. My heart races in my chest like a scared rabbit. I don't know who these people are, but they're serious, and I'm in trouble.

I yank hard on the chains. They hold, but the iron ring gives a tiny bit. I try again and get the same result. I'm not strong enough to yank the ring loose, so I inch close to it on hands and knees to inspect the clasp.

The van takes a left turn, probably onto Route 100. Left is toward town. The metal ring is connected to the van by two heavy screws. I clumsily reach into my front pocket and pull out the small screwdriver Troy gave me.

A whisper of hope flutters through me. I go to work on the right screw and hope they won't look back and see what I'm up to. I sneak a glance at the small window. They think I'm nothing but a helpless teenage girl. I need to be more.

The van moves slowly. They probably don't want to attract any attention. Still, I only have a few minutes. Once they clear town or they arrive where they're going, I will have no chance. I twist the screwdriver using all my strength. My hand aches as the small tool digs into my palm. Sweat pours down my face as the screw gives—slowly at first, and then more easily. The van stops, and I jump away from the ring.

I glare at the small window and see Gold Tooth smiling back at me. When the van starts again, he blows me a kiss and turns away. I tug on the chains. Only one screw secures the ring this time. It lifts more than it did before, but the screw holds and so does the ring. I scoot over and try the screwdriver on the left screw, but this one is fastened too tightly for the small tool to loosen. The screwdriver bends in my hand and snaps. Terror rips through me. I'm more scared than I've ever been, but I can't give in to the fear.

The van stops again. We're at the center of town. One more stoplight and they will probably head for the highway. I need a new plan. Time is running out.

When I scramble to the side of the van, the two-foot chain pulls tight. There's an indent in the van's sidewall where the back wheel sits. It's large enough for my feet to wedge against. When we start moving, I jam both my feet against the indent, focus all my attention on my legs and push.

The ring loosens. I concentrate harder, first on the muscles in my feet, then legs, arms and hands. Strength I have never felt before flows through me. It's as if the muscles hear the desperate plea from my brain and oblige. I push with my legs and pull with my arms and strain every ounce of energy in my body. I focus on nothing but yanking the chain loose.

A soft groan escapes my lips. The ring springs free with a clank. My back bangs hard against the side of the van. I glance at the window toward the cab—nothing. Heavy Metal music floats back from the front.

Good, listen to the music. Don't worry about me. I'm just a helpless little girl.

Only one stoplight remains. I slide for the back doors, waiting, hoping for a red light, hoping for a chance. If the van doesn't slow, we'll speed out of town and it'll be too late. I've been stuck at this light more times than I can count. I just need a little bit of luck.

The van slows, the brakes squeak, and my hand clutches the latch. I count to three and turn. The door opens, and I jump out. My shoulder hits the pavement hard. The car behind us blasts his horn, slams on the brakes, and locks his tires, burning rubber in the process. I roll toward the sidewalk, jump to my feet and run.

The pavement pounds hard against my feet, and my shoulder stings with jarring pain. A few faceless people float past me on the street. My hands are still cuffed, but the two-foot chain falls away behind me.

I look over my shoulder toward the van. The passenger door flings open. As I turn back in front of me, I crash right into the chest of Mr. Cordingly of all people. He catches me before I fall. He frowns and is about to say something nasty when he looks me over and notices the cuffs, my ripped shirt, and bloody shoulder. He looks behind me and sees the van, and a steely look settles into his eyes that I've never seen before.

"Run! They have guns!"

Cordingly pushes me behind him. "I will not. You are a student under my care." He slides between the van and me. "Go. I will stop them."

For an instant, I don't know what to do. What chance does he have against Gold Tooth? But he makes my decision for me when he steps forward to meet Gold Tooth who's sprinting toward us. I turn and run, pumping my legs as fast as possible. The street blurs past me when a gunshot rings out. I stumble for a step before I regain my balance and keep going. I don't look back. There's no need. Tears spring to my eyes when I take a hard left down a side street. My lungs ache.

My vision blurs and my legs start to burn when a dark sedan pulls to the side of the road next to me. The door opens, and a face jumps out of the car.

"Here, Juliet!" The voice is foreign, but I know that face. It's the same face from Mom's photograph. I dive into the sedan and slam the door shut.

The back windshield explodes. My father stomps on the gas and tires screech as we race away. He jerks the car hard to the right. The backend fishtails, but we're in the clear.

"We have to go back for Troy."

"Who's Troy?"

"He's my best friend." My entire body feels as if flesh and bone have been replaced by led and bolts. I can't move my arms or lift my head. "He's at Roundtree's house."

My head explodes in white light. I fight hard, but my eyes close, and when they do I see nothing but blackness.

CHAPTER 21

I hear garbled voices that sound as if they're whispered outside on a windy day. "You should have shown her the letters, Summer... she doesn't even know..." I try to hear the rest of the conversation, knowing it's important and about me, but the wind picks up and blackness returns.

Mom talks to a doctor. "When will she come around? It's been two days." She sounds scared. I want to tell her I'm okay, that she doesn't have to worry about me, so I try to pry open my eyes, but the lids are impossibly heavy.

"It is up to her," a soft voice says. "She still has a high fever."

I fall into all-consuming blackness again. I don't know how long, but eventually the darkness turns to color. Troy sits with me on the cliff high above Slippery River. The sun is bright and the colors vivid. He frowns.

"What's wrong?"

"You need to embrace your inner swan," he says casually, as if he's making sense.

"What do swans have to do with anything?" Before he answers, a red-shouldered hawk calls from high above. The red feathers on its wings are flames that glisten in the sun. The colors twist together, and suddenly I am the hawk—well, not really. I'm still me, but I can see what the hawk sees.

He circles above Devil's Peak. There's a ledge high up toward the summit. The hawk circles lower again, and the sunlight glitters off the twisted arrows symbol carved into the stone.

The hawk squawks, and the world twists back to the way it was—Troy sits beside me again. I reach for his hand, but he pulls his out of reach. "You can't be ashamed of who you are. You're part of the Tribe."

My face flushes with heat. "I know, but Bartens is different. How can I fit in? I can't..."

His eyes narrow and his face pinches together. "You want to be just like Tiffany and Morgan, don't you?"

"No, that's not it!" I shout, but part of me *is* jealous of them, wants to be accepted by them, wants to belong in their world. I despise myself for feeling that way. I hate them, but they have everything I'm supposed to want. My emotions jumble together. It's impossible to know what's real and what's imaginary.

"When you reject the Tribe, you reject me."

"You don't understand. I just want a future." My shoulders fold down, and I lean back against the cliff face. Tears moisten my eyes. I look away, not wanting to see him so cross.

"I understand, Little Bird," he says, but his voice sounds old and weathered like my grandfather's voice. When I glance up, Sicheii sits with me.

I try to slide away, but there isn't enough room on the ledge to go more than a few feet. "What have you done? Those men wanted to take me. They were going to kill me. They said they need something from you."

"It is not what I've done, but what you haven't done. The fault lies with you." He stands. There isn't much room on the ledge. His toes dangle over the edge.

My heart leaps. Sicheii's gray eyes look dark and disappointed. He switches his gaze to the river below.

Worry whips through me. "Don't jump. I'll do better. Tell me what to do." The wind picks up, and his straw hat blows off his head and floats toward the river.

He frowns. "It might be too late. I warned you." He jumps without uttering another word. I lean over the edge and stare down toward the river, but he's gone. I see the hawk again. This time, he beats his wings, just one powerful stroke and flies off into the distance.

A cold breeze brushes against my face. I feel an urge to jump. My feet inch close to the ledge. A small stone careens toward the canyon below. The wind gusts. The pull to jump is too strong. He *wants* me to leap. I'm certain of it, as certain as heat on a summer day. I bend my legs and spring forward. The river rushes toward me. I scream and open my eyes.

Mom holds my hand. She looks old. Her hair, pulled back in a low ponytail, appears dull and listless. Her face is colorless, with wrinkles forming at the corners of her eyes. When she notices my eyes have opened, she smiles, and her face transforms like the sun breaking through clouds on an overcast day. Some of her youth and beauty return. She squeezes my hand tighter.

"Welcome back, sweetie," she whispers as if she's concerned she might chase me away if she speaks too loudly. "How do you feel?'

Where am I?

I glance around and find myself in a private hospital room. An intravenous line is plugged into my right arm, my shoulder aches, and my mind feels sluggish as if I'm wading through a marsh. Rain darts against a dark window. The staccato pelting sharpens my thoughts.

"I'm okay. Just a little tired. What happened?" I attempt to sit up, but my body feels heavy and lethargic. I only manage a half-shuffle to shift partway up when the pain in my shoulder barks. The lines in Mom's face deepen.

"Don't worry, Mom."

She squeezes my hand. "Don't try to sit up so fast."

I shake my head as memories return and bolt upright as if someone has thrown a bucket of ice water in my face. "Where's Troy? Is he okay? We've got to find him."

"He's fine, Jules." She stands and leans in close, gently stroking my cheek. "He has a broken nose, but it will heal."

"What about Mr. Cordingly? Is he all right?" I remember the protective look in his eyes and the gunshot. Mom's expression and her ghostlike color tell me the answer even before she says anything.

She shakes her head. "He didn't make it."

The air is knocked out of me. I gasp for breath. Mr. Cordingly saved my life. He traded his life for mine.

"Does he have a family?" The words sound lame. He sacrificed his life for mine and I don't even know if he has a family.

"He has a brother back in England, but other than him, he had no one." Mom tenderly brushes some loose strands of hair from my face. "Don't blame yourself, honey." She tears up. "If it wasn't for your father... I don't want to think what would have happened." Her voice cracks.

I breathe deeply, the air filling my lungs. My father saved me. He must have gone back for Troy.

My father?

When I look up, I see him standing behind Mom with his hand on her shoulder, Mom's fingers circling on top of his.

What in the world is happening?

"Jules, this is your father." She squeezes his hand again as he slides around her to the side of the bed. His long, thin fingers grab the guardrail, and his pale complexion contrasts with Mom's dark skin.

"Hello, Juliet." His voice is soft and sweet, which is not at all like I imagined it. He stands a full head taller than Mom and wears a t-shirt that fits comfortably over his lanky frame. His bright sapphire eyes sparkle, and he has the same longish, pointy nose as mine. He smiles at me and my mind careens in circles. The clatter in my head grows louder, as if a child just received a drum set on Christmas and is playing in my head.

I fight through the racket. "What are you doing here?" The anger in my voice surprises me. *After all, didn't he just save me?* I should be thankful, but sixteen years of anger bullies any other feelings out of the way.

"When I heard about the murders, I came right way," he says. "I knew Jake was mixed up in it just like before. I was worried about you. I needed to protect you."

The drumming in my head starts to sound like voices, but I can't hear what they are saying. "Just like before?" I fight through the clamor, but it's maddening. "What are you talking about? What's Sicheii involved in?"

The door opens. Sheriff Daniels and Deputy Johnson step into the room, each holding a hat by their waists. They have solemn expressions on their faces and move slowly, as if they are inching toward me with bad news. Mom gives them a cautionary glance, and they stop. Worry darkens her eyes.

She says, "Sheriff Daniels believes that grandfather might be involved with these recent deaths in some way. They are looking for him and want to ask you some questions, if you are up to it."

But I'm not up to it. Acid churns in my stomach, bile rises in my throat, and the voices practically scream in my head! I jam both of my hands against my ears to drown them out, but it doesn't help. Pain rips through me. I screech.

Mom jumps back.

A doctor races into the room.

"What's wrong, Jules?" Mom sounds just like another one of the voices in my head.

"The voices are so loud!" Tears flow down my cheeks freely. A dam has broken that I'm not sure will ever stop.

"What voices?"

"The ones in my head. They keep coming back. I just want them to go away." They're so deafening, I jam a pillow against my ears, but that does nothing to quiet the noise. The sound comes from inside my head.

How can I quiet that?

Her face turns white and the next face I see, a man's, is unfamiliar. He says something to a nurse who enters the room, but the voices are too loud for me to hear them.

I'm afraid of what might happen next, so I shut my eyes tight, and the blackness returns. This time, I welcome it.

CHAPTER 22

I wake to find Mom staring out the window, her shoulders stooped, her hands pressed against the wall. My head throbs dully, but the voices are soft like water gently lapping on the sides of a small creek, so I shift in the bed and hope they don't get louder.

She must have noticed that I'm awake because she turns, a forced smile stuck to her face as she twists her hair. "Are you feeling better?" She's worried about me. Strain shows in her eyes, the thin tight line made by her lips, and her fingertips that twirl the ends of her long hair. She really wants to ask me about those voices I've been hearing, but she's anxious about bringing up the topic. That's okay with me. I want to know what's happening with Sicheii before we talk about me.

"I'm feeling better."

Mom visibly relaxes. Some of the tension leaves her shoulders and neck as she strides to my bedside.

Before she asks me any follow-up questions, I strike first. This is my window of opportunity, so I need to take advantage of it. "What's going on with Sicheii, and why does the Sheriff think he's mixed up in these murders?"

She looks away. Her eyes rest on the doorway. It looks like she's hoping a doctor or nurse will show up to rescue her.

I *need* to know what's happening. Sicheii's in trouble and it has something to do with those two thugs who grabbed me, so heat starts to flush my face. "Tell me what's going on!" The words come out in a low growl.

"Don't get worked-up, Jules." Mom sighs. "I'll tell you everything I know. Do you want something to drink first?"

My throat is desert dry, so I nod. Mom hands me a plastic cup of water with a straw. My eyes lock on her until she starts to talk. It takes a full minute, but she buckles. I knew she would.

"I don't know how much you've heard about these... deaths." She doesn't want to call them murders because she's worried it might upset me. Since I don't burst out in tears or pull my hair out of my head, she continues. "Old Man Roundtree, Samuel Brooks, and Stuart Baker have all died in the past week."

"Judge Baker was murdered?" Stuart Baker was a long-time local judge and as white as snow. As far as I can tell, he didn't have a drop of Native American blood. *How does he fit in with the twisted arrows?*

"Yes, sweetie. He was killed three days ago." She squeezes my hand. "Sheriff Daniels believes your grandfather may be involved."

"Why?" There's a difference between lying and keeping secrets. At least I think there is. I decide to keep the twisted arrows secret because I don't want to give anything away that might implicate Sicheii—not even to my mom. "They should be looking for those guys who attacked me and Troy. They're probably the killers."

"The Sheriff and the other deputies are searching for them, sweetie, but they don't think those two are involved in the slayings. A team of burglars has been targeting houses after someone's died or gone on vacation. The Sheriff believes you and Troy just interrupted a burglary."

"He's an *idiot*." I sip water through the straw. I'm not going to tell Mom or the Sheriff that Slicked Back Hair wanted Sicheii. That will have to be a secret for now because it means he's in the middle of these crimes in some way. I need to talk to Sicheii before I start to make him seem more suspicious than he is already. "What evidence do they have against Sicheii?"

Mom frowns, but I fire a hard stare at her. I count to ten in my head and she cracks. "They found an antique hatchet in Grandfather's apartment with blood on it."

"Anyone could've put that hatchet in his apartment," I blurt out, immediately suspecting Lisa. "Why would he keep something like that?"

"I don't know, sweetie, but they found some other evidence at Baker's house."

"Like what?" The skin on my face is on fire, and the plastic cup bends under my grip.

"They found strands of long white hair. The results of the DNA test aren't back yet but they think it's your grandfather's hair."

"What does Sicheii say? Have you talked to him?"

She shakes her head and squeezes my hand. "No one's heard from him. I've checked with everyone."

I don't like the defeatist sound in her voice. She sounds like she believes the worst, which is not like her. A hatchet and a hair shouldn't be enough to convince her that her father murdered three people. I study her for a second. She starts twirling her hair again. "What else aren't you telling me?" Then I go with a hunch. "What does this have to do with my father?"

Mom's face freezes.

Bingo.

Her eyes twitch toward the door. "I'd better find him so we can explain together."

My father's name is Ayden Connors. That's the one thing I've known about him my entire life. Everything else is a mystery, like the water in the bottom of a deep well. Anything could be down there because it is too deep for the light to reach.

My throat tightens and my heart pounds as if it will explode as Mom leads him into my room. Ever since I was little, I dreamed of the moment when I would first meet him. I know this isn't technically the first time we've met. He saved me in Old Town, and he *was* in the hospital room the last time I woke up, but those times don't count. I never got to talk to him or really *see* him.

As a young girl, I often fantasized that he was innocent, hoping that one day the truth would be discovered and he would rush home to be the father that everyone else had. Once, right after my fifth birthday dinner, I asked Mom a few questions about him, and she shut me down. She took hold of my hand, told me he was guilty of his crime, and I should do my best to forget him. We were better off without him. "He's bad," she said.

Of course, I couldn't forget about him. Who could forget about their father? But it was clear she'd never fill in the blanks, so I asked Sicheii a few times about him, but he always answered my questions with stories about spirits—usually the Great Wind Spirit. It didn't take long for me to be left with only my imagination, so I invented many different versions of my father. They varied from *Prince Charming* to *Jack the Ripper*.

So when he strolls into the room behind my mother, I feel this crazy nervousness mixed with part giddiness and part dread. What if he was innocent after all? What if he proved to be a greater disappointment than I already assumed? What if he doesn't like me? *What? What? What?*

He walks stiffly, his blond hair cut crew-cut short. Small thin wrinkles line his face, and a scar meanders two inches down his right cheek in a thin white line. His back is slightly bent forward as he walks. He is five inches taller than Mom, and his arms are corded with muscle underneath a simple blue t-shirt. They approach the side of my bed with him a step behind Mom.

"Juliet, this is your father, Ayden."

He moves next to her. A shy light smile brightens his face with only the edges of his lips bending upward. It's definitely not a *Jack the Ripper* type smile, but it's not a *Prince Charming* smile either. I realize he's probably somewhere in the middle of those two extremes like everyone else.

"Hi there, Juliet." He has a distinctly Irish accent, and his glacier eyes sparkle with a bit of mischief. "You are even lovelier than your mother."

Years of emotions bubble up inside of me like an active volcano. It's all too much. "Don't *hi* me! I'm almost sixteen years old and not one letter. Not one phone call. *Nothing!*" Spit flies from my mouth, and the plastic cup crumples under my grip. Water splashes over the sides.

Ayden steps backward, a shade lighter than he was a minute earlier and Mom steps forward. "Don't become so upset, Juliet." She touches my arm. "It's not all Ayden's fault."

My jaw drops. "Don't you do that!"

"Do what, Jules?"

"Don't defend him after all these years! You're the one who said he was *bad* and that we were better off without him."

Mom shifts on her feet uncomfortably as her fingers twist the ends of her long hair. "I don't remember saying those things, and there are reasons why you never got any correspondence from Ayden."

"Reasons! It's been almost sixteen years. Did he forget how to write in jail?"

"Actually, he might have written you a few times." She averts her eyes away from mine.

"What are you talking about?" My heart sounds like a war drum. Mom's a bad liar like me. I can tell that she's upset, so I hold my breath and wait.

She bites her lip. "Ayden wrote you one letter each week. I just never gave them to you."

My mouth opens, but it takes a while for the words to spill out. I'm so furious I can barely breathe. "After all this... I can't believe you... You've been lying to me... *I hate you!*"

Ayden leans closer. "Now don't be too hard on your mom, Juliet. She was only doing what she thought was best."

"*Out!*" I point toward the door. "Both of you! *Out!*"

Mom twirls her hair. I chuck my pillow at her, hitting her square on the face. Ayden grabs her arm and pulls her in the direction of the door.

Mom's face goes white, but the twinkle in his eyes brightens.

CHAPTER

Befuddled. Confused. Shocked. Upset. Stupefied. Dazed. Really pissed off! I feel them all as if my emotions are ingredients in some awful angry stew that I'm forced to eat.

I've spent almost sixteen years living in a world without a father, believing he wanted nothing to do with me, that he was *bad*. But now I find out Mom kept him from me, hid his letters, and lied to me my entire life. And now she seems to like him? She holds his hand and smiles at him?

Argh!

I punch my pillow. Words, thoughts, and emotions swirl in my mind like a dust storm. Everything I thought was solid crumbles beneath me. One moment I'm the angriest I've ever been, and the next I'm elated with a sense of giddiness bubbling inside of me as if my heavy emotional stew has turned into a carbonated soft drink. It's ridiculous. I feel like two different people. I'm more comfortable being angry, but the giddy Juliet keeps nudging her way into the picture.

My father wrote me letters.

What should I do? I have a father, and he wants to be part of my life. Was he innocent of his crime? Perhaps he isn't bad at all. If Mom could have hidden all those letters from me, she could have easily lied to me about him.

But he *did* spend fifteen years in prison for manslaughter. He *was* convicted. Someone died. And what does all this have to do with Sicheii? The dust storm rages on.

My thoughts settle on Sicheii. *What's he mixed up in?* I can't believe he tortured Roundtree. But I hesitate, caught by a whisper of doubt that trips me up. Could he do something so extreme? Part of me says absolutely not, but another part is unsure. He's always been mysterious. His beliefs are rock hard. What if they were challenged? What if he had to kill to keep the world in some type of balance only he could see? Would he murder to do that? Sicheii's core is strong. I've never seen him waver from doing what he thought was right. He never even hesitates. But torture is a totally different extreme from murder.

I am lost in the middle of the dust and debris of my own thoughts when the door opens. I expect my mother to step through the doorway with an explanation I don't want to hear, but Ayden stands at the threshold instead. I raise my pillow threateningly, and he tosses both of his arms up in surrender.

"I'm unarmed. I come in peace. Don't fire." He smiles at me. "Can I come in?"

I lower the pillow but keep it close just in case.

He ambles to my bedside. "I've waited so long to meet you. I'm sorry it has to be here in this place. But we can't make our own world. We have to live in the one we're given."

"I can't believe you wrote me letters and that *woman* hid them from me. I could strangle her!" I look down and my hands are indeed strangling the pillow.

Ayden's face softens. He rests his hand lightly on the side guard. "Don't be too hard on your mother, Juliet." The short sleeve on his t-shirt rolls back an inch, revealing the edge of a tattoo. It looks like a skull. "She had her reasons to keep me away from you."

"There's no reason for lying to me! I deserved to see those letters. I thought you wanted nothing to do with me. Do you know how hard that was?" My face burns and probably turns red. With the color comes voices, mumbled, jumbled voices, which grow more numerous and louder. I ignore them. "I thought you hated me, that you wished I was never born. You have to be angry with her, too."

"At first, sure, I was angry with Summer, but I could never stay angry with her. Not when we were kids and not now."

Not when they were kids?

I assumed Ayden was a one-night stand, a momentary lapse of judgment, but now it's obvious there's a more substantial connection between them. A thousand questions threaten to spill out of my mouth all at the same time when Ayden lifts both of his hands up, palms out.

"I know you must have questions. Let me tell you the truth, and you can decide for yourself."

I nod and do my best to keep my mouth shut and quiet the voices in my head. If I try hard, sometimes they grow weaker.

"I met your mother in elementary school. We hit it off instantly. I can't say it was love at first sight, but we were close from the beginning. We were so different, it was easy to see why your grandfather disliked me from the first."

"Why would Sicheii dislike you?"

"Oh, he had his reasons. My brother was six years older than me, and by the time I was in sixth grade, he led a gang that dealt drugs. I helped him. At first, it was no big deal. I'd just deliver a package, collect some money. But that was only at the beginning. By tenth grade, I had a clientele of my own. The money was easy."

I sit up higher. "My mom was dealing drugs?" The idea is so foreign it might as well have come from a different planet.

"No, Summer never dealt drugs." Ayden jabs with his pointer finger to make the case. "She was always better than that, better than me. She kept a distance from that side of my life."

"But she knew what you were doing?"

"We were in love." Ayden shrugs. "When you're in love, you overlook the other person's faults, especially when you're young. And I had many faults. Still do." A sly smile whispers across his face.

"Sicheii must have known about you."

"Your grandfather has a way of knowing everything. He warned me to stay away from Summer, but it would have taken a bullet to keep me away from her. Summer felt the same way."

"But how—"

Ayden lifts his hand to silence me. "My brother got busted when I was sixteen. He got caught dealing and had to go to the pen for five years. I took over the gang."

A faraway look clouds his eyes. "I didn't know what else to do. My brother needed me to run things. I couldn't let it all break apart on him." He pauses for a second. "Oh hell, I'd be lying if I didn't say I wanted to be the *man*. The money was good and the power was, well, I got a bigger high from being the boss man than from anything we were selling."

Ayden clutches the side guard with both hands. His knuckles start to turn white. "I did bad things those years. I'm not going to lie to you. I hurt people. Your mother didn't know what I was doing."

"She must have known some of it."

"She never knew any of the details, but I guess she didn't ask that many questions either. For a few years, it all worked, and then Summer got pregnant with you." Ayden smiles. This time it's such a full, genuine smile I return it with one of my own. "You changed everything for me. I wanted out. I wanted to open a bar, have Summer work the books. I would be the bartender. We could have a happy ending, even a white picket fence."

"What happened?"

"I needed one last score to make enough seed money to start the bar. I even had the place picked out on the edge of Old Town. We decided on a name: *Second Chances Saloon*. I planned to sell a mountain of blow to some college kids. I cut a deal for everything we had left."

"So you would've had enough money to buy the bar and come totally clean?"

Ayden smiled. "Well, not totally. My brother was going to lend me some of the dough. I'd stop dealing drugs, but in return for the loan, we'd launder some of his cash through the place. Just enough to pay him back."

"Mom knew about that?"

"Yes. Summer wasn't happy with it, but it would get me out of dealing and it would only be temporary. But we never

164

got that far. Before I sold the coke to the college kids, rumors started circulating — rumors about your grandfather and Roundtree."

"Rumors about what?"

"This was a long time ago." Ayden twists the side guard. The cords in his arms and neck stiffen. "There was a rumor that Roundtree had developed a new super drug with your grandfather's help. This new drug was going to make everything else obsolete. I was in the business and had a reputation at that point, so it interested me. Besides, it was important for me to know who was dealing, you understand."

He focuses his eyes on mine, and I nod.

"I probably wouldn't have paid the gossip any attention, but these dodgy guys from out of town show up asking questions about Roundtree. They wore suits. They looked like they had money." He shrugs.

"You confronted Sicheii with this rumor?" I can't imagine Sicheii involved in drugs. Roundtree maybe, but Sicheii never.

"No. I didn't. Things might have turned out differently if I had, but I talked to Summer instead. *That was a mistake*. She got really cross with me. She thought I was making it all up, that I wasn't serious about getting out of the business. We fought hard. It was quite the dust up. We had never fought before that, but she stormed out on me. I was so bloody angry. She should have believed me. She was eight months pregnant."

His face twists and his nose flares. He's reliving the argument he had with Mom at that moment, the emotion still raw even after all these years.

"Later that night I was working Old Town, killing time. It wasn't such a ritzy place back then, and there were many shadows and hiding places. I was waiting to meet the college kids for the final score when your grandfather shows up heading to his gallery. He was in a hurry, but his strides were off. He stumbled a bit as he walked, so I followed him.

"When he reached the front door, the light from the gallery brushed against him. Dried blood crusted on his hands and splashed against his shirt. I stayed in the shadows as he went inside. This was none of my business. I wouldn't have said anything, but a second later, one of those guys from out of town appeared on the street, hustling toward the gallery. I'm not sure why I jumped in his way. I was young and acted without thinking.

"Maybe I thought if I helped your grandfather, he would cut me some slack and make things easier for us. Anyway, this guy barreled into me. We both tumbled to the ground. The wanker got up and started berating me! I've got a temper, just like you. No one is going to yell at me like I'm some punk. We started to tussle. He had a gun. I had a knife. I got to him first. The police found me standing over him. He was dead and I was still... kicking him." Ayden stops, his jaw clenched tight. He looks me in the eyes, and his face trembles a little.

"I later found out that two of the outsiders were killed in Roundtree's house. Roundtree claimed he killed them when they tried to rob him." Ayden shakes his head. "Roundtree was old even then, so I can't imagine him getting the drop on those two by himself. They looked like pros to me. So you see! When I heard about Roundtree's murder and then Brooks, I knew it had to involve your grandfather. The outsiders had asked about him also."

"How did you find me?"

"Your Mom gave me the information to track your cell phone. I followed the signal to Old Town."

One part of Ayden's story jumps out at me like a bronco. "You killed that man in self-defense. You were innocent of manslaughter!"

Ayden frowns and releases the side guard. "Don't start making me out to be something I wasn't now. I was a bad kid. He might have had a gun, but I wanted to kill him." He glares at me. "I *wanted* to kill him. Besides, it was only a matter of time. I should have been thrown in jail long before then."

"Didn't Sicheii say anything in your defense?"

He laughs coldly, his voice frigid. "Your grandfather testified against me. He said he saw the fight and there was no gun. The police never found the weapon. He turned Summer against me. She had to choose between us, so she chose him."

Ayden runs his hand through his short hair.

I must have made a face because he says, "Now don't get like that with your mother. I was a bad kid. She made the right choice. She did what was best for you both."

Ayden didn't blame Mom, but I sure could.

How could she turn on the man she loved?

CHAPTER 24

I lie on my hospital bed alone, happy for the solitude. After Ayden finished his story, I told him I need some time, some space to sort things out. He nodded at me before he left. I'm sure he wanted a different reaction from me, but I don't know what he expects or what I'm feeling. Everything is so new and raw. I need time to sort through my feelings—time to think. He wasn't the horrible villain I sometimes imagined, but he was a drug dealer and a killer. Even if he killed that man in self-defense, he still confessed he wanted to do it.

I wrestle with my new reality when a doctor strolls into the room with Mom a step behind him. His gray curly hair, short wiry beard and mustache look as if they are made from wool. He's shorter than Mom and waddles as he walks, probably because he carries a few extra pounds around the middle. His white lab coat flops open and hangs at his sides. He couldn't button it if he tried. He looks oddly familiar, but I doubt I've ever seen him before.

He smiles as he approaches the bed. He has a friendly, reassuring smile, if such a thing is truly possible. It makes me like him before he utters a word. He holds a clipboard in his hands, but he doesn't look at it. "Hello, Ms. Stone. Is it okay if I call you Juliet?"

I shoot icicles from my eyes at Mom, who maintains her distance, a step behind the doctor with a stony expression carved on her face. Her hand reaches for her hair to twirl it, but by force of willpower, she returns it to her side, its mission unfulfilled.

I look back at the doctor. "Juliet is fine."

"Good. You can call me Doctor Dan, if that is okay."

"Sure."

"Now tell me about these sounds you have been hearing. Your mom says you described them as voices?" His voice rises at the end of his statement, which transforms the assertion into a question.

My self-preservation instinct kicks in. This isn't an ordinary doctor. The badge hanging from his lab coat reads *Dan Epstein - Psychiatrist.* I don't like where this is heading.

I hesitate before answering. "I don't think... I said anything about voices." I glance toward the door. "I just had a headache, that's all." I don't like the way he said *voices.* I certainly don't want to be the kid who talks to voices in her head. Visions of a straight jacket and padded walls darken my imagination and future. Bartens sucks, but it's a lot better than a psychiatric hospital.

Doctor Dan doesn't say anything. He just waits. After a long moment, I look back at him and his small, moss colored eyes.

He sighs and smiles at the same time. "I can't help unless you're honest with me. Are you hearing them right now?"

I really wish I were a better liar! Even with all the experience I've had lately, he still sees through me in a second. "Yes. I don't hear them all the time, but recently they've been louder." My skin turns clammy.

"Do these sounds talk to you? Do you understand what they are saying?"

"No. I never understand them." My voice is husky and coarse like sandpaper. I do my best to keep tears from my eyes.

Doctor Dan places his hand on my arm. "Don't worry, Juliet. We'll find out what's causing your condition. Hearing noises is a common problem, especially when someone has been through a lot." He squeezes my arm.

I feel better. I hadn't realized how much the voices have been bothering me until now. I can't hold back the tears any longer, so they start to fall. Mom bites her lip and looks at her feet.

"Is it always the same sound you hear or different ones?" Doctor Dan reaches into his lab coat, pulls out a wad of tissues and hands them to me.

"I think they change." I wipe my eyes with the tissues. "I usually feel emotions when I hear them, like anger or fear or excitement."

"That's good. How long have you been hearing them?"

I think for a second. "I don't remember exactly. Maybe they started two months ago. At first, the sounds were like white noise. I figured it was no big deal, but it's been getting worse. Now they sound like voices, but I still can't understand them. They're starting to make me crazy."

"You've been hearing voices for two months and you haven't mentioned it to me, Jules?" Mom squeaks. "Why not? We could have done a strategy session."

"I don't want a *stupid* strategy session. I want them to go away. Besides, you're always too busy. Working. Hiding letters. And let's not forget all the lies you've been telling me!"

My dinner sits uneaten on the bedside table. Mom left with Doctor Dan and then returns right away with worry etched on her face. She sits at the edge of my bed. "Since when do you keep secrets from me?"

I roll my eyes. "Really, Mom? You've kept the letters from Ayden secret from me for sixteen years."

"That's not the same thing, Jules." She twirls her hair. "I thought I was protecting you. At first, you were too young to understand. With time, it became too hard to change. The lie was easier than the truth. I've saved the letters." Tears glisten in her eyes. "You can have them when we go back home."

"So that makes it all better? I've thought my father wanted nothing to do with me for my whole life, that he hated me, and now I can just have the letters and all is forgiven. You're kidding me, right?" I'm about to really launch into it, but the noises in my head start to thunder, and I feel an overriding sense of melancholy, which tempers my anger and saps my energy.

"I'm sorry. I made a mistake, but we can't have any more secrets. I need to know everything that's going on with you to help with these *voices* you're hearing." She keeps chattering for a while, but I tune her out and turn my energy to quieting the noise in my head. When it seems like she has finished, I smile weakly at her and tell her I want to take a nap.

Doctor Dan returns an hour later without her. He's carrying a chocolate glazed donut in his hand, which he gives to me.

"How did you know this is my favorite kind?" I ask. Mom believes sugar is poison, so she never lets me buy donuts or other sweets. The only exception is ice cream and flavored ices. It would be impossible to live in Arizona without them. Sicheii, on the other hand, has no problem with desserts. We used to sneak around Old Town without Mom knowing. It was our secret. Sicheii's always been good at keeping secrets.

Doctor Dan grins as I take a healthy bite into the pastry. "Us psychiatrists never reveal our secrets."

We talk for a while. He asks general questions, like "How is life at home? Do you have many friends? How is school?" It seems stupid to lie to him, so I answer his questions truthfully.

I ask him some questions of my own. "What the heck is wrong with me? When will the voices go away? Why's this happening to me?" He doesn't really answer any of my questions. I don't think he can, so it's a test of sorts. He is honest at least.

He takes three vials of blood and promises to come back and see me tonight. He gives me two pills to quiet the noises in my head so I can sleep. He doesn't call the noises *voices*. I notice that right away. He always refers to them as sounds or noises. Who knows what that means, but it seems important.

When he leaves, I start to wonder where the television remote control went when Troy, Ella, and Marlon stroll into my room. My heart skips a beat when I see Troy. Fresh white tape stretches over his swollen nose, and black circles darken both of his eyes.

"Troy, I'm so sorry! I should never have made you go to Roundtree's. This is all my fault."

"You're not the one who hit me with that flashlight." He shrugs. "I could have ducked."

"Besides, he looks cuter with a crooked nose," Ella says. "It gives him character. How are you doing?" Her eyes quickly scan my body and linger on the discarded IV bag by the side of the bed.

"I'm fine, really." There's no way I'm telling them about the voices or Doctor Dan. "I should be out of here soon."

I notice Marlon eyeing my unfinished dinner. "Are you going to eat that Jell-O? Red is my favorite flavor."

Some things don't change, even in hospital rooms. "Go ahead."

Ella and Troy step to the side of the bed while Marlon dawdles behind with the cup of Jell-O in his hand. He looks for a spoon, doesn't find one, and sucks the Jell-O out of the plastic cup in one noisy gulp. Finished, he smiles at us. "Did you know there were only four original flavors: lemon, orange, strawberry, and raspberry?"

"Where'd you learn that?" Troy asks.

Marlon shrugs. "Snapple cap."

Ella ignores him. "Did you hear about Judge Baker?"

I nod. "It's odd. I don't think he has any Native American blood, and the twisted arrows thing seems to be all about the Tribe. Are there any rumors about who killed him? It has to be connected somehow."

"Nothing new," Troy says as his eyes dance around the room. "I gave the Sheriff a description of the guy who clobbered me at Roundtree's house, but it was dark and I couldn't really remember what he looked like. I just remembered that he had oily hair."

"I gave descriptions of both guys to the Sheriff this afternoon, but I doubt they were much better. One of them had a gold tooth."

"I don't remember two guys."

"You were flattened by the time Gold Tooth showed up behind me." I sit up high in the bed and smooth the cotton blanket over top of me. It's rough against my fingers, nothing like the blankets at home, but I'm happy to have something to do with my hands. "I got to meet my father," I say, dropping the bombshell.

Ella's mouth makes an O shape. Troy crosses his arms against his chest, and Marlon munches on a cold roll leftover from my dinner.

"He's not really what I imagined." I tell them everything Ayden told me, and I toss in the hatchet and Sicheii's hair the Sheriff found at Judge Baker's place.

"They must suspect the two guys that kidnapped you for the murders," Marlon says. "They were at Roundtree's house and they're dangerous."

"Yes, but just because they were at Roundtree's house after Troy and Juliet got there doesn't mean they're the ones that killed Roundtree," Ella says. "It doesn't necessarily connect them to the other two."

"The idiot Sheriff thinks we interrupted a burglary and they're unrelated to the murders," I say.

"He could be right," Ella says as she crossed her arms against her chest. "The hair and the hatchet don't look good for your grandfather. Still, what's his motive and what's this secret society all about? They're just some old guys, as far as I can tell. I don't see the connection, although Marlon found another one of those twisted arrows symbols."

"I saw it in Joe Hunter's general store right by the cash register," Marlon mumbles with his mouth full of roll.

"Did you see Hunter reach for his shirt collar when we confronted him? He must have wanted to make sure we didn't see his tattoo," I add.

Ella whispers. "Do you think your grandfather has something to do with these murders?" "I don't know what to think." I lean toward them and speak quietly. "But the guys at Roundtree's house said they wanted to use me to capture Sicheii. I haven't told that to the Sheriff or even my mom. Sicheii's wrapped up in these murders somehow."

"That doesn't mean your grandfather killed anyone." Ella touches my arm. "I haven't found out anything new about Dent's article, although *The Sentinel* ran a story that said Dent died in a car crash. His car flipped off Eagle Ridge Road and burst into flames when it hit the gully."

"That's always been a dangerous road. They probably didn't have the guard rails in back then," Troy says. "What do we know about this Ayden character? He seems suspicious."

"Only that he saved us!" I shout surprised at how quickly I became angry. "If he didn't go back for you, who knows what would have happened?"

"It sounds like someone's framing Jake to me. This Ayden guy might be holding a grudge. I mean, he obviously has a beef with Jake and Roundtree from way back. I'll bet Judge Baker was the one who sent him up the river. He's already admitted killing one guy. He could be behind these new ones."

"Troy!" snaps Ella. "That's Juliet's *father!*"

"He's a drug dealer, Ella. It seems very coincidental that he shows up in town just when all these murders are going down. I'm just saying, he seems very suspicious to me."

"Stop it, Troy!" I yell.

"How could you take this guy's side over your grandfather's?" Troy's eyes narrow. "Jake's been there for you and your mom your whole life. This other guy just showed up a couple days ago. We don't know anything about him."

Ella glares at him.

"I'm not taking anyone's side, Troy. Sicheii's caught up in this somehow. We need to figure out how."

Troy huffs and turns his back on me. I want to strangle him. He's being pigheaded.

"We can check out part of Ayden's story," Ella offers. "I'll search the Internet and see if anyone else was killed when your father was arrested."

"That won't tell us much," Troy says, his back still turned to us.

Before I can say anything else, Ayden appears in the doorway and hesitates when he sees my friends. He looks at me. "I didn't realize you had visitors. I could come back later."

"No, come in. I'd like to introduce you to my friends."

Troy turns to face him, his expression cross. Lines that don't normally crease around his eyes and mouth develop. Deep rivers dig into his forehead.

"Guys, this is my father, Ayden." I can't believe those words came out of my mouth – *my father.*

Ayden thrusts his hand out. Marlon and Ella shake it. Troy looks at it as if he's contagious with the plague or something.

Ayden keeps it outstretched for a few uncomfortable seconds. When it's clear Troy won't shake it, he brings his hand down to his side and smiles broadly. "I understand, Troy. I have some work to do to earn your trust."

"You certainly do," he grumbles.

"I'll leave you to your friends, Juliet." Ayden turns and leaves.

"I wonder how he got that scar," Marlon says.

Ella stomps down hard on his foot. "Ouch," he says and hops on one foot. "Why'd you do that?"

"I imagine he got that scar in prison," I say.

"Well, he seems nice to me. It's great that he's back and wants to connect." Ella shoots Marlon a dangerous look, and he retreats a step back. "When are you going to be sprung?"

"I don't know. I still have a little fever. And you know *my mom*. She quarantined me last year, thinking I had the chicken pox when a few freckles showed up." I would probably be leaving tonight if it weren't for the voices.

How long do they lock you up for hearing voices?

Locked up might be a little dramatic, but that's what it feels like.

We chat for a few minutes, but Ella gets antsy, shifting her weight on her feet and looking around. I can't blame her. I hate hospitals too, so I take pity on her and fake a yawn. "I'm getting a little tired. The doctor gave me some sleeping pills a little while ago, and they seem to be kicking in."

Ella jumps at the bait. "We'd better roll." She leans toward me and rubs my arm. "Besides, you don't have any more food left for Marlon. If we stay much longer, he'll be forced to eat the tray."

Marlon waves and they rush from the room.

After Ella and Marlon leave, Troy slides to my bedside. "I'm sorry I jumped on Ayden. He helped us, but that's not enough for me to trust him." Troy frowns and looks at me with wide, soft eyes. "Some guys just aren't meant to be dads."

He's talking about his own father. "Is your dad still hassling you?" I don't know when we agreed *hassling* was our code word for *beating*, but I can't say *beating* and I thought things had improved between them.

Troy shakes his head, but his eyes are sad. "He hasn't touched me since my fourteenth birthday. You remember the rock climbing accident when I broke my arm."

I nod. I'm the only one besides Troy who knows the truth.

"Birthdays were always the worst for me. I don't know why. Maybe they remind him that I was born. He thinks I'm just a leech that sucks away his money and his life. I've heard him argue with my mom enough times about it when he's drunk. I'll leave that house soon, maybe live above my uncle's garage. I'd have left already if it wasn't for my mom. She's begged me to stay."

He shrugs. "Jake spoke to my dad the day after my fourteenth birthday. They were sitting close together in my living room, and since then he hasn't hit me once. I don't know what he said or did, but that was the last time my father's *hassled* me or my mom."

My heart swells. I had no idea Sicheii spoke to Troy's dad. He does many things as a medicine man, but that's his world, not mine. "I wonder what he told him."

"Maybe he threatened him with an antique hatchet?" Troy shoots me a half smile. "Just go slow with Ayden. Not all dads are good."

Troy is only being protective, and I love him for it. "Ayden was a drug dealer and has a slippery past. I'll take it snail like slow with him. He has to earn my trust also."

Troy nods, and his eyes widen and moisten. A thick silence separates us. "I should have done a better job of protecting you. I don't want to think about what could've happened." He reaches over and sweeps a strand of hair from my eyes. When his fingers brush against my forehead, a jolt of electricity pricks me.

Does he feel the same thing?

"I can't believe that guy flattened me with one swing of the flashlight. I'm such a loser."

"He hit you on your weak spot. You've always had a glass nose." I smile and suddenly wish I looked better and straighten the blanket again. "Did you meet Sicheii at Slippery River like he said in the note?"

Troy shakes his head. "When they released me from the hospital, they were worried I might have had a concussion. Mom went all smothery on me. She wouldn't let me leave her sight until my uncle grabbed me at two to work in his garage. He promised to keep an eye on me for the rest of the day. By the time I got to the garage, it was too late to go to the river."

"I don't know, Troy. The evidence is starting to pile up against Sicheii. The twisted arrows seem like trouble to me. Whatever secrets they're hiding, they seem willing to kill to protect them."

A nurse walks past the empty doorway.

"I hope he hasn't done something we'll all regret."

CHAPTER 25

The time on the television reads nine forty-five. I chased Mom and Ayden from the hospital for the night a few minutes earlier. She wanted to stay, but I threw her out. I really don't need her hovering over me, fussing about what I've eaten or haven't eaten, and she could use the rest. Besides, every time I look at her, I think about those letters she hid from me and my blood heats up. She started to protest, but Ayden took my side and we teamed up against her.

"Let's talk about these noises you've been hearing, Juliet." Doctor Dan sits with his back toward the window, his clipboard flat on his lap. A brown crumb probably left over from his dinner is tangled in his beard, hanging precariously on the left side of his mouth.

"When are the noises loudest?" Doctor Dan slides his chair next to my bed by shuffling his feet forward. The chair scratches against the floor.

"Usually when I'm angry."

Doctor Dan scribbles on his clipboard. "Good. That should narrow it down."

I smile. "Not so much. I'm angry a lot."

"Oh." He frowns and the sudden downturn of his lips frees the crumb. "Are they louder when you're near other people or when you're alone?"

I hesitate for a second, having never thought about that before. "Always when other people are around. Usually the more people, the louder they get." They were blood spurting from my eardrums loud the other day when plenty of people crowded around me.

I want to ask him why he calls these sounds noises instead of voices, but I'm uncertain what rules govern our relationship. He must have recognized the expression on my face because he pauses and leans back in his chair. His green eyes are flecked with gray. They seem intelligent and earnest at the same time. "This *is* a two-way conversation. You are allowed to ask questions."

"I notice you don't refer to these sounds as voices. You call them noises. Why?"

He tugs on his beard. "That's because I don't know what they are yet. Usually when people hear voices, the voices are their subconscious telling them to do something, like some course of action they really want to take, but are afraid to. In your case, the sounds are not decipherable. Therefore your subconscious isn't suggesting you *do* anything. Your situation doesn't fit the normal scenario. These noises might not be voices at all. I'm not quite sure what they are yet."

"Is that really bad?" I whisper.

"It is neither bad nor good at this point. We will have to discover what's going on together."

"Argh. I just want to fit in and be normal."

"Normal *how?*" He fiddles with his beard. "Bartens normal, or the normal life you had *before* you went to the private school?"

That's a great question. I wish I knew. "Beats me. I just want the noises to go away and for me to be normal like everyone else."

"There is no such thing as normal, Juliet. It's a fallacy, a fiction created by Hollywood or school or church or whatever. I'm sure a normal teenaged girl would never have escaped that van. Let's do away with normal as our goal, shall we. We are all unique. It's important we embrace our uniqueness and understand who we are."

Funny, but I could imagine Sicheii saying the same thing.

He leans forward. "Let's try something different. Accept the noises in your head. Don't try to make them into voices, but listen closely and tell me if any ideas form in your mind."

I nod, although my skin turns clammy. It seems strange to make the noises louder. I want them to disappear, and this feels like we're headed the wrong way on a one-way street. Still, I follow his instructions and concentrate on the sounds in my mind. The noise is not particularly loud, so I attempt to turn up the volume. It feels weird trying to understand the sounds as opposed to stifling them. The harder I concentrate, the louder the noise gets. I pinch my forehead tight and start sweating. The noise is just outside of my comprehension. It's maddening.

"Don't try to make the sounds into a voice, Juliet. Envelop them and embrace them."

I do just that. I stop turning up the volume and start sculpting the sounds in my head as if they're made of clay. I mold them, playing with them, probing them, twisting them. The number eight flashes in my mind, and I open my eyes. I didn't even realize they were shut.

"Yes, Juliet?" One of his bushy eyebrows arches upward.

"I don't know, Doctor Dan, it's probably nothing." I feel stupid. What does the number eight have to do with anything?

"Tell me what you saw. There's no wrong answer."

"The number eight flashed in my mind." I shake my head, confident I sound foolish. "I must have imagined it."

Doctor Dan's eyes twinkle brighter. He slowly reaches into his lab coat and pulls out an origami swan matching the one Sicheii had left for me at home the other day. He holds the paper steady in the palm of his hand.

"This is for you."

I look at the paper bird and back at him. "Where'd you get the swan?"

"An old friend gave it to me. It's for you. Take it." He slides his hand closer to me.

I don't want it. "How do you know Sicheii?"

"That's not important." He nods at the swan and encourages me to grab it.

I reach out and take the paper bird softly between my fingers.

He immediately rises. "I'll see you tomorrow." He turns and leaves me alone without waiting for me to open the message and without giving me a chance to ask any more questions.

I stare hard at the figure in my hand. I'm not sure what to expect. Part of me imagines that the stupid thing will start moving on its own, but the laws of nature still hold. There's no magic at work here. The bird just sits uncomfortably in my hand, unreasonably heavy.

I start to feel foolish. It's just a note from my grandfather. It cannot harm me. Perhaps it will offer some new evidence or explanation about the murders. Maybe the message proves his innocence.

Just staring at the thing is not an option, so I unfold it and find Sicheii's fine handwriting on the inside of the white paper.

Little Bird:
The Great Wind Spirit has blown. It is up to us to understand what she wants and to do her bidding. Our time has come.
The correct answer is eight.

Love,
Sicheii

The correct answer is eight.

How did he know the number eight would flash in my mind? What is he talking about with the Great Wind Spirit? He looks to many spirits as guides. The one he thinks is most powerful is the Wind Spirit. But what does that particular spirit have to do with these murders and me?

I read the note again and my gaze sticks on the dime-sized circle with twisted lines after his name. I move the paper close to my eyes. I'm certain it's meant to be the twisted arrows. What type of weird society did Sicheii join, and why am I in the middle of it? I crumple up the swan in my hand. I had expected, even hoped for some answers, and all I get are more questions.

The time for questions runs short. Whether Sicheii likes it or not, I'm going to find some answers.

CHAPTER 26

Dreams scare me. Not like clowns for some people or spiders or close spaces or heights, but they still scare me. The idea that my subconscious lives a separate life while I sleep freaks me out. It's hard enough to manage one life. Do I really need another?

Hospital rooms are a fertile ground for dreams. The same nightmare keeps replaying in my mind in a freakish loop.

I'm late for class. When I enter the classroom, everyone is sitting at his desk. Ms. Arnold points to a seat up front, her face angry and tight. She hands me a test. I forgot about the exam and didn't study. Morgan and Tiffany snicker from the back row. I slouch and glance at the paper. The words are written in an ancient Native American language I don't understand. Katie sits next to me and she's busy filling in the bubbles. I don't know what to do. That's when I wake in a sweat, feeling unprepared for upcoming events.

When I open my eyes, Katie is standing by my bed. She stares at me, holding the string for a Mylar *Dora the Explorer Get Well* balloon. For a second, I think I'm still dreaming. She waves at me with a stiff shake of her hand, looking painfully nervous. The balloon bobs up and down with each flick of her hand. Her Bartens uniform fits snugly, as if she's gained a few pounds since I last saw her.

"I guess they let anybody in here." I sit up.

She smiles shyly and ties the balloon to the foot of the bed.

"You brought me a Dora balloon?"

"I remembered those pictures of you with a Dora backpack when you were a kid. When I saw it at the gift shop, it seemed perfect." Katie beams at me.

"You're the best!" I smile. "It *is* perfect!"

"They almost didn't let me in." Katie brings her hands to her hips. "One nurse wasn't too happy about me visiting you."

"Tough. I'm happy you're here."

She tentatively walks to the side of the bed, her eyes curious. She's studying me, wondering if anything is seriously wrong. You can't see voices from the outside, so I figure I'll pass her inspection.

"How are you feeling?" she asks, her voice quiet.

"I'm fine." I shrug. "I should be released in no time."

"Did someone really try to kidnap you?" Katie's eyes widen and her skin turns pale. When her father was first suspected of fraud, many death threats were levied against her family. They hired the best private security team, but the money ran dry. Now only one bodyguard follows her dad around all day.

I nod and tell her about the murders, the ill-advised trip to Roundtree's house, Ayden's rescue, the letters, and even my conversation with Ayden about his drug dealing past.

Her skin becomes paler as the story goes on. When I finish, she's turned ghost white. "I can't believe your mom hid those letters from you. That's awful."

I eagerly agree with her. After a series of questions about my father, most of which I can't answer, she says, "At school, they told us Mr. Cordingly died during a robbery attempt. They're having a memorial for him today. They didn't say it was connected to what happened to you."

"That's a shame. I wish I could go. He died protecting me.... He was a true hero."

"I guess you never really know about people. Sometimes they do surprising things." A faraway look settles in her eyes. She could be talking about Mr. Cordingly or my mother, but she's thinking about her father.

She starts gnawing on her nails. "You know how I tell everyone that my dad is innocent?" She glances at me and I nod my head. "Truth is, I don't know. Lots of evidence is piling up against him, and I overheard him talking to his lawyer last week."

She looks up at me. Her hands shake, and I grab them. They're ice cold. "And he said — "

Her eyes moisten. "They were talking about countries without extradition treaties." She pulls her hands from mine and wrings them together. "My dad's thinking about running to Croatia."

I want to say something to lessen the hurt, but my mind is a blank. After all, what do I know about fathers? I just stare at her quietly instead and wait. Sometimes just being there is all you can do. I hope it's enough.

It takes a minute for her to return to the present when she wipes the tears from her eyes with the back of her hands and refocuses on me. "I found the article you wanted." She removes a folded piece of paper from her pocket and hands it to me. "Someone deleted it from *The Sentinel's* server after it was posted in the archives. I hacked into their system and retrieved the original article. It's not long."

I had forgotten she was going to dig it up. I unfold the sheet of paper.

"A secret society among the local Native American population has long been rumored to exist. The above photograph was taken at one of their secret meetings. The leader of the society is apparently Charles Roundtree or "Old Man Roundtree," as he is called among his followers. The existence of the society is not surprising, as rumors go back for decades about their organization, but their purpose is truly shocking. They call themselves the Order of the Twisted Arrows. Stay tuned to my column as I detail their history and their dark purpose in the days ahead."

The article is nothing more than a teaser, but my eyes focus on the words "their purpose is truly shocking." Cold sweat breaks out on my face.

What did Dent uncover, and did the secret kill him?

I glance up at Katie. "It looks like there was more to this story. Did you find anything else?"

She shakes her head. "Nothing else shows up on their server about this society or on the Internet. Apparently, only this article was ever reported."

"I'm not surprised. The reporter died in a car crash the day after it was published."

Katie's mouth momentarily flutters open. "You don't think this secret society really exists, do you?"

I consider telling Katie about the tattoos and the twisted arrows symbol that keeps popping up, but I don't want to involve her so directly in this mess. Besides, I have no idea what the symbol means, and she has so many other things to worry about with her dad. I simply say, "I'm not sure. With Sicheii anything is possible."

"You don't think your grandfather has anything to do with these murders, do you? He owns the most successful gallery in Old Town." Katie is always very conscious of what people *do*. She still has a hard time believing successful people can be criminals. I'm sure it's her upbringing. Mine is very different. Sicheii taught me to look past appearances and focus on the person underneath.

She points to the date at the top of the page. "This article was written almost thirty years ago. I know your grandfather is in the photo, but he would never be involved in murder."

"I don't know what to believe." I tell her about the hair and the hatchet and Sheriff Daniel's suspicions. The picture isn't a good one.

"Those can all be explained, and I don't trust the Sheriff or the authorities one bit." Katie glances at her watch and her lips turn downward. "I have to go."

I check the clock next to the bed. "You have an hour before school starts. That's plenty of time."

"I know, but the angry nurse said I could only stay fifteen minutes. He wasn't happy I came to visit in the first place."

"What angry nurse?" I sit up straighter and my chest tightens.

"The one with the English accent and the gold tooth."

CHAPTER 27

Doctor Dan bursts into the room with quick purposeful strides, his lab coat flapping in his wake, kinetic energy engulfing him. He waves his arms as he speaks and looks a little like a ruffled penguin that's trying to take off. "Good morning, Juliet. I'm happy you're up. We have an appointment in my office. You'll need to put on your street clothes." He looks like an unmade bed dressed in the same clothes he wore yesterday, only now his shirt and pants are more wrinkled and his beard more unruly.

The urgency in his voice propels me into action. This must have something to do with Gold Tooth.

He glances at Katie. "I'm sorry young woman, but visiting time is over for this morning. You'll have to go." He points to the door with a stern expression pinching his face.

She frowns at him and flings her arms around me, which temporarily squishes the breath out of my lungs. "I'll be back later," she whispers before she spins and walks out of the room. I have the feeling I won't be here when she returns.

I grab my bundle of clothes from the closet and hustle to the bathroom.

"You need to hurry, Juliet. You have some visitors we would like to avoid." The playfulness from yesterday has vanished from Doctor Dan's voice, which has hardened into steel.

I fumble with my jeans in the tiny bathroom but manage to slip them on straight. My heart pounds. I can't go back to the van.

When I open the bathroom door, Doctor Dan is peering out of my room and down both sides of the hallway. His head swivels back and forth as if he's watching a tennis match.

"Katie said she spoke with a nurse with a gold tooth. One of the guys who tried to kidnap me has a gold tooth. I'm guessing it's not a coincidence."

Doctor Dan glances at me. The corners of his eyes are webbed, and tight creases form at the end of his lips. "I'm afraid you are correct, Juliet. We have to go to my office on the second floor right away. They'll be looking for you here." He surveys me up and down. "You'll need to put on some shoes first."

Stupid! I had forgotten about my sneakers. Luckily, they're in the closet.

"Why don't we call the Sheriff?" I finish slipping on my sneakers and tie the laces.

"There's no time. The hallway is clear. Walk right behind me. Don't look directly at anyone. Our destination is the elevator at the end of the hallway to our left."

He shuffles from the room at a brisk pace. I follow close behind and focus on the back of his flowing lab coat. I wonder whether Gold Tooth or Slicked Back Hair is about to pounce from one of the doorways. Neither of the two nurses on duty lifts their heads. When we reach the end of the hallway, he jabs the elevator call button three times and shifts nervously on his feet in front of the shiny stainless steel doors.

No one notices us. Once the elevator door opens, we squeeze on. He presses two, and I turn to face the doors and the hallway.

I gasp. The air freezes in my throat. Gold Tooth saunters through the doorway at the opposite end of the floor. His right hand is tucked inside his white nurse's coat where I imagine he's hiding a gun. The doors close, and the elevator drops.

I don't think he saw me, but it takes forever until the elevator door opens on the second floor. When it does, the hospital has been transformed into an office building with a narrow hallway, white wooden doors on both sides, and yellow walls.

Doctor Dan leads me off the elevator, moving at a more measured, confident pace than he did when we raced from my room. The hallway is empty at this early hour, and he stops at the third door on the left side of the hall, removes a roll of keys from his lab coat, unlocks the office, and holds the door open for me.

His office is small and exceptionally neat for the wrinkled doctor. A simple oak desk sits at one end by two windows. A computer screen is perched toward the left side of the desk. The rest is smooth wood without papers or files of any kind. A black pine bookshelf blocks most of the other wall with an assortment of hard covered books stacked neatly on it. They're all psychiatric textbooks that I can't imagine anyone reading.

"Take a seat, Juliet." Doctor Dan waves at one of two leather high-backed chairs in the corner of the office.

I have no intention of sitting. I grab him by his coat. "Tell me what's going on. Why did my grandfather give you that note, and how did he know I was going to guess eight?"

He smiles. "You are going to have to ask him."

"Is... he... coming here?" The words catch in the back of my throat. I release the lab coat. I'm not sure I want to see Sicheii before understanding the twisted arrows and what's going on.

"Not exactly." He glances at his wristwatch. "Wait here." Without warning he leaves and shuts the door behind him. The lock twists and the deadbolt latches in place.

Click.

Really? I try to turn the doorknob but the door is locked and there's no way for me to unlock it from the inside, which is really strange. *What do I know about the doctor? Why did he lock me in the office? Was it for my protection or to keep me here?*

I turn and survey the sparsely decorated room. Something odd starts nagging me, like a stick poking me in the side. *What's missing?* I stroll toward the windows and turn in a tight circle surveying the room. There are no personal effects of any kind: no pictures of the doctor or his family, no mementos or stupid desk toys, no diplomas hang on the walls—*no diplomas.* My heart quickens. I've never been in a doctor's office without diplomas.

I step behind the desk and open the drawers—nothing, no files or office supplies. When the light streams through the windows, I notice the outline of half a dozen rectangles on the walls where frames have recently been removed. A frost inches up my spine. This isn't Doctor Dan's office. This is an empty office waiting for a new doctor.

Who is Doctor Dan? Where did he come from?

My pulse accelerates into a rapid drumroll. Strange sounds fill my head, anxious sounds. I spin and examine the windows. They're standard white vinyl windows with plain glass.

The noises grow louder. The walls start closing in on me. I'm trapped. I yank on the windowsill and it's locked. I glance at the door, certain that Gold Tooth or Slicked Back Hair is about to burst into the room.

Panic starts to overwhelm me. My feet turn numb. All I see is the inside of the van and the metal ring. I tug and the ring won't let go of the chain.

I shake my head to clear it. I need something sturdy, so I grab a stainless steel trashcan underneath the desk. It feels heavy. The voices grow louder. They almost scream at me. They can't take me again. There's an alley below the window that's only ten feet down.

Screw it!

I heave the trashcan against the glass with all my strength and it shatters. Shards rain down onto the empty street below. I hear footsteps. Someone is in the hallway, just outside the door. Sweat stings my eyes. I can't go back in that van.

The doorknob turns. I wiggle my way out of the window feet first and hold onto the sill, suspended in midair. The plastic edge of the windowsill digs into my fingers and my shoulders ache.

When the door swings open, Lisa is standing there with Doctor Dan right behind her.

"Juliet!" she shouts.

I hold my breath and let go. A second later, I land lightly on my feet in the alley, and race toward the main street.

When I reach the corner, I notice the palm of my hand is bleeding. I reach for my phone to call Troy, but it's not with me.

I peek over my shoulder. Lisa is sprinting after me.

CHAPTER

28

Wild thoughts race through my mind.

Who can I trust?

Why would anyone want to kill me?

How do I find Troy?

I pump my legs and make a quick right in front of the hospital. I almost barrel into an old woman with a cane and wide brimmed straw hat, but swerve at the last second to avoid her. Breathing heavily, I start to gather up some real speed when a crack on the sidewalk trips me up. I lose my footing and stumble forward. About to face plant onto the concrete, I slam into a mailbox, which knocks the wind out of me. I stagger back a step and suck in air. Stars circle in front of my eyes. My injured shoulder screams at me.

Lisa has to be gaining ground on me, but I can't get enough air to start running again. Panic creeps into my thoughts as does images of the inside of that van. I'll never be able to escape from there again.

A white Toyota pulls up beside me.

"Get in, Juliet." Ms. Arnold waves for me to hurry.

I glance over my shoulder. Lisa has reached the main street with Doctor Dan red faced and huffing behind her. There's no sign of Slicked Back Hair or Gold Tooth or the white van. But how far behind can they be?

I yank open the back passenger door, jump in, and slam it shut. Ms. Arnold stomps on the gas and the tires screech. Lisa stops running and angrily places her hands on her hips. Bent at the waist, Doctor Dan gasps for air. I exhale deeply in one long gust. They won't capture me, at least not yet.

"What's going on, Juliet?" Ms. Arnold's eyes, dark and small, flicker to the rearview mirror.

"I needed to leave the hospital in a hurry."

"Why?" She takes a hard right and the tires protest again, but she keeps the car from skidding into oncoming traffic. "Does this have anything to do with your kidnapping?"

"I thought the school was keeping that quiet." I assumed everyone at Bartens believed I got hurt as part of a failed robbery attempt.

She takes a quick left and slows the car. "Some of us know better than the school's story." She shoots me a meaningful look. "Does your mom know you left the hospital?"

"No... no one knows."

"Okay, Juliet. Let's go to my place so we can check out your hand. That cut looks nasty." She tosses me a hand towel with little green tennis balls embroidered on it. "Use the towel to put pressure on it."

A shard of glass has sliced into my palm, leaving me with a two-inch gash. The glass is gone, and the wound is already clotting, but I push the towel against the blood anyway. "What were you doing at the hospital?"

"I was on my way to visit you before school starts." She smiles with only the corners of her mouth. "Good thing I saw you."

A few minutes later, she parks in front of a small brick apartment building on the outskirts of Old Town in a neighborhood locals call *Yuppyville*. She bounces out of the car and holds the door open for me, a concerned look in her eyes. "How's that cut?" She peeks at the towel.

"The bleeding's stopped. It's no big deal. It doesn't hurt."

"Great, let's go." She shuts the door behind me, checks both sides of the street, and opens the glass door to a high-class apartment building.

My sneakers squeak against marble tile, and my fingers brush against mahogany walls. Ms. Arnold hustles us toward the elevator with one arm around my shoulders, presses the call button and waits impatiently for the elevator to arrive. When the door opens, she pushes me in and jabs the button for the top floor.

The shiny steel doors act like a mirror. She's dressed casually in a t-shirt, shorts, and sneakers. She bounces nervously on her toes, her eyes never meeting mine. When the bell rings, the door opens and she unlocks a cherry wood door with a shiny brass placard that says "PH-1" on it toward the top. When I step inside, she bolts the door behind us.

"There's a bathroom on the right." She takes brisk steps and points to a white door. "Clean the cut and I'll find a bandage."

The cold water feels good against my hand. My breathing steadies. Why would Doctor Dan and Lisa work with Gold

Tooth and Slicked Back Hair? What do they want with me? Nothing makes sense. Sicheii's led me down a rabbit hole where I can't find my footing. I'm going to strangle him when I see him next!

Ms. Arnold returns a moment later with a large Band-Aid and some antibacterial cream. She clicks her tongue as she bandages the wound. "Do you know where your grandfather is? Everyone seems to want to talk to him."

I shake my head as she leads me into the living room. The blinds are drawn even though light streamed through them just a minute ago.

"I'll make you some tea and then you'll tell me everything." She disappears into the kitchen.

I pace the living room in small steps. Questions pop into my mind quickly like I'm playing *Whack a Mole*. The only problem is I don't have any answers to bash the mole in the head, so questions keep jumping up all over the place and crowding around me. In the end, all my thoughts return to Sicheii.

What has he gotten us into?

Almost by osmosis, I start to notice the apartment around me. The place is gorgeous. The duplex has floor to ceiling windows, hardwood floors, a gourmet kitchen, and a giant sized living room. It looks like a model apartment from one of the design magazines my mom reads. How can Ms. Arnold pay for an apartment like this at what Bartens pays her? The teachers all complain about the awful pay. Never directly to the students, but you would have to be deaf and clueless not to overhear the conversations.

She appears at my side, holding a cup with steam swirling above it. She smiles as she hands it to me. "Drink it. The tea will make you feel better."

I take the cup and sip. "Thanks. This is a really cool apartment."

Ms. Arnold glances around the place as if she's looking at it for the first time. "I'm just house sitting for a friend. Take another sip."

Feeling like a student in her class, I comply. The tea tastes sweet, as if she added a tablespoon of honey, but it doesn't taste like honey exactly. It leaves a bitter aftertaste on my tongue.

"Come sit on the couch." She pats a black leather sofa and we sit close together. I get the feeling that something is off. I can't put my finger on it. A sensation creeps along my body that starts at my toes until my head starts to swim.

I notice her t-shirt and shorts, and they strike me as odd. "You're not dressed to teach."

"I was taking the day off."

"I thought you were going to teach after you visited me." I don't like the expression on her face. Her eyes look calculating and detached. Noise starts to flood my head. "Maybe I should call my mom." My tongue feels thick and fat and my words come out slow and slurred.

She takes the cup from my hand. "That's not a good idea, Juliet." Her voice starts to twist towards me as if floating through a tornado. She leans in close to my face, her lips only inches from my ear. "Do you know what you are?"

I lean back. "What're you talking about? I'm not anyone special." My head spins groggily. Her face turns fuzzy and then refocuses.

"You really don't know, do you?" She chuckles. The sound grates against my nerves. Her face turns fuzzy again, and this time, it doesn't clear. "They haven't told you." She strokes my cheek with her fingers.

I look at the cup and three stare back at me. I try to yell but can only sputter, "What... have... done," and that takes an eternity. My body folds back into the couch, my breathing labored. I'm a fool for trusting the wrong person.

She sits up straighter. "I wasn't at the hospital to visit you. I was watching for your grandfather. They think he is the one we need. They believe he holds the key the Seeker is after. I don't think they're right."

I open my mouth, but the drugs in the tea have stolen my voice and my tongue flops out, leaving me voiceless.

Her face twists and turns as if her features are reflected in one of those oddly shaped mirrors they use at carnivals. "You are the key," she says and leans close to me. Her fingers lift my chin. "You are the Alpha." Her hot breath brushes against my cheek. I want to pull back, but I've lost all control over my body.

My mind staggers in drunken circles. *What's she talking about?* I'm just a normal teenager. All I've ever wanted to be was normal, but my eyelids start to close on their own, and it takes all my will to keep them open.

"I've been observing you. You're special. You moved so fast you were a blur when you attacked Tiffany the other day. No one moves that fast, and the ring from the van was bent. It would take two hulking guys to bend that ring.

"They think the Alpha has to be a boy. Ha! *You're* the one we need. You contain the secret. The Seeker will be so pleased. He will reward me generously. This apartment will only be the beginning. I'll be wealthy beyond your imagination. You *must* be the Alpha."

I smell her perfume—roses with a slight hint of tobacco. The smell makes me ill. Bile fills my throat. I try so hard to stay awake, but my eyes close and won't open. Just when all turns gray, I hear splintered wood. Ms. Arnold screams and jumps off the couch. I try to twist, to see what's going on, but my body is too heavy and my eyes stay closed.

Strong arms lift me. Familiar arms, and I smell incense.

Gray turns black.

I can see, yet I'm not awake. I'm dreaming, but it feels more real, more solid than my usual dreams, almost like I am reliving a vivid memory. Two suns light a cloudless sky with a bright red hue. Beams of light beat down hot on my face.

I stand on a cliff of bluish rocky soil. Below me is the beginning of a battle. Short, wide people with bushels of curly black hair on their heads and faces wield wooden spears. Leather skins cover only a small portion of their bodies. Thick-knotted muscle bunches on their arms and legs and backs. At least a thousand adults brandish spears. They look angry, nervous, scared even.

They're not human. They have bent backs and only a few teeth, which are filed to sharp points. Their eyes burn blood red. Both men and women have curly black beards. Only the small ones – the children - do not. The adults form a ragged line six deep in front of round, blue, clay huts that I guess are their homes, while the children stand fifty feet behind them, bows and arrows with shiny metal tips clutched in their little hands.

The second group is tall and thin and hairless. Their features are fine and handsome, and their eyes shine an electric shade of violet. Dressed in light, almost translucent tunics that hang to their knees, they could pass as extraordinarily beautiful humans, but they're different. Marching forward in perfect formation of neat squares five rows deep, each warrior holds what resembles a glass sword with light glimmering off the sharp edges. They have no fear. They move as if they are conducting a harmless training exercise. All the fear emanates from the short brutish people even though they outnumber their opponents two to one. Nothing separates the two forces except flat, bluish rock.

The children shoot a wave of arrows that take flight like a flock of birds that whistle through the air.

The oncoming army never slows their gait. When the arrows start their downward plunge, they fall harmlessly to the ground five feet in front of the approaching warriors as if all their momentum was somehow stolen away before they could do any harm.

One of the short, brutish warriors jumps in the air and waves his spear in looping circles over his head. He must be the leader of his people. He wears a long leather cape and stark white horns protrude from the curly hair on his head. I can't be sure, but the horns are probably from an animal—decoration or a symbol that he's in charge. He turns to face his people, screams a high-pitched battle cry that echoes in the rocky canyon, and his army surges forward. The ground shakes from their sandals and anger and fear.

The taller soldiers never break formation or change their

pace. When the two forces collide, it's no contest. The glass swords carve through spears and into flesh. They cleave away muscle and bone as easily as the arrows had flown through the air. The horned leader is the first to fall. Blood splashes the ground. Screams echo and death spoils the air.

Within minutes, piles of dead, brutish warriors litter the battleground — hundreds of dead. I want to scream for the battle to stop, but I have no voice. I can do nothing as the remaining brutish people turn to retreat. Parents frantically wave at their children to flee. The attackers race forward. Their long legs carry them past the brutish people in a blur as they swing their glimmering swords of death.

A horrifying scene of carnage plays out below me. I hope the children will be spared, or can escape, but they are neither fast enough nor shown any mercy. Most run and are struck in the back. A few try to fight, swinging their small bows as clubs. They are no match for the beautiful soldiers. I try to look away, but I cannot turn. In a few minutes, the entire village is massacred. Not one member of their tribe stands.

I search for the dead among the taller warriors. Surely a few have been killed, but only one man appears injured. A spear has pierced his side. He wobbles on his knees. Four compatriots stalk toward him. The tallest of the four swings his glass sword; the injured man's head topples from his shoulders. I wince at the brutality of the scene and wake.

Scorching air roasts my flesh. When I open my eyes, there's nothing but darkness. Not normal darkness, but disorienting total darkness, as if all light has been sucked out of the world. *Am I awake? I can't tell.*

I push away the horrible images from the battle, and memories of Ms. Arnold and the apartment shove their way into my mind. I sit up fully awake now. I'm on a rough mattress and hear a nearby shuffling sound in the darkness.

I'm not alone.

My heart skips a beat and my mouth goes dry.

"Who's there?" My voice sounds timid and my eyes strain against the darkness. I expect Gold Tooth or Slicked Back Hair to answer or grab me. I'd run if I could see where to go.

A shadow strikes a match and tosses it on a small stack of dry wood, which instantly bursts into flames. The sudden flash burns my eyes. The flickering firelight provides enough light for me to see. I'm sitting at one end of a small oblong structure made totally of clay.

The shadow moves and I look into gray eyes framed by long white hair, and a deeply tanned, lined face. The flickering firelight plays games with his eyes, turning them wild.

My heart jumps. "What's going on, Sicheii? Where are we?"

He moves close beside me. "We are at my sweat lodge, as the Great Wind Spirit has commanded." He speaks matter-of-factly as if he is merely reporting the weather. I know he has a secret sweat lodge. All medicine men have one where they ask the spirits to cure people or speak to them or whatever weirdness they do in private. I've never asked to visit his or even seen one before.

"Who are these people that are after us?"

Sweat glistens off his chest and the twisted arrows tattoo over his heart. "That's a very complicated question." He lifts the back of his hand to my brow and frowns with his lips and eyes. "You have the fever. We don't have much time to talk."

"Tell me what's going on!" The words escape fast as I ball up my hands into fists. He's so infuriating.

"You are a very special young woman. You are not ill as your mother suspects." His face twists sourly; his displeasure at Mom reflects in his eyes. "These voices you hear are a gift from the Great Wind Spirit. You can understand the thoughts of those around you, human and animal. You must embrace this gift and learn to control it to break the fever. It's your first test before you receive your other gifts."

"What do you mean gifts?" I huff. "I don't want any gifts. What's wrong with everyone?"

"The time for childish games is over, Juliet." Sicheii touches me on the arm. His fingers are cool to the touch, and the simple gesture steadies me. "You know differently. You can't deny your uniqueness any longer. You must be a rock."

"How did you know I would see the number eight when I was with Doctor Dan last night?" I have so many questions, I'm not sure why this one jumps to my lips. Still it did, and it spilled out.

He smiles. "I told him to clear his mind and think only of that number. I knew you would read his thoughts."

I slump my shoulders and sit heavily on the mattress. "You've gone insane." Still, as crazy as he sounds, he does make some sense. How else would he have known I was going to say eight? Eight isn't even my favorite number. My favorite number is six.

A mischievous smile springs to his face. "You know the truth. You just have to let yourself believe."

Could I have gifts? I've never been special — just an average student, a good lacrosse player but not great, an average looking girl — nothing special.

"What do I have to do?" I sound mousy and small, as far away from special as imaginable.

206

Sicheii glances back at the flames for a moment before his eyes meet mine. "Every animal has the spark of life given to it by the spirits. That spark is unique to the creature. Your mind is more finely tuned than others. You can pick up their sparks and hear the thoughts behind it." He smiles. "If you concentrate hard enough on the voices, you can understand them like a radio receives stations. People generally think in words, but animals see images."

I recall the day Troy and I found Roundtree dead behind his house. I saw those cuts on his chest. They weren't my imagination. They could've come from the goats. *Argh!* This is so weird, but there's truth underneath the weirdness. "How do I tune my brain? Do you have this *gift*?"

He shakes his head. "The Great Wind Spirit chose you. You are Chosen. No one else has these gifts." He passes me a glass of water. "As our leader, Roundtree knew more. He had the Ancient Book of Gifts, but he refused to give it to me. All I can do is help you with the old ways: through the stones, the prayers, and the ancient medicines."

"How come you didn't tell me about this earlier?" I practically growl at him. "Why does everything have to be a secret?" I feel heavy and tired like a pack animal that has carried supplies for too long.

"I am only an agent of the Wind Spirit." His face softens and his shoulders go limp. "This is how it's written. Besides, you would be in danger if others knew about your special nature before you accepted your gifts."

"Did you kill Roundtree and the others?" The words come out pillow-soft. I have to ask. I study his eyes, but the firelight dances in them, so I don't see the truth.

"There is no time for that." Tension jumps into his body, his back stiffens, and his jaw clenches. "We must concentrate on you and controlling your first gift. Later we can talk about all you need to know."

"Great."

He turns and shouts in the old language to the fire-keeper outside. Every sweat lodge has a fire-keeper. He or she keeps a fire burning, makes sure the stones smolder, keeps everyone safe, and protects the lodge from outsiders. Even though this is a secret sweat lodge, I'm not surprised he has a fire-keeper. I wish I can understand what he said, but I've never tried to learn the language.

He ambles toward the opposite end of the lodge where a leather hide acts as a door and takes the handle of a long shovel and lifts three smoldering stones. Thin wisps of smoke circle above them. He meticulously places the three stones into the fire and creates a perfect triangle. The stones sizzle in the fire pit. He tosses sage, cedar, and sweet grass on top of the hot stones to purify the smoke. The heat spikes. He returns the shovel to the fire-keeper and closes the leather hide.

Before he returns, he chants an old song and shakes a leather and wooden rattle. He asks the Great Wind Spirit to guide us and protect us. The flames dance upward for a heartbeat, and I see the adobe bricks that make the sweat lodge and the grass that's been used as mortar.

As the flame burns brighter, the air turns hotter. *Why make it hotter?* The air is practically on fire as it is. I bring my hand to my mouth to thwart some of the heat. The sweltering temperature blasts me in suffocating waves. When I take in air, the heat burns my lungs, and my skin feels like it's on fire.

He returns to my side and frowns. "You have the fever. You must concentrate hard on your gifts. You cannot fail." His eyes lock onto mine; they look like diamonds, sparkling in the firelight, hard, severe, untamed.

My head swims, but I don't like the jagged edge to his face and the desperation in the tilt of his head. "What happens if I fail?"

"If you fail to control your gift, the fever will consume you, and the Great Wind Spirit will take us both."

I struggle to stand, but my arms and legs are loosely tied to a wooden post by heavy rope.

CHAPTER 30

"Are you insane? Untie me!" I pull hard against the rope with both arms, but the restraints hold, and the cords dig into my wrists, so I stop. "It's hot in here, and I don't feel well." My head reels, thoughts collide against each other, none make any sense. The herbal incense and the fever burning through my bloodstream send my mind careening out of control.

Sicheii scowls at me, as if I had given him the wrong answer to an important question. "You must quell your anger to survive. There's nowhere else for you to go. White medicine can't cure you." He brushes a couple of stray hairs from his eyes. "It is written The Great Wind Spirit requires you to face this test in a sweat lodge. You must search within and embrace your gift. It's the only way to break the fever. You must control the gifts the Wind Spirit has given you."

"Help!" I shout at the gate, hoping to reach the fire-keeper. "Help me!" I repeat the cry four times. Each time, my voice loses more steam.

He glances from the leather door to me. "You will find no help from outside, Little Bird. You must look within. You must ask the Wind Spirit to guide you." He moves toward the gate where he takes another handful of herbs from his leather pouch.

"Please, Sicheii, let me go!"

He ignores me, begins chanting again, and tosses more herbs on the flames.

The fragrance fills the lodge. The air is heavy. *Is he crazy? Could he be right?* My thoughts spin and spin and spin. I see the photograph of the secret society from the article, Roundtree's dead body, the twisted arrows tattoo, the look on Ms. Arnold's face after she drugged me. The heat rises and the smell of incense fills my lungs. I sag down on the mattress, my body a led weight. He circles the fire, round and round, and ignores me as if he's alone. My anger bursts into all-consuming rage like a wildfire. I need to let it go, but I can't.

I collapse on the mattress and slip in and out of consciousness. Dreams twist and torque through my mind. One moment, Troy is next to me. He seems sad, with moist eyes and a deep frown. The next moment, a hatchet slices open my chest.

Morgan and Tiffany show up in one of my visions. They laugh at me and call me *Indian trash*. They tell me I'll never be welcome in their clubs.

Ella tries to explain something important about the murders while she drives her Ford recklessly, and Katie is crying. I can't console her. I fail her.

Lucid times mingle with the visions. Sicheii gives me water from a glass. The visions and reality twist together so neither is recognizable. Anger is my only constant companion, consuming me, sucking away my energy.

I must have fallen into a deep sleep because I find myself in a vast city made of crystal. I feel different, lighter. It's serene and otherworldly. The anger has finally vanished, a weight lifted from my body.

I twirl in a lazy, looping circle. Tall structures soar upward in all directions. Paved roads sparkle with silver and crushed stone, and small circles of sapphire colored grass appear randomly. Crystal structures stretch off into the distance as far as I can see. The city should teem with life, but I find none. No vehicles or people or noise of any kind.

I wander down the widest of the ghost streets and pass buildings of increasing size and elaborateness. They're completely foreign looking. Some curve with vast arches, while others point with jagged edges. Most are translucent, but a few are opaque and block out the light. A sun, larger but dimmer than ours, floats high in a greenish sky with three small moons that circle close to it in the distance.

Where am I, and how did I get here?

As I travel down the wide avenue, the buildings become spaced farther apart until a circular stadium shines in the distance. The first traces of life sprout as I move closer to the stadium—signs appear. Not paper signs, but screens with fixed images. Most have a purple triangle with a yellow circle in the center. An "X" drawn in red crosses out the entire symbol. A few have an image of a beautiful looking man. He's hairless with fine features. Purple islands float in the otherwise blue ocean of his eyes. They seem to glow dangerously. The same red

"X" crosses through his face. He isn't human. He's one of those warriors from my prior dream who ravaged the short, brutish people.

I feel as if I'm floating above the street as I go. Before realizing it, I cross the arched entranceway into the stadium. It is vast, much larger than any stadium I have ever seen. The sides stretch as tall as the tallest building in Phoenix. Energy, anxious and angry, buffets against me as I push open gray crystal doors and enter the main floor of the arena.

Inside the crystal coliseum is a field of knee high, wispy, blue-green grass surrounding a wide stage six stories tall. On the stage sit three tall, hairless, almost human looking people. Two are men and the third is a woman. They wear white and silver tunics that shimmer with the symbol of the triangle and the circle on their chests.

Six others sit on glass thrones that tower over those with the symbols — three men and three women. Their tunics glisten with golden specks and each has a crystal pendant shaped like a disc hanging from their neck. I cannot tell their age. Their lack of hair and fine features disguise them, but the man and woman in the center throne chairs are clearly well aged, with lines around the eyes and stooped backs.

The oldest woman shouts, her face red as spit flies from her mouth. Her hands clutch the side of her throne chair, the muscles on her forearms tense. I tear my eyes from her and glance up into the stadium, where I see thousands and thousands of these people. I can't tell one from the other, but a quarter of the stands are full with those who wear tunics with the triangle and circle symbol in one section. Separated from the rest, they're guarded by others who hold clear crystal swords.

The sun reflects off the weapons and makes it appear almost as if the guards hold staffs of light.

When I return my gaze to the stage, the old woman stops yelling and glances at her comrades who sit on thrones beside her. A sly, confident smile graces her face. A decision must be reached. Her chair is a few feet taller than the rest. Each of her comrades nods his head and beats his chest with a fist. They are all in agreement.

When the last one does the same, the old woman faces the three sitting before her, her expression severe. She grabs the crystal pendant around her neck and it turns blood red. She waves her other hand and the tunics of all three are ripped. A red slice appears across their foreheads as if she has cut them with an invisible knife.

The stands roar. Not a cheer or shout or cry, but the sound of thousands and thousands of people beating their fists against their chests and stomping their feet. A wave of energy, like a current, races through my body. Those in the stands with the symbols on their chests stand stoically. I squint and see their tunics rip. Blood splashes across their foreheads.

The ground beneath me sways. I open my eyes.

Sicheii gently shakes me. "You cannot sleep now, Little Bird." I sit up and he says, "You must concentrate on the voices."

My head whirls unsteadily, and Sicheii's face changes into that of Doctor Dan. "Turn your attention to the sounds. Embrace them, Juliet. Feel them intensify, shape them."

Is this reality or another dream?

"What do I do?" My voice sounds weak and pathetic, and I despise it. My right heel stings, and I remember the story Sicheii

214

told me of my birth. I feel the connection between that story and the voices as if tied together by a silk cord.

"You don't have much time left," Doctor Dan says. "Concentrate on the voices, embrace them, fine tune them with your mind like you did the other night. It's the only way."

I close my eyes and my body wobbles. I reach into my mind for the voices. Determination replaces my fear. I will not die here. I focus on the loudest voice. It sounds like a radio station that isn't quite tuned in, full of static and gibberish.

My skin burns. I refuse to open my eyes for fear I might see flames engulfing my body. My attention focuses on the sounds. They grow steadily louder but no more comprehensible. My body rocks. I almost topple over and have to put my hands down on the mattress to steady myself. If I fall, I will never rise again, but I will not fall. My eyes stay clenched shut.

I play with the noises and mold them, twist them. They start to come into focus. The unintelligible words begin to sound like Sicheii's voice. My lungs are on fire. I gasp for breath.

I open my eyes. Sicheii's face is close to mine. He takes shallow desperate breaths. "Déélgai," I say. "Déélgai, you crazy old man."

He bends backward at the waist and lets out a full-bodied "WHOOP." A smile beams brightly across his face. "What does déélgai mean, Little Bird?"

Déélgai is an ancient word, but I understand its meaning. I not only hear the word but see the image from his mind. "Swan... Sicheii. It means swan."

"Yes it does," he says. He lifts the back of his hand to my head. "The fever has broken. You've passed your first test." He feathers his fingertips against my cheek lovingly.

"Great, now get me out of here." Other words and images flash in my head. They are Sicheii's. His relief and love wrap tightly around my body like a wool blanket. I so want to be angry with him, but how can I?

He cuts the ropes from my wrists. I try to stand, but my legs are too weak, so he lifts me. "How long have I been here?"

"Almost three days." He carries me through the sweat lodge and into the cool night air.

A shadow hovers close to the campfire—the fire-keeper in the distance. I don't need to see him to know who he is.

CHAPTER 31

Sicheii carries me to a rusted 1970s RV. He kicks open the screen door and gently places me on a plastic kitchen chair. The camper smells old and musty and acrid as if the vehicle is displeased we are using it and hopes to drive us away with its foul stench. The Formica kitchen tabletop peels in long, curved strips. Age yellows the once white kitchen cabinets, which hang crookedly on rusted hinges. Thankfully, the light is dim.

"Let me find you something cool to drink. You need to hydrate." Sicheii swings open the door to the mini-fridge, pours two glasses of iced tea, places one in front of me and downs the other in three noisy gulps.

I stare at the condensation that clings to the outside of the glass. My throat is scorching dry and the tea's amber color inviting. My fingers wrap around the glass and I peer inside. What else is in the iced tea? Another drug or test, maybe? A fire burns through me, so I toss the cold liquid in his face.

He smiles in return. "The anger is never far from the surface with you, is it?" His long, white hair and bushy eyebrows resemble a wet mop as iced tea drips from his face in little streams.

"What have you done to me? I could have died!"

Sicheii sighs. "I've let you fulfill your destiny." He takes the empty glass from my hand. "If I refill this glass, will you drink the tea?" He stares at me, eyes boring into mine, making no effort to dry his face. One drop of tea clings to his eyebrow until it gives up and falls to the kitchen table below.

Despite my anger, I fight hard not to grin. "Yes, Sicheii, I'll drink the tea."

He moves slowly, shoulders slumped, and dries his face on an old green towel. I wonder if he has spent the entire three days in the sweat lodge with me, worrying and praying to the Great Wind Spirit. He looks much older than he did a few days ago.

He returns, and this time, he brings the pitcher with him. He hands me another glass of iced tea and places the half-full pitcher on the cracked kitchen table. I can't recall ever being so thirsty before, so I eagerly take the glass and chug. The cold liquid flows down my parched throat, refreshing and reviving me. I don't even mind the little splash that sloshes down the side of my face.

I refill the glass. "Everything started the day I was born, right? You did something weird to me in the hospital. These voices are connected with that story you told me on my thirteenth birthday."

He shakes his head. "That is only the middle of your story. Your destiny goes back over 200 years. The Wind Spirit spoke to our ancestors and described what had to be done. They recorded the encounter in the Book of Knowledge. Only a few of us were allowed to be secret keepers. Only a few knew and understood what was required. Only those who could be trusted."

"Only those with the twisted arrows tattoos," I say, interrupting him, and the light in his eyes burns brighter. "Yes, I know all about the tattoos and your little club."

"The Order of the Twisted Arrows is no little club, Juliet. We are sworn to carry out the Wind Spirit's wishes." He pours himself another glass from the pitcher.

"So I'm the secret you've been trying to keep." I hunch back in my chair. "The entire mystery this whole time is about *me*. All these people, sworn to keep *me* a secret."

"The Order goes back over two hundred years, Juliet. This secret has been carefully guarded and only entrusted to a few select individuals. But yes, it all culminates in you. This is the only way our people can survive."

"What does any of this have to do with the survival of our people?"

"The Wind Spirit demanded that we inject her essence into the Chosen to let the spirit bind with the Chosen's spirit. This way, the two spirits can twist together and the Wind Spirit can empower the Chosen with gifts you will need to save our people from death."

"So that needle you stuck me with was filled with the Wind Spirit's essence?" I shake my head. "You injected something *weird* into my blood."

"Yes, but it was not some drug. It came from the Wind Spirit and was handed down to us over two centuries."

I drink the second glass of tea. This time, I take my time. I need a little space to wrap my mind around what he is telling me. "Why did you choose me? Someone else must have been more worthy. I'm not special."

"I didn't choose you. If there were any other way, I would have found someone else. I know this is a big responsibility, but the Wind Spirit was specific. She told us the exact star configuration when the Chosen would be born and instructed us that the Chosen had to be one of our descendants." He shrugs. "You were born at exactly the right time and were the only eligible candidate."

He opens his hands on the table palm out. "You see, the Wind Spirit chose you over two hundred years ago. There was nothing I could do but accept your destiny."

I groan. "You could have told me. You didn't need to lie to me my whole life. First Mom, and now you. Why is everyone lying to *me!*"

"It's not my place to question the Wind Spirit, Juliet. We are bound to keep your role secret until you face your first challenge. There was no other way." He clenches his right hand into a fist and taps the table. "Besides, secrecy is critical. Others seek to destroy you. They will kill you if they have the opportunity."

"Great. The story only gets better. Does Mom know about this?"

"No. She would never have understood."

"You said reading thoughts was only one of my gifts." I push my glass to one side. Intrigued, I wonder if there is some benefit for being the Chosen whatever. "What other gifts are you talking about? Anything useful?"

He frowns. It is a full-face frown; the many lines in his face turn downward together. "I don't know. Roundtree had the Book of Gifts. I tried to persuade him to give it to me, but he said he had hidden it in a safe place." His hands smooth back his hair. "I warned him, but he would not yield or relinquish the book to me."

"What does it say? You must have read it."

He shakes his head. "It is not for any of *us* to read. The Book of Gifts can only be read by the *Chosen*."

"Did you kill Roundtree?"

Sicheii's face turns red. "Don't ask questions you already know the answer to!"

He rarely gets angry, so the outburst surprises me and the force of his words makes me lean back in the chair. I stare hard at him and try to fine-tune my brain like a receiver to read his thoughts. Words and images come, but they come so quickly they jumble together. I sense sadness and guilt, but I can't tell what it all means. A flame behind his eyes scares me, and for the first time, I really wonder whether he was involved in the murders.

I snap from my trance, tired and weary. The effort to manipulate his thoughts and images sap the rest of my waning strength. I feel as if I'm made of stone and lean on the table with my head hung low. "What do we do next?"

He smiles, and his face returns to his old self, confident, happy. "We eat. I'm starving." He looks through the RV's rusted window. "The fire should be perfect for a barbecue."

CHAPTER

Alone, I close my eyes. I'm not sure how much time passes, but it seems to cease. Weariness has seeped into my body beyond flesh and blood and bone and into my soul like a slow trickle of water has seeped into a sponge until it can't absorb another drop. I would be content to sit in the plastic chair with my head resting awkwardly on the peeled table for the rest of my days.

But the smell from the barbecue triggers an animal survival instinct. Steak sizzles against stone slabs and my stomach jumps. It's the only part of me with any life. If my stomach wasn't tethered to my stone-like body and had free will to act on its own, it would do cartwheels at the thought of eating freshly grilled steak.

I lift my head and find a shadow figure by the door — the vague form of the fire-keeper, nervous, anxious. He knocks softly.

I narrow my eyes. Blood rushes through my veins again. "Come in, traitor!"

The door opens, and Troy skulks into the RV, his shoulders stooped with his eyes focused on his feet.

"You knew about this madness and you didn't tell me? How could you?" My mouth hangs open. I have a hard time believing Troy is complicit in Sicheii's schemes, yet he stands before me as his fire-keeper.

Troy raises his eyes, eyes I have stared into so many times before. Always, I believed in a best friend and imagined a future. Now I see a liar.

"Jake explained things to me six months ago. They needed new blood for the Order and wanted me to look after you... protect you."

"You've been lying to me for *six months!*" I shake my head and rub my hands through my hair. "I can live with my mom and even Sicheii, but not you." A hole opens in my heart. A sharp pain stabs through me that almost doubles me over with cramps, but I grip the table hard and stay upright. Bits of Formica from the table snap in my hands.

"Once I knew the truth, I was bound to stay silent, Jules." He steps toward me and rests both his hands on the edge of a kitchen chair on the opposite side of the table. "If I had told you, you would be in danger."

"You let me think I was going crazy to protect me? Lift up your shirt." I know what I'll find on his chest, but I want him to lift his shirt anyway.

He hesitates. "There's no need to do that, Jules. I've always been on your side." Guilt weighs down his voice, making it slow and lumbering like a buffalo.

I glare at him. "Lift up your shirt."

Troy frowns and lifts his t-shirt. A twisted arrows tattoo blazes on the smooth brown skin on his chest.

223

"No wonder you were reluctant to help me this whole time. You knew what the ink meant. You realized what was happening. Did you kill Roundtree? Maybe help my grandfather as he tortured him?"

"No, Juliet. I had nothing to do with Roundtree's death and neither did Jake. The Seeker's people tortured Roundtree. They were looking for you." Troy waves his hands. "He knows about you now and won't stop until he gets you."

"You are a *liar*! Why should I believe anything you say?"

"I'm your best friend, Jules." Troy tries to smile, but his mouth won't budge beyond a thin grim line. "You have to trust me."

I shake my head and turn away from him. I can't look at him. "I don't know what you are, but you're not my friend. Friends don't lie to each other, not about something like this. Get out. I never want to see you again. Go be with Candy. I'm sure she misses you!"

I stare at the grimy window until I hear the screen door swing open and close a few moments later. The weariness returns, and I bang my head against the table.

Clunk.

I don't know what to think.

Clunk.

Everything is mixed up and everyone has been lying to me.

Clunk.

I feel alone. Troy anchored me, his friendship has been the rock I've built my life around. I'm not sure what happens next and that scares me. I never thought I'd have to think about life without him.

Sicheii calls from outside that the food is ready. I debate whether I should get up or stay and melt into the smelly, broken

224

kitchen table forever. My belly grumbles and makes the decision for me.

It takes considerable effort to leave my chair, but I can't stay in the dirty kitchen forever. I push on the table with my hands, find my feet, and trudge outside. The night sky is clear and the campfire flames are low and dance a slow waltz. Sicheii has changed into a blue linen shirt and his favorite straw wide-brimmed hat. He laid out a red woolen blanket a few feet away from the fire where he's placed two large, sizzling steaks on a white ceramic serving platter.

I trudge toward the blanket, dragging my feet across the ground. Dirt drifts in the still air behind me. Sicheii smiles when I sit cross-legged next to him.

Troy hasn't left. He sits near the fire watching and sulking in the darkness. I want to ask him to leave, but I don't have the energy, and part of me wants him to stay.

Sicheii prays to the Great Wind Spirit for delivering me out of the darkness. I tune him out. I should wait for him to finish, but I don't care about hurting his feelings at the moment, or the Great Wind Spirit, or any of this mess, so I grab the plate, a fork and knife, and dive in.

My grandfather has many shortcomings, but he's a magician around a fire-pit. The meat bursts with flavor. It's been a lifetime since I last ate. A little energy returns to my body, and I sit up straighter and glare at him. "So who decided to kill John Dent? Was it Roundtree? Did you need to kill him to keep your secrets?"

He chuckles and wipes grease from his mouth with a white cotton towel. "You are so quick to believe the worst in me that you refuse to see the obvious in front of you."

"What does that mean?" I am tired of his riddles. "Just tell me the truth this time."

"We didn't kill John Dent." He smiles. "When he broke his story about the Order, we took him in and told him the truth. He was in danger and saw the grievous error he had made and decided it was best to disappear."

"Sure... I saw his grave."

"He's not dead. He changed his name and went back to school. You met him as Doctor Dan Epstein."

I slice off another piece of steak and slip it into my mouth. So *that's* why Doctor Dan looked so familiar. He was the grown up person from the picture on his mother's mantel. I add him to the long list of people who seem to have no problem lying to me.

"What about Ayden? You knew he killed that man in self-defense. You could have prevented him from going to jail."

Sicheii places his fork on the serving dish. He hesitates for a couple of seconds as he thinks about what to tell me.

"I'll know if you're being honest. I'm the Chosen, remember?" I have no idea if I can tell whether he speaks the truth through my gift, but a good threat works even if it only has the illusion of being carried out.

"Yes, you are," Sicheii replies. "Ayden was a dangerous drug dealer. He was no good for you and Summer. You could never be safe around him, and we needed to keep you safe."

"So you let him go to jail?" I clench my hands closed.

"It's not as simple as that. The Seeker was on to us. He had sent three men to investigate our town. They made a connection between the Order and Roundtree. The only way we could cover up the situation was to have those deaths appear like a drug deal gone bad. We planted enough evidence and covered our tracks well enough that we fooled him, at least temporarily. Your father had to pay that price to keep you safe."

"But he was innocent." I toss my fork onto the plate with a loud clang. "He spent fifteen years in jail. I could have grown up with a father!"

Sicheii touches my leg. His eyes convey real sorrow. "I'm sorry you didn't have a father growing up, Juliet. I did my best to fill the void, but Ayden was not an innocent man. He had committed many crimes for which he had not been punished. Life has a way of catching up to you, and this time, it caught up with him."

I swipe Sicheii's hand from my knee and eat in silence. Frogs call out in the distance. An owl hoots and ruffles the leaves in a nearby tree.

Troy shivers when he hears the owl. He believes that owls warn us about upcoming death. His eyes scan the nearby trees as he looks for the bird.

"We need to make plans, Juliet," Sicheii says. "I don't know what your teacher told the Seeker, but we have to assume he knows you are here or will figure out how important you are soon. He won't stop until he captures you. Besides, the rest of your gifts will come quickly, and I don't know what they are or how to help."

"Gifts," I snort. "I don't want any more gifts."

"You are Chosen," Sicheii says, his voice low, deep, and full of concern. "You don't have any choice. If we knew where Roundtree kept the second book, we would know more."

"What happened to Ms. Arnold?" She was my favorite teacher, the only person other than Katie I trusted at Bartens and another one who lied to me.

"She is being held in a safe place. She can't hurt us now." Sicheii stares hard at me. "We need to focus on you and your gifts. They are the key to fulfilling your destiny. You must embrace them before the Seeker finds you."

"Who is this Seeker you keep talking about?"

"I don't know exactly." He sighs. "He's sent here by Coyote to find you and harm you. We need to keep you secret until you are ready to face him."

"I don't care about the Wind Spirit or these gifts or the Seeker." I stand. "I want nothing to do with any of this. I'm done. I'll run away if there's no other way."

"Jules, you can't ignore your responsibility," Troy says from the darkness, his voice soft like a summer breeze. "Without you, we'll all perish."

"I guess you'll have to think of something else." I turn my back on them and stalk toward the RV. I'm so tired. The only thing I want is a bed with sheets. It doesn't matter what type of bed.

I'm sure of only one thing though. I don't want to be the Chosen.

CHAPTER 33

Light fights through a dirt-encrusted window and tap dances across my eyes. I jam the pillow on top of my face in hopes that the past few days will prove to be nothing more than a nightmare, hoping that when I wake, Mom will hover over me as she did before, anxious to start her trip.

Of course, Mom doesn't appear, and there's no redo. The world doesn't work that way. We have to live in the imperfect and face our faults and mistakes and those of others.

I growl and toss the pillow aside. The bedroom is tiny, just large enough for one twin-sized bed, a small table, and an elfin-sized closet, which I refuse to open. Who knows what Sicheii has stuffed in there? I don't want to find out. The more I learn about my grandfather, the weirder he gets. I can only take so much and have reached my limit.

I know I'll never go back to sleep now. My mind is awake, even if the rest of my body wants a few more hours of rest. If I try to sleep, I will just lie in bed and become angrier with each minute that passes. I refuse to buy a ticket for that Ferris Wheel. I hop from the bed and catch a glimpse of myself in a dusty mirror. I'm still wearing the same jeans and t-shirt from when I left the hospital. Dirt and grime blot my face, and my hair is a greasy, stringy mess. I look like a wild child, raised by wolves. A sly smile crosses my face as I wonder what Tiffany and her pack of sharks would think if they saw me now.

I brush hair away from my face and move stiffly to a small bathroom, eyes half closed. I let my dirty clothes drop to the floor, swing the shower curtain open, and work the controls. The hot water feels good as it bounces off my head and forms little rivers down my body. My eyes close and my mind roams. The voices are there, just under the surface. Now that I understand how to manipulate them, I play with them. Two distinct voices bounce inside of my head, one from Sicheii and the other from Troy. I ignore Sicheii and dial down the volume much like the control on my iPhone, and focus on Troy's instead. I listen intently, increase the volume, and shape the sounds until words form.

He worries about me, worries this Seeker is dangerous, worries I might run off. He wants to protect me.

I pull back and quiet his internal voice. It doesn't feel right to listen to his private thoughts. It's like I'm reading his diary without his permission. And in truth, part of me is afraid to know what he thinks about me anyway. My feelings for him have always been complicated, always deeper than friendship alone, but he's never shown any sign that he shares those feelings. Now his betrayal looms so large it crowds out my affection as if it's a roadblock I can't pass—not yet anyway.

I breathe deeply and push Troy from my mind with a mental shove. Other concerns are more pressing at the moment. I must sift through lies and truth and find my way. The water turns cool as I wash the rest of the grime from my body. A neat stack of clothes waits for me on the sink. On top is the *Beatles* t-shirt Troy bought me as a Christmas gift. The local radio station ran a *Beatles* weekend in the beginning of December, and I got hooked. Troy bought me an *Abbey Road* t-shirt a few weeks later for the holiday. He can be thoughtful that way.

I smile despite myself and lift the shirt to my face. It smells fresh, like the detergent Mom uses. I forget for a moment I'm angry at Troy and Mom and Sicheii. I dress in the fresh clothes, swing open the screen, and enter the hot Arizona morning to face two people whom I love, but who felt it perfectly fine to lie to me about the most important aspects of my life. My anger returns and my face flushes.

Both Sicheii and Troy turn to face me. They stand near a small campsite with two sleeping bags neatly folded behind them. They both slept outside with the bugs while I snoozed in the bed in the RV. They would sacrifice everything for me if they have to, but I've never asked them to and I don't want it. I just want to go back to an ordinary life.

When I trudge toward them, they both stand, bodies rigid as if they are waiting for bad news. I nod toward a plate of scrambled eggs, which looks cold with a slight film on top, but I'm hungry. "Is that for me?"

"Yes, it is." Sicheii waves at a blanket not far from the fire. "Take a seat."

I sit cross-legged at the edge of the blanket. Sicheii hands me the plate with the eggs, and Troy places a glass of orange juice next to me. They stand near me as if I'm their queen and they my subjects. It weirds me out a little.

"Sit down." I look only at Sicheii. I can't look at Troy, not just yet. "And if you lie to me again, I'm gone."

They sit on the far end of the blanket as I eat my breakfast. When the eggs are gone, I glance at Sicheii. "So tell me about this Seeker. Who is he and what does he want from me?"

His lips curve downward and the lines on his forehead bunch together. "He is Coyote's pawn. You are the Chosen who will defeat the Seeker, using the gifts the Great Wind Spirit has given you."

"You have no idea who or where he is?"

"No, except for the description from the Book of Knowledge. The Wind Spirit tells us he will be cloaked in beautiful clothing, tall and fine featured with eyes that could melt ice."

"That's not a lot to go on. I hoped for something like a jagged scar across his forehead or a skull tattoo on his arm." I pause for a second. "You said I need to prevent the extermination of our people. What do you mean?" I have so many questions, but extermination sounds bad so I start there.

"Coyote and the Great Wind Spirit are locked in a battle over our fate. Coyote believes we have treated Mother Earth poorly. He wants to end our time on Earth and return her to nature, to a time before the First Man. Coyote is using the Seeker for his purposes. You must kill him. If you fail, he will lead an army of demons who will destroy us."

"Seriously, an army of demons?" Intense pressure squeezes my chest, and I resist the urge escape. "Where is this Book of Knowledge you two seem so enamored with? I need to see some proof of this Great Wind Spirit thing — something tangible."

Sicheii nods toward Troy who jogs to the RV. As my eyes linger on his back, Sicheii says, "Don't be so hard on him, Juliet. He's only living up to his oath. All he wants is to keep you safe."

"He's supposed to be on *my* side!" I am shouting now, the veins on my neck pulsing. "He's been lying to me for months! He's supposed to be my best friend, the one person I can always rely upon." Unwanted tears brim my eyes.

Sicheii touches my leg. "Blame me then. I shouldn't have involved him, but I needed the right person, someone the Order could trust."

I jerk back my leg. "Don't think I'm not mad at you either! I'm your granddaughter. You could have trusted me." I wipe away tears that have not yet fallen.

"This has nothing to do with trust." He lifts his hands palm upward and the wind gusts as if he caused it to blow. "I did what was best for you and our people."

I huff and watch Troy return from the RV. He holds two bundles covered in black velvet. He refuses to lock eyes with me, keeping them on the ground until he stands over us and hands the bundles to Sicheii.

He unwraps a small package and removes a leather notebook. The tattered journal is no larger than a child's diary. He hands it to me with both hands.

I look at it suspiciously and remember the dream with ancient Native Americans, jewels, and the campfire from only a few days ago. This could be the same book the old man had at that meeting. The leather is old and dry and cracking. Inscribed on the cover is a simple golden square slanted on its side — the Tribe's symbol for the Wind Spirit. I open the journal and find neat looking symbols written in black ink. The pages are yellow and brittle.

I laugh a full body laugh. "What in the world is this?" Tears roll down my face. "I've never seen anything like it. Who could understand this?"

Sicheii frowns. "The book was written over two hundred years ago by an esteemed medicine man chosen by the Wind Spirit. The symbols are an early version of our language. Only those in the Order can discern its meaning now."

I carefully flip through the yellowed paper. "Six pages? *The Book of Knowledge* is only six pages long! You have to be kidding me. I wrote a history paper that was longer than this last week!" I study the first page. "I thought the Chosen was supposed to be able to read it. I have no idea what these symbols mean. The journal could be a cookbook for all I know."

Sicheii smiles as he reclaims the leather journal. Nothing fazes him. "I said only the Chosen can read the Book of Gifts. The Book of Knowledge is for the Order to understand."

"Well, if the Book of Gifts is written with those symbols, I'll never understand it." There's more. I stare at the second bundle. Anxiety ripples through me.

What do I want? Do I want proof that this crazy story is true? Something more solid than my ability with these voices, or do I want something easily dismissible? Something that makes me laugh and means that I am not special or Chosen and everything is a big mistake.

"I see you are interested in the second bundle." Sicheii lifts it with the tips of his fingers and folds away the black velvet cloth. "We call this the Seeker Slayer. The Wind Spirit gave it to us. The Seeker Slayer has helped convince Troy about the truth behind our Order." Sicheii smiles. "It has convinced many people of our truthfulness."

Sicheii removes a crystal object from the velvet wrappings. The crystal is shaped like a capital T. The long part of the T is the size of my palm. Light sparkles off the antiquity, ricocheting within the internal structure much like a diamond—only this is no diamond. Slight traces of teal and emerald reflect from inside the crystal. The twisted arrows symbol blazes on the long portion of the T in shining silver.

I know Sicheii wants me to take the relic, but my hand hovers in the air. "What's it made from?"

He shrugs. "The Seeker Slayer is not from this world but comes from the land of spirits." Sicheii smashes the end of the crystal on the slab of stone he used for cooking, and the stone splits. The crystal stays whole without chipping or cracking. "The structure is harder than a diamond."

"They had it tested at the University and it doesn't match anything in their database," Troy says as he leans forward. His eyes plead with me. He wants me to believe this tale, that he was right to side with my grandfather. I ignore him.

"Why do you call it the Seeker Slayer?"

"Only the Chosen can wield this weapon. You will use it to kill the Seeker." Sicheii pushes the crystal closer toward me.

"I don't want to touch it," I say and shrink away from him. I don't know why. Maybe I fear what the relic represents, its weirdness, and its otherworldliness. If I take it, I suspect there's no going back. "It doesn't look like a weapon to me."

Sicheii's voice is patient and strong. "You've passed the first test, Juliet. You have accepted the first gift. You must accept this weapon. It's the only way."

I glance at Sicheii and then at Troy. I wish I had a plan, a way to go back to a normal life. "I just want to be an average, normal person. I've never asked for this."

"I know, Jules," Troy says. "None of us asked for this, but what if it's all real? What if this is the only way? Those guys at Roundtree's house were real enough." Troy manages a half-grin. The skin under both of his eyes is still dark and his nose swollen.

I inch my hand toward the relic. It pulses with energy as I move closer. I steel my nerves and grab the crystal in my right hand. A soft shock and a vibration run through my body as if invisible fingers tickle me and grab hold of me. The air above the crystal shimmers and reforms into a three-foot blade made from the same material as the hilt. Etchings glimmer down its center.

I have seen swords like this one before: in my dreams.

CHAPTER

I drop the crystal sword, and the blade disappears before the hilt touches the ground. Sicheii smiles, and Troy's face turns ashen. I want to run, to leave this place and the sword and Sicheii and even Troy behind, but my eyes are locked on the crystal hilt. My breathing is shallow and raspy as air sticks in my lungs.

I am *not* special. I am not the smartest or the strongest or the fastest or the richest person. I'm an average girl born between two worlds—one rich and the other Native American. I'm the victim of a cosmic mistake.

Still, I close my eyes, and visions of Gold Tooth and Slicked Back Hair and Ms. Arnold darken my thoughts. They think I'm special, and as long as they do, everyone I care about remains in danger.

I push bile back down my throat. I must be more than a scared teenaged girl if I'm going to survive and confront this Seeker, this menace, this future I don't want but has been thrust upon me.

"What was that?" I hope Sicheii has more insights and will share the deeper meanings behind what's happening than he has thus far. I search his lined face for answers and realize his knowledge is limited. He has no more secrets to reveal.

"The sword is called the Seeker Slayer," Sicheii answers. "The weapon is blessed by the Wind Spirit. You must use the sword to destroy Coyote's pawn."

"Does it come with an instruction manual?"

He shakes his head.

I stare at the crystal hilt as if the relic is a living thing. *What does all this have to do with my dreams? How is the Wind Spirit connected to the tall and beautiful looking people with the crystal swords?* Sicheii's description of the Seeker fits one of the tall warriors from my dreams, but that's crazy. They were just stupid dreams, crazy images from my imagination.

They weren't real, or were they?

I remember to breathe, and with air, resolve slowly nudges aside some of my fear. I can't ignore the people looking for me, the crazy sword that only appears when I touch the hilt, or the voices and images I hear and see. Even if this whole thing is a big mistake, I'm not going to make it easy for this Seeker to harm me or anyone else I care about. I have to find a way to protect them.

My legs start bouncing up and down. They're filled with a kinetic energy. "Let's go. We can't sit around here all day." I jump to my feet. "We had better find that Book of Gifts before the Seeker finds me."

"I tried to force Roundtree to divulge its hiding place to me, Juliet, but he refused. I don't know where to search. I've prayed to the Wind Spirit for guidance, but she won't answer."

"I know where Roundtree hid the second book." At least, *I think* I have a good idea. I smile and turn my back on them. For once I know something they don't, which feels good. "And you had better bring that crystal thing with us. You never know who we might run into. A magic sword could come in handy."

I head toward the RV and wonder where my grandfather parked his car. There's no way they took the RV into the desert; both front tires are flat. I cross the front of the rusted metal house and find an old green SUV.

"Where's the Porsche?"

"The desert is no place for the Porsche. I may be odd, but I'm not crazy." Sicheii chuckles. "Besides, don't you think the SUV is a little less conspicuous?"

"Maybe just a little." At least we won't have to cram into the sports car.

I slide into the passenger seat, and Troy hops in back with a backpack slung over his shoulder. He doesn't need to tell me the Seeker Slayer is in the bag. I feel its presence.

Sicheii settles behind the wheel and turns the key in the ignition. The SUV starts with a slight wheeze and a sputter. "Where to?"

"Roundtree's house. The Wind Spirit showed me a sign."

Who knows?

Maybe the Wind Spirit caused that flashlight to shine on the tiny twisted arrows symbol in Roundtree's living room.

The drive to Roundtree's house is uneventful and quiet, so I have time to wrestle with my thoughts. I don't believe in fate, that our destinies are predetermined in the stars. Troy doesn't have to stay in this sleepy town to work for his uncle. He can forge his own future. Still, I find myself written into an ancient story I cannot escape.

I am the Chosen, whether by mistake or not. The Seeker is real. I don't believe in demons, yet events are happening that have no other explanation, so how can I dismiss the idea altogether? I am the mystery behind the Order of the Twisted Arrows. The center of the mystery that people have died to discover and to keep. Whether I want it or not, those deaths force a certain grim responsibility onto me.

Sicheii parks in front of Roundtree's house, where this story started for me and ended for Roundtree. We amble out of the SUV. With no one in sight, I lead us around the side of the house toward the back door.

Most of Roundtree's blood has washed away, but crimson stains darken the dirt at the base of the maple tree. The stains cause me to shiver and remind me of the seriousness of our situation. This isn't some adventure for children. These people won't hesitate to kill us.

I turn the handle to the back door, and it opens with a creak.

Light flows through the windows in little streams. Dust particles swirl in the air.

"What are we looking for?" Troy asks.

I ignore him. He hates the silent treatment, and I'm not prepared to let him off the hook so easily, so I creep toward the living room in silence. Sicheii follows behind, a thin smile stuck on his face.

The last time I was here, Troy almost died. I sneak a glance at him and shudder. For a second, I expect the van to pull up, but shove that thought from my mind. I have to be stronger than the van.

I lift the charred hide I noticed the last time we were here and show it to Sicheii. "This was more than just an old painting. This had a picture of a Seeker on it, right?"

He nods. "It was made around the time the Order was established. I bought it when it was brought into the gallery. I'm not sure what it meant. Roundtree and I prayed on it and even spent a couple of days in the sweat lodge, but the Wind Spirit failed to give us a vision. We were going to give it to you when you were ready."

"So that's why they burned it. They didn't want any evidence of a Seeker around."

At least one small mystery is solved. Still, it won't help us find the Book of Gifts, so I move to the center of the room where Gold Tooth threw me to the floor and glance in the direction where I saw the twisted arrows symbol, but nothing unusual glimmers against the wall.

Blood rushes to my head. I didn't imagine the symbol. It was here! The room looks the same as it did the other day. There's no sign anyone else has been here. No one could have removed it.

Maybe I'm just not looking in the right place. What was I doing when I saw the symbol?

I close my eyes and remember. Gold Tooth had tossed me to the floor. I stoop low, bending at the knees. The light reflects off a speck of silver in the corner of the wall. I smile and point. "Look over there, Sicheii. You'll find the twisted arrows."

Sicheii glides toward the wall and swivels his head toward me.

"Look close to the ground, right in the corner."

He stiffly squats and, after a few seconds, his fingers brush against the silver twisted arrows symbol. "Well done, Juliet. The Wind Spirit has spoken true."

Troy and I join him. He tries to pry open the wood paneling with his hands, but his fingernails slip against the smooth wood. "Get something hard, Troy. We need to break through the paneling."

Troy finds a heavy metal bookend on the floor shaped like a bison. He returns and bashes the bison against the cherry wood three times before the wood splits. Sicheii touches his arm to stop him, brushes away the splinters, and finds a small leather notebook hidden within a hidey-hole in the darkness.

He smiles and lifts the leather notebook toward me. I hesitate for a second and sigh. I want this all to go away. The small notebook looms large. It's real, and if it's real, everything else is. I don't want to touch it, but whatever this craziness is, I need to find the rest of the puzzle pieces, some of which are in this notebook, so I grudgingly take it from him. The cover has the same silver rectangle symbol for the Wind Spirit etched on it as the Book of Knowledge.

I try to flip open the book, but it's sealed with wax.

"The Book of Gifts is only to be read by the Chosen. It has been sealed for over two hundred years," Sicheii explains.

"Terrific." I use my thumbnail to cut through the wax and open the notebook. I expect to find pages with the unreadable symbols like those in the Book of Knowledge. Instead, the book is really a box, which holds a small crystal vial the size of my palm. I shift the box and a clear liquid sloshes to one side.

"What's this?" I ask Sicheii.

The liquid inside the vial turns red and starts pulsing.

My heart skips a beat and so does the red fluid.

CHAPTER

Each pulse of light from the vial coincides with my heartbeat. When my heart quickens, so do the pulses.

"What should I do with it?" I ask Sicheii.

He bends his neck back, closes his eyes and begins to hum, softly at first, and then progressively louder. After two minutes, he makes a loud popping sound, opens his eyes, turns toward me and shrugs. "I got nothing. What do you think you should do? You are Chosen."

"Thanks." I frown. "I think I'm supposed to drink the fluid. The pulsing light seems connected to me." I lift the box with the tiny bottle close to my face. No design graces the surface, just the smooth edges of the vial and the pulsing light from the liquid. There's no top, so how am I supposed to pour the liquid out to drink it?

"Let me try the potion first," Troy offers. "It might be dangerous. Coyote is a trickster. This might be a trap." He sticks his right hand out, palm up.

I swing the box away from him. "You had your chance to protect me. You should have considered that before you lied to me." He steps back as if I had slapped him.

I reach into the box and lift the vial with the tips of my fingers. When my fingers touch the glass, the pulsing stops, the fluid turns blood red, and the top of the bottle disappears.

Everyone makes life-changing decisions. Sometimes you don't realize how important the decision is when you make it, like when my mom slept with Ayden. She didn't know she would become pregnant, yet it happened anyway, and her life was forever changed. Other times, you know the importance of the decision before you make it, like when Sicheii injected me on the day of my birth. This is one of those times. I decide to be bold and bring the edge of the vial to my face, feel the smooth surface against my lips, and tip it upward.

The liquid is thick and syrupy and tastes like roses. Upon contact, my tongue, the roof of my mouth, and the back of my throat all freeze. I swallow and the frigid sensation spreads throughout my body.

I start to shiver. The cold threatens to overwhelm me and I crumple to the ground. A million tiny bees sting my insides at the same time, and I squeal.

Everything changes.

I have only been in the ocean once, when I was eight. Mom and I stopped in Santa Monica before going to Disneyland. I wore a pink two-piece with Little Mermaid characters on the bottom and seashells on the top. The air smelled of salt water, suntan lotion, and fun. People laughed, music played from a nearby portable radio, and a man sold ice cream from a box he had strapped over his shoulders.

I stared out at the waves, lost in the beauty of the ocean when the man called out, "Ice Cream!" I turned and saw a boy my age race toward him with money squeezed tightly in his fist. He stumbled on the sand and face planted. I looked at my mom, who was frantically pointing toward the ocean. I turned and a wave blasted me in the face. I flew backward, tumbling along with the wave and sand and seashells, drinking in the ocean water in gulps. As suddenly as the wave hit me, it receded, taking water and sand and shells with it. A moment later, Mom grabbed me. I'll never forget those two feelings—the first, a sudden explosion of energy and the second, a draining sensation as the wave retreated.

The same thing happens now. A million thoughts and images flash through my mind, flooding me with energy much like that wave. Then the energy leaves me just as suddenly as it came. The crystal vial drops from my hand and rolls toward Troy along its side until it clunks against his sneaker.

The bottle has turned black and has cracked.

I close my eyes and my world turns black as well.

CHAPTER

I wake and find myself in a well-worn leather chair, Roundtree's ravaged living room scattered around me. Troy stands close, his arms crossed over his chest, eyes full of worry. He shifts his weight from leg to leg.

"I'm all right," I say, my voice husky as I rub my aching head. Stars float in front of me, and my mind feels sluggish as if it's working with a few seconds delay.

"What happened? Are you hurt?" Troy asks, his voice sounds as if it passes through a tunnel.

"It's obvious what happened." Sicheii smiles. "The Wind Sprit blessed Juliet. She is the Chosen and will deliver us." His voice is wrapped tight with confidence and years of certainty.

A weird sensation rifles through me like someone is tickling my brain with a feather. I shake my head, clear my vision, and chase the stars away. "I'm not sure what happened. One minute, I was freezing cold, the next - stinging pain everywhere, and then I was flooded with... thoughts." I don't know a better way to describe the rush that whipped through me.

"Thoughts?" Troy asks. "Do you remember them?"

I frown. "Some of them." I rub my eyes. The tickling stops and my mind clears.

Sicheii leans forward, his voice breathless with anticipation. "Did the Wind Spirit show you the rest of your gifts?"

"It doesn't work like that, Sicheii. It only reveals the gifts my body is ready to accept." I'm not sure how I know this but I do. Part of me is amped from the fluid, and the other part is scared like I'm a child who learns how complicated and unpredictable life really is for the first time.

I glance at Troy. I'm still angry with him, so my tone is frosty. "Toss me that bison you used to break the wood."

He retrieves the solid brass bookend from the corner of the room, dusts off a few loose splinters, and hands it to me. I concentrate on the muscles in my hand, wrist, and arm. I feel nerve endings fire and direct the energy to my hand. When power pulses through my fingers, I wrap them around the head and bend it back as if it were made of tin.

Troy's mouth drops. I flip the disfigured bookend back to him and beam a full-faced smile.

"How did you do that?" He tries to bend the head back, but as big and strong as he is, the head is stubborn and stiff and stays in place.

"I can direct the energy in my body to specific muscles, strengthening them. It acts like a weird energy funnel. I must have tapped into that ability when I bent the ring in the van to escape." I shrug, but my legs buckle, and I plop down onto the leather chair. "It must take a little getting used to."

"What about the Seeker? What are we to do about him?" Sicheii asks.

"Avoid him. He is extremely dangerous. He will be tall and beautiful and will have gifts also—strength, speed, the ability to read people, and the power to move objects with his mind. I'm warned to avoid him until I retrieve the Book of Wisdom. He won't hesitate to kill me."

"What's the Book of Wisdom?" Troy asks.

I glance at Sicheii, and his body goes rigid. "I don't know, Juliet. I've never heard of another Book."

"It is the third and final Book. It completes the story and tells me everything I need to know."

"Why didn't the Order know of this book? Where is this book hidden?" Sicheii scowls, his eyes narrow, and the muscles in his jaw clench. Indignation flows from him. I sense emotions faster than reading thoughts. The stronger the emotion, the easier for me to read, and Sicheii is pissed. He feels betrayed.

"The Wind Spirit meant no slight against you or the Twisted Arrows Order by keeping the third book secret, Sicheii." With strength now returned to my legs, I rise from the chair and step close to him. I take his large, calloused hands in mine. "You are most trusted by the Wind Spirit."

I make this up because he needs to hear me say it. I just now realize how much he has sacrificed to keep the Order's secrets. His entire life has revolved around those secrets. He could have had a different life, one far from here. He has kept things from me, important secrets, but he did it to protect me, to keep me safe, to let me satisfy the destiny he believes I must fulfill. Unlike Mom, he acted out of pure love and obligation. He deserves to believe he has done the right thing. I can't change the past, so I forgive him and give him the present.

"Only I can find the third book. When I'm ready, its location will be revealed to me."

Sicheii nods. The tension releases from his jaw and his body uncoils.

I feel someone approaching like a psychic radar system. Every living animal casts off a certain spirit energy. The human spirit is different from other animals, and each individual human spirit is further distinct from other humans like fingerprints. If I concentrate hard, I can identify a person by their spirit energy. It's another gift.

I look toward the back door. "We have company." The spirit energy flows toward me like a fog rolling over a lake.

Sicheii glides toward the window and peeks out.

"It's Lisa," I say, as her face appears in my mind.

A second later, she swings open the door and bounds into the room, sweeping her eyes over Troy and me. She glares at me, but the expression is only fleeting as her eyes search out Sicheii. Apparently I'm not the only one who holds a grudge.

"Jake, we have a problem." Dark circles smudge under her eyes, and small lines crack from the edges of her lips.

"What's wrong?" His boot crunches a broken picture frame as he steps toward her. The photo in the frame shows Roundtree sitting on a rocker with a young girl in his lap. Even though she is young, I can tell the girl is Lisa.

"It's Summer." Lisa brushes her straight black hair from her face and pushes it behind her shoulders. "She's gone missing."

"Missing?"

"I tried her cell phone, and she didn't answer. I drove to her house to check on her, but she's gone. Ayden doesn't know where she is, and he's worried. He hasn't seen her since this morning when she went to the store."

"Maybe she's just running errands and the battery on her phone died," Troy says.

My stomach lurches and a dark feeling drapes heavily over me, squeezing my chest and throat. "Mom always carries a back-up battery just in case work calls. Something must be wrong."

Sicheii rubs his hands through his long white hair. I have never seen him do this before. He is uncertain.

"Do you think the Seeker has her?"

He glances at me. "It's possible. I asked her to leave town, but she refused to go without you."

My heart lumps in my throat. The last time I saw Mom, I was angry with her and tossed her from my hospital room. I still want to be angry at her a little longer for keeping those letters secret, but now I'm terrified that she might be harmed and I'll never see her again. For sixteen years, it was just us three. My hands go numb when I ask, "What did you do with Ms. Arnold?"

"We're holding her until we decide what to do with her."

"We'd better hurry." I march toward the door. Moving makes me feel a tiny bit better. When I think of Gold Tooth and Slicked Back Hair with my mom, my hands ball into fists. I need to act and Ms. Arnold is the only loose thread we have.

"We've got to find Mom. I won't let them have her."

CHAPTER

Fear comes in many flavors. I seem to have experienced them all in the past few days: fear for your life, fear he won't love you back, fear you won't belong, or you will mess up, or get in trouble, or can't help a friend when she needs you. I thought the fear that raked through me in the van was the worst until now.

Now that I'm afraid for my mom, I realize there are worse fears still. Some people become paralyzed by fear, unable to think, move, act. Not me. Fear propels me. It couples with my anger and forms a turbo boost.

We split up in two cars. I drive with Sicheii, and Troy goes with Lisa. We head to Old Town where our investigation into the murders began. Sicheii parks the SUV in the back of the parking lot farthest from his gallery and we start on foot. We avoid his gallery just in case the Seeker has people watching it.

I walk beside his long, loping strides. He moves briskly, but not hurriedly. Only those who know him well would notice the tension in his jaw and the urgency in his eyes.

I study those we pass: dozens of tourists, one with a brand new cowboy hat with the tag still dangling from it, another one who's sunburnt and carries a shopping bag from the *authentic* boots store. Still, I have to wonder if any of them work for the Seeker. The voice in my head tells me to be wary. He will have resources, perhaps unlimited wealth.

We scoot down Front Street, which runs parallel to Main Street. The buildings are all made from brick just like those on Main Street. The art galleries and restaurants are similar in appearance, but not quite as upscale or large. When we pass 2nd Street, we take a left onto 3rd. The neon sign for Aunt Maye's Big and Tall Western Outfitter greets us. Sicheii presses the button to J. Dent's apartment and the buzzer rings almost immediately to let us in.

Sicheii takes the stairs one at a time. He moves stiffly as he pulls himself up by using the handrail. I don't know exactly how old he is. I guess I should, but I don't, and for the first time, he seems aged. His energy is waning. The events of the last few days have taken a toll on him. He needs rest.

Lisa stands in the doorway and holds the door half-open. Sicheii nods, and she steps aside.

Jane Dent's apartment looks the same as I remember. Only this time, her son, Doctor Dan, slouches by the windows, peeking through the curtains. He wears blue jeans and a blue check collared shirt that balloons slightly at his midsection and falls untucked below his waist.

He turns toward me as I follow Sicheii into the apartment. He grins, but the smile is forced. His mustache and beard are gone. "Nice to see you again, Juliet," he says.

I glance at him and the photograph on the mantelpiece. Now that the truth is out, the resemblance is obvious. I should have realized it before. "I see you've shaved."

He touches his chin. "I only wear the beard and mustache when I don't want to be recognized. It's an abundance of caution after all these years, but old habits linger."

I remember the pained expression on his mother's face when we questioned her. "Does your mother know you're still alive?" I scan the room, expecting to find her.

He releases the curtains, allowing them to fall and fully block the windows. "Yes. Only a few know the truth. I don't visit with her much for obvious reasons, but we stay in touch." For her, that must be a big loss. There's no way she faked the look of sadness that crossed her face.

Troy slides into the living room from the kitchen with a sandwich in his hand. I shoot him a dangerous look. The last time we were here, he knew the truth and stayed silent. Another lie.

Dan locks eyes with Sicheii. "Jake, I don't like this situation at all. We're too exposed here. They could find us."

"The Seeker has no way of knowing about you or this apartment. You are safe here." Sicheii settles his hand on his shoulder. "I've kept you safe all these years. You have to trust me. How is our guest?"

Dan reluctantly turns his back on the windows. "She's mildly sedated. You can question her. She should be able to answer."

"Good," Sicheii glances at me. "Shall we find out what she knows?"

I nod. Doctor Dan returns to his pointless vigil by the window. He pulls the curtains back an inch and looks for signs of danger he probably won't recognize if he sees anyway.

Sicheii leads me to a back bedroom. Ms. Arnold is handcuffed to a brass bed, a piece of gray duct-tape stretched across her mouth. Her eyes are closed and puffy and her skin a sickly pallor. A small trace of crusted blood sticks to her temple.

The room is small. The only other furniture besides the bed is an oak nightstand. There's just enough room for Sicheii, Lisa, and myself to stand in the room. Troy has to straddle the doorway.

I shake the footboard and her eyes open. When they find me, they widen and sparkle.

Sicheii slides next to her and leans close to her face. His voice is rich with malice. "I'm going to remove the tape. If you yell, it won't be good for you. Do you understand me?"

Ms. Arnold nods with a small bounce of her chin, and he rips off the duct tape with one hard pull.

She sits up and pulls her knees to her chest, ignoring everyone in the room but me. Her eyes sweep over me in a slow arch. "I knew you were the one from the start. I should have told the Seeker months ago."

"Did you tell him about Juliet?" Sicheii leans toward her.

When she glances at him, her eyes flicker. He scares her. "I called him before you barged into my apartment."

I grip the footboard hard and twist my hands over the brass. "Where did they take my mother?"

She chuckles and Sicheii slaps her across the face. Hard. A red mark appears on her cheek where his hand struck her. She ignores him and zeroes in on me. "The Seeker will have her by now, Juliet. You are the only one who can save her."

"Tell me where he's hiding."

Her voice rises. "Who said he's hiding? You are making a mistake." She sounds giddy with a crazy kinetic energy. "All of you." She cackles. "You should join him. He will win. He is too powerful. You can't stop him!"

"Tell me where he is!"

Ms. Arnold rattles her cuffs, her voice shrill, spit flying from her mouth as her face reddens. "He's right where you would expect him to be, you stupid little girl!"

"And where is that?" My knuckles turn white. How could I have trusted her? I am such a fool.

She pauses, and the light temporarily dims behind her eyes. I reach into her mind, and increase the volume on her internal voice, molding the sounds, sharpening them. I concentrate hard and feel my body shake, but her thoughts stay muddled. It must be the medication. I bear down harder. Air gets stuck in my lungs and a flashing white light burns my eyes. A thunderclap breaks in my head, and her thoughts are revealed.

I pull back from the bed, woozy. "He's at the casino."

Ms. Arnold goes limp, her breathing shallow. She's unconscious. I wonder if I broke her somehow.

I should feel bad, but I don't.

CHAPTER 38

We all make choices and decisions. Life is full of little compromises— like you want to get an A in Geometry, but your favorite TV show is on, or you want to lose weight, but that ice cream calls you from the freezer.

But there are some compromises we cannot make.

I've never considered myself a particularly brave person, but I won't let them hurt my mother—not if I can stop it.

"We have to save her," I say, my back to the fireplace in the living room.

Sicheii runs his hands through his hair again. Indecision creeps back into his eyes. "The Wind Spirit warned you to avoid the Seeker until after you've found the third book. You cannot confront him now."

I start to tap my foot, and my hands find my hips. "I don't care what the Wind Spirit said or what you say, Sicheii. I'm going to save Mom. I won't leave her for those people." A chill shivers through me like a late frost surprises an early blooming flower. I see the inside of the van and the sneer on Gold Tooth and Slicked Back Hair's faces and suspect that the Seeker will be worse. I don't want to imagine what they might do to Mom.

"We need a plan," Troy says. "If we act quickly, we can have the element of surprise on our side. The Seeker won't expect us to know where to find him."

"The Casino is a big place," Lisa says. She steps toward me, her expression grim but eager to confront the Seeker. She looks like she wants revenge. "We'll need to know where he is in the Casino."

"You had a special relationship with Roundtree, didn't you?" I remember the photo from Roundtree's house.

"He was my godfather, so I have good reason to find this Seeker."

"He'll be in the Villas," Doctor Dan offers, his back toward us as he continues looking out the windows. "You need a special pass to gain access into that part of the Casino, and it provides the most privacy."

Troy smiles. "Ella's mom works nights at the Casino. She has an access card that gets her into the Villas. She cooks private meals for the whales."

"I forbid this." Sicheii crosses his arms against his chest. "We must honor the Wind Spirit's wishes. Juliet cannot go looking for the Seeker or Summer until she is ready. I will go alone."

"You will do no such thing. You heard what Ms. Arnold said — only I can save Mom." Heat flushes my face. I'm not a child any longer. The days when my grandfather could stop me from doing something are over.

Troy steps in between us. "I'll go with Jake. He's right. This is too dangerous."

"The Order has been keeping these secrets for over two hundred years. Others have died to honor the Wind Spirit's wishes," Sicheii argues. "You can't throw that away now that we are so close. We can save Summer without you."

I look back and forth between both of them. Each loves me in his own way. I don't need any special gift to know how they feel. It's etched across their faces, in the light behind their eyes, and in the worry lines on their foreheads.

My anger snaps like a dry twig. How can I stay vexed at those willing to sacrifice their lives to protect mine?

I take Troy's hand and relief washes over him. "I know you would go and do your best, but that won't be good enough. I have to be the one to save Mom." I squeeze his hand tight and see his expression melt like snow on a warm day. "I won't be able to live with myself if something bad happens to her, knowing that I could have saved her. I know you understand. You would save me if you had to."

I swing my eyes to Sicheii, who stares at me hard. It is the same expression he used to chastise me when I was little. It won't work now. "I'm sorry, Sicheii. I'm sorry you've sacrificed so much and have had to do things you regret. But that wasn't my decision. I'm grown now. I'm Chosen. This is my decision."

He isn't convinced, so I try to reach him on a different level. "I feel the Wind Spirit in this. It can't be a coincidence that Mom's been taken now that I have the sword. This must be what I'm supposed to do. It's a sign from the Wind Spirit that my time has come and that I have to rescue Mom." I know it's a lie, but some lies are good. Well, if not good, then necessary. If he thinks the Wind Spirit wants me to go after Mom, maybe he'll go along. I try to look sincere.

His arms drop to his side, and a tentative smile nudges across his face. "You believe the Wind Spirit is calling you? You can feel her with your second sight?"

I nod, worried my voice would betray the truth.

"It is written you will slay the Seeker and save our people from the army of demons. If now is the time, then we must pursue our fate. You will slay the Seeker and the demons will be defeated."

People are willing to believe crazy things if they really want them to be true. Usually he is hard to fool, but he wants me to fulfill this prophecy so badly this fib works on him.

Troy interlocks his fingers with mine. This isn't the first time we've held hands this way, but it feels different, stronger, more substantial than ever before. I feel heat where his skin touches mine. I absorb the contours of his fingers, the callouses in his palm, the strength in his hand. It's almost as if our flesh has molded together and formed one hand, stronger and better than the two.

"We will all go together," he says. "We just need a plan."

"Troy, you call Ella. Ask her to *borrow* her mom's access card and meet us here. I'll call Ayden. He needs to know what's going on."

Sicheii groans and turns his back on me.

I don't care. I'm done with secrets. Ayden is my father and deserves to know the truth—at least, the truth about Mom.

CHAPTER 39

"What are you going to tell Ella and Ayden when they arrive?" Troy asks. We sit in the corner of the living room on the couch close together, our knees touching. He smiles. "The whole story might be a bit much for them to believe right away."

"I could always take out the sword. That's pretty convincing." I smirk.

Troy grins back, and his eyes light up the way I'm used to seeing them. "It won't be good enough for Ella. You know how her mind works—"

"It spins a mile a minute."

"Yes. She'll try to find some *rational* explanation for all of this." He rolls his eyes. "We could be stuck here for hours. Marlon will raid the kitchen and tell us more ridiculous facts he's learned from Snapple caps."

"I'll figure out something, but I'm going to tell them the

truth the first chance I get." I hate the idea of lying to them, but Troy is right. We have to move fast.

The buzzer rings. When I open the door, Ayden hesitates at the doorway, his eyes silently asking if he can enter.

"Come in."

He strolls into the apartment, his shoulders swaying as he moves.

"We were so worried about you, Juliet." He inches toward me as if he wants to hug me, but he doesn't have it in him yet, so he stops in his tracks and looks down toward the floor.

"I'm fine." I smile back at him. "I'm feeling much better than before."

"Are you still hearing the voices?" He whispers as if he does not want to disturb this secret conversation I might be having.

"They're all gone, but that's not important now." This is the first lie I've told Ayden, but it's a white one. "Mom's been taken. We need to rescue her."

Sicheii enters the living room from one of the back bedrooms, and a cold frost follows him. Ayden's eyes lock on his, laser tight. He seems to grow taller, and his chest puffs out. "What is *he* doing here?"

Sicheii stops ten feet away from us. "Where else would I be?"

Ayden turns toward me, his hands curled tight. "Juliet, I can't be here with him." His voice is low and rumbly, and his cotton t-shirt rubs tightly against his shoulders. "He's robbed me of everything."

"You did that yourself," Sicheii says. "We don't need him. He's *unreliable*."

"You didn't give me a chance!" Ayden explodes and inches toward Sicheii. I sense the aggression in the air as if two rams are about to butt heads.

"You had many chances and you couldn't change. I warned you." Sicheii's face turns red and the veins on his forehead pulse. "Don't blame me for your own faults!"

I step between them, separating the two bulls. "We need to work together. It's the only way."

"But—" Ayden growls.

"But nothing! I know what Sicheii did to you was wrong. He should have told the truth." I place my hand on his arm, which is tight with anger. "But you admitted you had done bad things. If you hadn't gone to jail back then, who knows what path you would have followed?" The tension relaxes in his arm.

I turn to face Sicheii. "And *you've* robbed me of a father." Tears rush to the surface of my eyes. "I need you both to get Mom back. I can't lose her." Sicheii's eyes soften, but I don't care. I rush from the room and into the main bedroom, slamming the door shut hard behind me.

I have a difficult time breathing as tears rain down my face. Mom's been missing for hours, and my imagination whirls at a breakneck speed. An unlimited number of nasty things could have happened to her by now.

Knock. Knock.

The door swings open. Ayden stands in the doorway. "Can I come in, Juliet?"

I nod and he steps into the room and shuts the door behind him. "I'm sorry. You and Summer come first. I've been angry with that old tosser for a long time. It seems like it has been the only constant in my life. First, his meddling with our relationship, and then his testimony at my trial."

"Can you put your feelings aside for now? We need you."

He walks to the bed and perches next to me. "Yes, I promise not to kill the old goat until after we retrieve your mom." He beams a half-smile at me. "That's the best I can do."

I stick out my hand, and he shakes it. "Deal."

"Now tell me what's going on and where we can find your mother."

I look into his eyes, and the stranger I had just met a few days earlier morphs into my father. Unfairly separated from his daughter, he missed out on so many memories, memories he can never get back. I had not made up my mind what to tell him until now; he deserves more than a bunch of lies. I have an inkling he will believe me, that he will trust me if I tell him the truth.

So, I start with my birth. He tenses up when I show him the scar on the sole of my foot, and I continue to explain everything I know. I include both the sweat lodge and the fluid from the crystal vial, explain Sicheii's theory about the Wind Spirit and Coyote and see skepticism in his eyes and in the line of his clenched jaw. I linger on Gold Tooth and Slicked Back Hair. He needs to know how dangerous they are.

He only interrupts me once, when I tell him that I alone can kill the Seeker. He pulls a .38 from behind his back. "A well placed bullet should kill the bloke."

I shake my head. "He can create a force field around himself which will stop bullets. Only my sword will penetrate." At that point, I remove the crystal hilt from Troy's backpack. When my fingers wrap around it, the blade appears. His eyes widen and he leans back on his hands.

I slash the sword through the air with a series of rapid sideswipes, upper swings, thrusts, and twirls. The blade moves in a blur, whistling as it goes. It feels slightly awkward at first, and then I let my subconscious take over. When I act without thinking, my body moves fluidly, faster than before. I finish my display, rewrap the sword in the felt, and sit beside Ayden and wait. I hope he's convinced. It's all I have.

"When did you learn how to do that?"

I shrug. "The fluid has given me that knowledge. I don't know how it works, but one moment, I don't even know how to hold the thing and the next, I'm Zorro."

His eyes turn inward as if he is calculating odds and probabilities. "This still sounds very dangerous to me. I'm sure Summer wouldn't want you rescuing her. I don't fancy you taking this on."

"It's not your choice. I want your help with Gold Tooth and Slicked Back Hair, but either way, I'm going in."

A trace of malice glints behind his eyes. "I'd be happy to meet up with those two. Are you sure you want to do this?"

I nod.

"When you do something dangerous like this, you have to be all in. You can't go halfway. You must be prepared to do whatever it takes, whatever is necessary to kill this Seeker if it comes to that." He nods at me knowingly. "Otherwise you won't have a chance. Can you do that?"

"I understand." At least, I think I understand. Either way I don't have a choice.

"When I was your age, I had to do some rough things when my brother went to jail. I was hoping you didn't inherit that proclivity from me."

"I can do this." I grab Ayden's arm with both my hands and grip it hard.

The buzzer rings. He jumps.

"That must be Ella with the access card."

Time accelerates.

The Seeker is out there, and I am going to find him. For sixteen years, it was the other way around. Now I'm taking the fight to him.

Blood races through my body and my heart thumps.

CHAPTER

40

Troy holds the door open and Ella, Marlon, and Katie walk into the apartment. When Ella sees me, she darts forward and embraces me in a miniature bear hug. I close my eyes. She smells like jasmine, her favorite perfume, and I smile. For a moment, I remember what being a normal, average teenager felt like, before I became Chosen or knew about the Seeker or the sword or the Wind Spirit or before Mom was taken.

That feeling lasts exactly one and a half seconds and is replaced with the knowledge that I am forever changed. I will never again be the girl who shrinks in the back of the classroom, who tries to blend in. I will forever be the Chosen, the Seeker Slayer. I will fulfill my destiny. I will be strong. I have no other choice.

I detangle Ella from me and she frowns. "Where have you been? Are you feeling okay? What's going on? Who just leaves the hospital and doesn't text anyone?" She sounds like a breathless train building up speed at a breakneck pace. "I was worried about you. How come you didn't text me?" She puts both hands on her hips and glares at me.

"I'm sorry, Ella. I had to lay low because those guys from Roundtree's house showed up at the hospital." All true, and I'm happy I don't have to start lying yet.

She gives me a quizzical look; her eyebrows arch above her eyes. "Your mom was worried also. She didn't know where you went."

"Mom's the problem. Those criminals who tried to kidnap me and clobbered Troy have taken her. We think they're holding her at the casino. They're probably camped out in one of the Villas. That's why we need your mother's pass. We need to find her."

She squints her eyes, uncertain whether to believe me. "Why don't you tell the Sheriff?"

"He won't listen to me. She's only gone missing a few hours and they suspect that Sicheii's involved in those murders."

She's about to say something, but she changes her mind and stares at me instead. She's examining me, and after a long moment her face twists in a smirk.

"What?"

"You look different," she says. "I can't put my finger on it, but you're not the same." She turns toward Marlon for confirmation.

Marlon nods his head. "I see it too. You look *badass*."

"*Badass?*" I say.

"Right," Marlon says. "Like how Troy's cousin, Landon, looked after he joined the Marines and got back from basic training."

"Yea, that's *it*—like you're about to bring a world of hurt down on whoever gets in your way." Ella grins. She's only half joking.

Katie steps forward. "It's probably just because she was in the hospital the last time you saw her."

From the expressions on Marlon and Ella's faces, I can tell they're not buying it.

Katie protectively wraps her arms around me and smothers me with a giant-sized hug. "I don't see how anyone can believe that your grandfather is involved in these murders. There's no way Jake could do such a thing." Katie's voice is stern. She's talking about Sicheii, but part of her is also talking about her father. With the evidence against her dad piling up and the conversation she overheard about him running, she needs faith in her father's innocence now more than ever, and the two things have twisted together for her.

"Thanks," I say, but Marlon and Ella share a look. It's only a second but Marlon's lips twist down at the ends and Ella's eyes sparkle dangerously. There's something behind that look. I'll have to ask them about it later, because Sicheii joins us from the back of the apartment.

"Does this thing with your mother have anything to do with these murders?" Ella asks.

"Well...." I don't know what to say. My newly developed ability to tap dance around the truth fails me.

Luckily, Ayden picks me up. "Summer's taking is all my fault. It has nothing to do with the murders. These guys are from my past." His face is full of remorse, with wide eyes and a deep frown. I find myself believing him even though I know better. "They are drug dealers who have issues with me from my prior life. They found out that I was released, and they're using Summer to force my hand."

Ella contemplates the new information the way she sorts out a tricky puzzle. She bites her lip, glances between Ayden and me, and makes up her mind in only a few seconds. "Okay, what can we do to help?"

"All I need is your mom's pass to the Villas. We'll take it from there."

Ella removes the security card from her back pocket but holds it tightly in her fingers. She turns toward Marlon and Katie, who both nod their heads. "I'll let you use my mom's pass, but only if we come with you and help."

"These guys are dangerous," Ayden says. "You shouldn't be involved. Once we spot Summer, we'll call the Sheriff." Ayden's such a convincing liar I wonder if he's been lying to me. He knows we'll never call the police.

Ella twirls the pass in her hands, a satisfied smirk on her face. I know that look. It's the same expression she gets when she knows she's won an argument. She won't give up until we agree. Time is ticking away, and the pounding in my head sounds fast and angry like my heartbeats. "Don't we have some place to go?" she says.

"Okay, you guys can stay in the car at the casino. If we need to leave in a hurry, you'll be ready."

She hands me the pass.

I don't want them to come, but what choice do I have?

CHAPTER

I jump in the white Ford with Marlon, Katie, and Ella. Ella revs the car down Route 100. When you know people well enough, looks and gestures can tell you more than words. Silent pleas like, "Let's leave this party," or "I'd like to punch you in the face, " or "Don't lie to me" are often as clear as if they were spoken.

"So what's with that look you shared with Marlon in the apartment?" I ask Ella.

Her eyes flicker across the rear view mirror and catch mine. "What *look*?" Her hands clutch the wheel tighter as she presses down harder on the accelerator. The tires squeal as she swerves around a Mercedes.

I grab the armrest, my fingernails digging in. "Slow down before you kill us. You're a terrible liar. Almost as bad as me. So, spit it out. What don't you want to tell me about my grandfather?"

The car slows, and Marlon turns his head to face me. "My brother says they have more evidence than just the hair and the hatchet against your grandfather for the Judge's murder."

"What else do they think they know?" I sound defensive even though that's not my intent.

"They have a witness that saw Jake leave the Judge's house around the time of the murder. He said Jake left in a green SUV." Marlon shrugs one of his beefy shoulders. "I don't know who the witness is."

"That doesn't prove anything," Katie says. "Eye witness testimony is the least reliable kind." Obviously she's been doing some research about evidence, but she loses a little of her conviction as she goes on. "Your grandfather drives a Porsche anyway. Everyone knows that."

I slouch back. "He also has a green SUV," I tell them, my voice just barely above the hum of the engine. We drive the rest of the way in silence until we reach the casino.

Ella swings the Ford through the entrance to the resort and parks her car in the employee's lot. Sicheii pulls his SUV next to her a minute later. They stare at the green SUV like it's a hearse. I can't blame them. I do it also.

The casino is part of a sprawling resort with one golf course, a lazy river, two pools, sixteen tennis courts, one casino, and a private stretch into the desert with dozens of thatch-roofed Villas. The main casino building itself is massive. It stretches fifteen floors high with a large ground floor for tables and games, four restaurants, and hundreds of guest rooms. I've been at the casino twice. Both times were a year ago. Mom and a friend she works with took me to the fancy Asian fusion restaurant. I thought the guy was cute and that maybe Mom had started to date him, but we later found out he was gay and just liked Asian fusion food.

We all roll out of the cars. Slung over my left shoulder is Troy's backpack, which feels burdensome with the crystal hilt weighing heavily in it. I can almost sense the weapon vibrating, calling me, warning me. I'm sure it's my overactive imagination, but it unsettles me. We need a plan and somehow I've become the leader. But before I devise one, a voice in my head seeks me out. It sounds sweet and sing-songy.

The verbalization is as clear as if I have ear buds on, but of course I don't. "Welcome, Juliet Stone. I so look forward to meeting you. I'm in Villa 11. Bring the old man. He intrigues me. Don't invite any of your friends. Your mom won't like that. Don't dawdle. She won't like that either. Do as I say and she won't be harmed."

Everyone's eyes are on me. For a second, I assume they heard the voice also, but that's foolish. I'm sure the Seeker's message was meant only for me.

"What do you think we should do?" Troy asks.

I'm grateful for the second to compose myself. I can think of only one plan. "We should break up into two teams. Sicheii and I will start on the West side of the property on the opposite end from the gate and Troy, Ayden, and Lisa should start on the East end of the property."

Ayden objects almost instantly. "I should go with you, Juliet. I don't trust the old man to keep you safe."

Sicheii growls behind me.

I raise my hand. "Each team needs at least one of us who has seen these guys. I've seen both Gold Tooth and Slicked Back Hair, and Troy remembers Slicked Back Hair." I add as much conviction to my voice as I can muster. "When someone spots Mom or anyone suspicious, text everyone else immediately." I almost forgot our cover story for Ella, so I hastily add, "that way, we'll all be able to make sure Mom is here before we call the Sheriff. Ella, Marlon, and Katie will stay by the cars, at the ready if we need help."

"Why does Troy get to go and I have to stay by the cars? I should come with you," Marlon complains.

"You've never seen either of these guys before, and we'll call you if we need you. That way you can help either team. You'll be just on the other side of the gate."

Marlon huffs and crosses his arms against his wide chest, but I doubt he really wants to join us. He's probably just acting tough for Ella. We all know he's really a giant marshmallow.

Some other minor protests about my plan erupt around me like brushfires, but I march toward the employee gate and ignore them. As the sun sinks below the horizon, the lights above the security gate kick on. Ella swipes her mom's card and the sturdy black iron gate opens.

Before we split up, Ayden grabs my arm. "Be careful, Juliet. Make sure you call me if you find anything. I'll be there in a flash."

"You'll be the first to know," I lie to my father. He won't be with me when I face the Seeker, but there's no other way to save Mom.. He releases me, and I feel like I'm about to throw-up. I point toward the West where I assume Villa 11 is most likely to be. "Let's go this way, Sicheii."

Troy whispers in my ear. "Be safe." His breath caresses my skin and I almost cry. His lips look like sugar. I shove him away and refuse to look at him. I can't face him. I can't be that girl.

Now, I have to be the Chosen, the Seeker Slayer. I need to find a way to be strong and independent if I have any chance at all. I need to be badass.

I tromp off down the gravel path with Sicheii striding next to me.

It's right that we face the Seeker alone. He got us into this mess, and together, we're going to have to pull Mom out.

CHAPTER

I march along the path just a pace short of a jog. Flickering street lamps light our way. Little wooden posts with Villa numbers point in different directions. I hesitate at the signs to make sure we head in the right direction.

"Which Villa are we looking for?" Sicheii asks.

"What do you mean?" I respond without breaking stride.

"Obviously you know where we are headed, so what number is it?"

"Number 11."

"That is a good number. I imagine the Great Wind Spirit has spoken to you." His weathered face beams with confidence, but I can't let him believe that the Wind Spirit is directing me. That is too much and too dangerous, so I stop and grab his arm.

"I heard the Seeker's voice in my head. He said to meet him at Villa 11 and to bring only you. Otherwise, he will hurt

Mom. I didn't hear the wind say anything."

He grins. "Oh, Little Bird, the Wind Spirit works in mysterious ways. Who made the Seeker reach out to you and reveal his position? I feel the Wind Spirit in this." He pulls his head back and breathes deeply. "I can smell her in the air."

I grind my teeth. "Great. The Wind Spirit wants us to march into the Villa where the Seeker and his lackeys will be waiting for us. It sounds like a stupid plan, but I don't see another choice. It's our only way to save Mom. He'll know if we bring others."

"We don't need another plan. You are blessed by the Wind Spirit, and your time has come."

A hawk circles high above us. It's a Red Shouldered Hawk, which is Sicheii's animal guide. He smiles when he sees it.

"Doesn't that hawk warn you of trouble?"

"Sometimes, Juliet. And other times, the hawk reveals my destiny. One circled overhead when I met your grandmother." We resume our trek toward the Villa.

I wish I had my grandfather's confidence, but doubt flickers like the streetlights just beneath the surface of my thoughts.

Villa 11 appears on our right. The white van is parked in the driveway and I shudder. I remember the last time I saw that van. Panic storms back into me. I have to fight through it.

I can't go back now. I must be strong. I am strong.

He turns to me. "Coyote has a silver tongue. Don't be fooled by the trickster's words. He will try to deceive you through his pawn. Stay strong. You are the Seeker Slayer."

"Yes, I am." I say with a surprising amount of confidence. I dig out the crystal hilt from my backpack and tuck it into the waistband in the back of my jeans and pull the bottom of the Beatles t-shirt on top of it.

My iPhone buzzes. It's probably a text message from Troy. I ignore it.

Sicheii puts his hands on my shoulders, his eyes wide and a little wild. "Lets go fulfill our destinies."

CHAPTER

The gate to Villa 11 is open. Gold Tooth and Slicked Back Hair flank both sides of the front door. We stroll up the driveway casually, our gait steady as if we are dinner guests.

They smile when they see us. Fear courses through me as I lumber up the three stone steps toward them. My body feels heavy, awkward, unsure.

Sicheii takes my hand in his big calloused one. It steels my nerves, and I move faster.

We stop when we are within a few feet of the two lackeys. A victorious grin graces both their faces.

Gold Tooth says, "You should have just come with us the first time, Love. Everything would have been easier."

"Now your poor mom is involved when all we wanted was the old man." Slicked Back Hair nods toward Sicheii.

"If all you need is me," says Sicheii, "then let them go and you can have me." He raises his arms parallel with the ground causing his linen shirt to flow loosely around him.

"It's too late for that, medicine man," Gold Tooth says. "The boss wants both of you now."

Slicked Back Hair opens the front door and waves for us to enter the house. We roll past them, but I stop in the doorway and sneer at Gold Tooth. "I won't forget what you did to Mr. Cordingly." I'm not sure why I say this, but the words spit from my mouth anyway. Both of my hands are bunched up tight.

Gold Tooth smiles a toothy grin, his one metal tooth gleaming in the moonlight. "I think you have bigger problems to worry about now, little girl." Still, a flicker of doubt dances behind his eyes. Maybe he remembers what happened to the iron ring in the van or maybe he's just curious or maybe I imagine it. Either way, Gold Tooth shuts the door behind us.

"I'm in the living room, Juliet Stone. I really can't wait to meet you." The Seeker sounds as if he is right next to me, whispering in my ear.

The Villa has hardwood floors and beige walls with floor to ceiling windows. The living room is off to the left so I start in that direction with Sicheii beside me. I breathe through my nose to steady my nerves and resist the urge to grab the hilt of my sword. I'd rather wait and surprise him. It's the only weapon I have.

When I push through a set of white wooden double doors, the Seeker is sitting on a bench behind a mahogany grand piano. My heart jumps. Two tall golden candles burn on both sides of the piano. A honey sweet scent wafts into the air, and a snow white Alaskan Husky lies on the floor by his feet. The dog barely lifts his head when we enter the room.

The Seeker wears a white silk shirt that flows past his waist. Loose fitting navy pants touch the tops of his bare feet, which rest casually on the hardwood floor. The shirt has an insignia on the chest of a purple triangle with a golden circle inside.

His light colored skin is almost albino and appears soft and smooth, but I can't help but stare into his electric eyes. There's beauty behind those eyes and intelligence and a certain hardness that can only come from a proclivity toward cruelty. His features are perfectly symmetrical with thick lips and a strong chin. I stop breathing when I realize he's studying me much the same way I am studying him. I feel heat where his eyes pierce mine.

His lips slowly curl upward around the edges until they turn into a wide smile. "They chose a girl." He chuckles. "And a rather small, average girl at that."

My face narrows and he casually waves his hand with a flick of his wrist. Long, thin fingers beckon us to come closer. "I'm sorry, Juliet Stone, but where I come from, women are not usually put into these types of situations. I thought they would have chosen a boy. There is, of course, the story of Agatha, who some believe was the greatest warrior of our people, but she is really a myth. Even if she did exist, I doubt half of what she was said to have accomplished was real. She has become a fairy tale for children. Still, they chose you and you are before me." He nods his head. "You clearly have courage. I'll give you that."

"Where is my mom?"

The Seeker's face turns hard, his voice terse. "Why ask me when you can tell on your own? You must be able to sense her presence."

I let my mind roam and immediately recognize her spirit. It comes from inside the house, and I can breathe. She's unharmed.

"You see, it's all the more rewarding when you discover things on your own. There are so many facts I need to tell you, Juliet Stone. I'm sure they haven't told you the whole story. They are so duplicitous in their ways, always hiding the truth, never letting anyone know the full story. They wish to trick you with falsehoods so you will do their bidding."

Doubt flits through my mind. They really haven't told me much. I don't even know who they are, not really. Sicheii believes the Wind Spirit is behind everything, but I have a problem believing in something I can't see or touch or feel. I've searched my mind for evidence that he is right. I've rummaged through my thoughts as if I were searching the Internet, expecting to find a voice that agrees with him or to just know he is right like I do about other things, but so far, nothing.

"Don't listen to his lies!" Sicheii spits out.

The Seeker's fingers flutter across the keyboard for a minute and play a quick paced tune, one I have never heard before. His hands stop as abruptly as they started. He glares at Sicheii. "You have been thwarting me for years, Jake Stone, medicine man. I admire what you've done. You're a man of action. I can use a man such as you. How about you work for me. Switch sides to the triumphant."

"Never! You are evil." Sicheii's hands turn to fists. "You are Coyote's pawn. You seek to destroy us."

The Seeker pounds out two dark chords on the piano. "Oh, seriously. You don't really believe in that nonsense, do you? I'm not the one who killed the Judge or Samuel Baker. You did that on your own."

"What?" I say.

"Jake Stone, you didn't tell your granddaughter. Shall I tell her instead?"

Sicheii glances at me, his eyes hard and unwavering. "They were weak. They would have broken their oaths before we were ready." His hands fall useless to his sides, and his shoulders slump. He looks unsteady on his feet, his age draping over him like a loose fitting jacket.

"They were your friends. They were part of your order."

"I had no choice. They knew what was at stake when they took the oaths."

I turn my back on him. I can't look at him. I don't want to see his pain or have him ask for forgiveness. It isn't mine to give.

"Don't be like that, Juliet Stone. He did the right thing," the Seeker says. "Charles Roundtree was stubborn and strong minded. My henchmen could not crack him, but we would have made the other two talk. I just wish we could have beaten him to it. We could have saved some time. Not that that matters now."

"Shut up, you devil!" Sicheii lunges toward the Seeker. I expect him to flinch or turn or react, but he stays perfectly still. Out of the corner of my eye, I see a chair fly at Sicheii. It crashes into his head and wood splinters. He drops to the ground hard, unconscious, six feet in front of the Seeker.

"Sicheii!" I yell and reach for him. I throw aside the splintered wood. Blood, thick and dark, seeps from his scalp down the right side of his face toward his ear. Air sticks in my lungs. I've never seen Sicheii hurt. He's never even been sick. Some part of me thought that so long as he was with me, everything would work out. He would find a way to make sure we were all right. Now he's still, his breath shallow and tentative.

I brush back his white hair from his wound. His hair is soft. My fingertips touch his cheek and blood spoils them.

I glance up at the Seeker. Anger races through my body and it trembles. I bite my lip and taste blood.

"You could have tried to save him, Juliet Stone. You could have used your mind to stop that chair. It wouldn't have worked. You are no match for me, but you could have slowed it down. You let him get hurt."

My hands ball up into fists.

"We all make choices. Do not be angry with me, Juliet Stone. You should be irate with yourself."

I slowly rise.

"Now listen to me carefully. He's not dead. None of the people you care about are dead... yet." He smiles, pets the dog with his long fingers and closes the cover on the piano's keyboard.

I want to smash the piano over his head.

"You have a decision to make, a side to take. If you choose poorly, they will all die a horrible death. Your grandfather and mother and Troy and Ayden. I know them all. Trust me; everyone you care about will meet a grisly end. Choose wisely and a world of riches will be yours, and they all will live."

Their faces flash through my mind. My phone buzzes again. I'm frozen.

"First, you must know the whole story."

CHAPTER 44

Truth is a tricky thing. Some people think there are absolute truths that are always correct. That's foolish. Truth depends upon your perspective. My truth might be different from Troy's, which may be very different from Katie's. Who knows what the Seeker's truth is? I'm not sure I want to know, but finding out his truth is the only way I will survive this.

He looks relaxed as he sits comfortably on the piano bench, his posture perfect. The purple flecks in his blue eyes bore into mine. Still, there is tension in his jaw and his shoulders.

"Why should I believe you?"

"I won't lie to you. A decision based upon falsehoods is built on shifting sand. It's useless. You can see where untruths have gotten your grandfather."

My eyes tighten into slits. "He never lied to me."

The Seeker's long fingers softly caress the top of his bald head. "Lies of omission are just as bad as outright falsehoods.

You know that. Don't play games." He pauses for a second and his eyes sharpen as if he's taken a whetstone to them and peers into my thoughts. "Anger is a good thing. If properly focused, it can help you achieve much. Alphians have hot blood. We've always been short tempered. Some believe extreme emotions are uncivilized, that we should *evolve* past those feelings. They're fools." He makes the word *evolve* sound dirty. "I wonder if your anger issues are Alphian induced."

"Alphian, what's that?" I have a sick feeling I already know, and it's connected to my visions.

The Seeker flattens his hands together and gently purses his lips against his fingertips. "They haven't told you much. I assumed the fusion would have informed you more. They obviously don't trust you. You see the differences between us? I will freely answer all you questions. Knowledge is power."

I shrug. I wish I understood what was going on but won't let him know that I'm lost. That would be weak. I can't be weak.

He sighs. "Alpha is the name of my home-planet. It's the first planet in the known universe to contain intelligent life — life with a soul. Humans on Earth are newborn babies when compared to Alphians. We are stronger, smarter, and more powerful than you and every other creature that has ever existed. My people split into two factions. Those of the old guard and us Deltites of the circle and the triangle." He points to the insignia on his shirt.

"There was a trial. Your kind were judged guilty." I remember the glimmering stadium from my dream. It was no dream, but a memory implanted in my body somehow.

"Not guilty, but innocent. You see, it's just a matter of perception. Alphians are superior to other life forms. It's our right, in our nature, to dominate other life, but we evolved beyond that over centuries. My group, the Deltites, wanted to bring back the old ways, the true ways, but the Elders refused. They banished us to a far-reaching part of the universe on a planet just barely able to sustain life. They should have killed us, but they were too civilized and weak and *evolved*." He snorts, but his eyes turn melancholy.

"We lost many of our faction during the early days, until the ship came. Adam, our first leader, predicted it would come, and he was proven correct. Alphians are curious by nature and many still secretly believed in our cause. After the first ship came, the rest was easy. We grew in numbers and our power multiplied."

"What does this have to do with me or Earth?" Sicheii twitches his hand, so I shift away from him. I don't want the Seeker to notice him move.

He chuckles. "You, Juliet Stone, are a pawn in their games. The Elders still underestimate us, but others realize the threat we've become."

"Humans are the closest in DNA to Alphians in the known universe. You are weaklings compared to us, much like a pet dog is to his master." He strokes the husky's fur. "But there are biological similarities that cannot be denied. Thousands of years ago, some Alphians even mated with your kind and the connection was close enough to hold. The result wasn't quite human nor Alphian, but a mix of the two. They were hybrids. Weak compared to a pure blood Alphian, but stronger than common humans. They were abominations, really, a defiling of our blood and uniqueness, but still they happened."

"Alphians have visited Earth before?"

"Most definitely! Earth is a rich planet full of resources. You're blessed with much, although you're content to throw it away in the selfish pursuit of the present. Still, we became aware of Earth only a few thousand years ago. What a pity we acted solely as observers restricted by the modern philosophies of the current Elders."

"What does that have to do with me?" Sicheii stirs, his leg shifts, so I step farther from him. The Seeker's full attention is on me. He doesn't notice.

"Good question. Those Alphians who fear us realized we will take Earth. Earth will be extraordinarily valuable to us. Earth will help us reclaim the universe."

"By killing us and taking over the planet!" Visions of the massacre of the short and brutish people flash in front of my eyes. They were merciless. *Would it be as easy for them to conquer Earth?*

"Don't be silly, Juliet Stone." He smiles. "We won't kill everyone. We aren't going to march down on Earth with an army. Earth is too large and well populated. Besides, there are easier ways to take the planet. We are infiltrating your institutions, both political and industrial. Our leader is close to achieving the influence he wants and needs. When he is ready, we will come and humans will unwittingly welcome us with open arms. An army of humans will come in handy, which leads me to your involvement." He pauses for a second and removes a crystal hilt like mine from his pocket and places it on the edge of the piano keys. My heart falters.

"I believe they injected you with Alphian DNA when you were first born. Your newborn body absorbed that DNA, allowing you to have some of our character traits. Although meager, they make you exceptional among humans. I am sure the old guard wants you to act as their agent, help them in leading a defense of the planet against us and thwart our leader's plan. Utter nonsense." He waves his hand as if he is shooing away a fly.

"I've lived on this planet for fifty years now as I wait for the invasion, waiting for enough progress to be made, waiting for our time to come. I still can't stand the smell." He nods toward the towering incense candles. "My wait is almost complete. Earth's time is quickly running out."

"So you want to kill me." My hand slides toward my back and my fingers inch toward the sword hilt.

"No, Juliet Stone." His voice rises and falls with amusement. "They've fused certain information with you. Information that, once we know it, will make it easier for us to take the planet and defeat whatever plans they might be developing. Once the information presents itself, you only need to tell us."

"I just have to betray my entire planet and race so you can make everyone slaves!"

"Humans are lost anyway. I will let you and your loved ones live. I'll also give you power and wealth. You will live like a queen, wealthier and more powerful than all the students at Bartens combined. Why not take our side? It is the only logical choice. Deltites are meant to rule. Choose the Alphians and everyone dies a miserable death, and we still control Earth—only more humans will die in the process, starting with your family." One side of his lips turns up, giving him a sinister half-smile.

He will kill everyone I care about if I don't help him—Troy and Mom and Sicheii and Ayden and all my friends. What chance do I have against him? How can I stand up to him? Only one decision makes sense. I can make a deal. Would that make me bad?

He snaps his fingers and the husky sits at attention. He smiles at the dog. "She's a beautiful animal. Primitive but beautiful. She's happiest with a strong master. She wants to follow my directions."

I know he's talking about humans. He thinks we're no better than dogs.

His smile widens as both sides of his lips curl upward. "Well, Juliet Stone? You obviously see the wisdom of my choice. You only have one chance to accept my offer."

The husky barks as Sicheii staggers to his feet. He clutches a stone knife in his hand, dried blood smeared against the side of his face. "You can't have her, you devil. Don't listen to him, Juliet." Sicheii's voice is rich with defiance and years of sacrifice. He lunges forward, knife held in his outstretched hand.

The Seeker moves in a blur and grabs the hilt of his crystal sword. The air shimmers, and the blade appears as he thrusts it through Sicheii's chest in one smooth motion. Sicheii swings his stone knife, but he is too far away to reach him. All the strength leaves his body, and the knife clatters across the wooden floor as he falls to his knees.

"No!" I scream. The world spins, and my heart feels as if it's about to explode. I can't lose him now, not when I just learned all that he sacrificed for me.

The Seeker slides his sword from Sicheii's chest.

Blood bubbles from his mouth.

"What a fool. I overestimated him." The Seeker stares down at Sicheii. His features are hard like stone. He's evil. He might not be Coyote's pawn, but he is the picture of evil.

I race to Sicheii's side and stuff my hands into the wound, hoping to stop the flow from the cut, but sticky blood seeps through my fingers. "You'll be okay. We just need a... doctor." My voice cracks. His life is slipping from him. I feel numb. I want to scream, but no words come out.

"Even rocks crumble eventually, Little Bird." He grabs my wrists with both of his hands. "I'm so sorry I've gotten you into this. I did what I thought was right. You're stronger than he is. You just need to see it. For all of us."

Sicheii shoots me a look right before the light leaves his eyes. It's the same look he's thrown at me my entire life. I used to be scared of that look. I feared it was some type of rebuke or reflected some disappointment that I didn't live up to his standards. Now I realize it was just his way of saying he loved me.

A hole rips in my heart and the pain singes me down deep past flesh and bone. He won't be with me anymore to teach me or show me the world in a different light. I'll miss his weirdness. I wish I had known that before.

I rise on steady feet. The Seeker gazes at me. Blood drips from his blade—my grandfather's blood. I'm not sure when I grabbed the hilt of my sword, but I hold it steady. The crystal blade appears out of thin air.

"I see you've made your decision. You're no smarter than he was. What a pity. You are truly just a silly little girl."

"I am Juliet Wildfire Stone, Jake Clearwater Stone's granddaughter, the Chosen."

CHAPTER

The Seeker closes the distance between us with two quick steps, slashing his sword in a flurry of sideswipes. My hand moves fast, parrying the cuts just before they score. He is strong, and my arm shakes from the force of his blows. When the blades clash, they clang and the room fills with the sound of breaking glass.

I sense his confidence as he presses the dizzying attack—six, eight, ten strokes. I retreat under the barrage. Sweat stings my eyes. He dips the edge of his blade on a backstroke against my side. The edge cuts my shirt and draws a trickle of blood. The blade feels cold as it kisses my flesh, almost as if it's made from ice.

Just as quickly as he started the attack, he stops and smiles. "Being fused with the knowledge of swordplay is one thing, but there is no substitute for real combat. You move stiffly and awkwardly, Juliet Stone. I fear you won't present me with much of a challenge."

Adrenaline races through me and my vision tunnels around him. I'm thinking too much. I have to let my hand move on its own, let the knowledge the fusion gave me work, unhampered by thoughts.

I dart forward and slash at his side. He sidesteps me, lets me rush past him and slices me on the leg. I stumble into the piano bench and topple it over with my foot. Luckily, I maintain my balance and spin back at him.

He chuckles. It sounds like fingers scraping against a chalkboard.

I breathe heavily. I want to rush him, hurt him for killing Sicheii, but next time he will kill me. He's too good. Too fast. Too strong. I need an advantage.

I back up and start talking to buy time. "You said you've been here for fifty years, but you don't look that old." Of course, I have no idea how old Deltites are supposed to look.

The Seeker grins, his blade held steady in front of him. Candlelight flickers off its edge and the drops of blood that still cling to it. "We don't age at the same rate as humans. We are not children. We can use our minds to control our body. I wonder if you have that ability." He shrugs. "I guess we will never find out."

I scan the living room and search for something to use. I spot the candlesticks. What good will they be if the sword doesn't work?

The Seeker attacks when my attention drifts. He feints a forward side slash. I move my blade to cover. He twirls and cuts me across my left shoulder. I feel ice again and dart behind a chair, keeping it between us. My chest tightens and my eyes widen. Oxygen bursts into my lungs in uneven gasps. I can't let the panic grip me—all will be lost. Too much is at stake, too many people rely upon me, so I beat it down.

"There is no place for you to hide." He kicks the chair between us, and it explodes toward me, crashing into my head.

I see stars and stagger backward. Blood drips from a cut on my forehead and seeps into my eyes, blurring my vision.

"I'm going to kill you now." He laughs and it sounds as if he's scratching his fingernails across a blackboard.

I fear he's right when I notice the husky standing behind him, watching us.

Sicheii's voice speaks to me. "Use the dog. Use your gifts."

I feel the dog's energy and in an instant, I am the dog. I see the Seeker's back, confident and strong. I force my anger into the animal and direct it at the Seeker. "Attack!" I command the husky and retreat from the animal's mind.

The dog launches himself at the Seeker and sinks his teeth in his right thigh, catching him off guard. He spins and the husky clamps down even harder, snarling and angry. The Seeker screeches and swings the sword down at the dog. He hacks him a second and a third time. The dog's snow-white fur turns red as he butchers the animal.

I leap forward. The sword flies in my hand. I rake the blade against his back.

Twisting, he knocks my sword to the side. His beautiful face contorts angrily. The beauty is all gone, replaced with a vile puckered ugliness. Angry red splotches spring to his cheeks.

"You witch!"

He reaches behind his back, and when he brings his hand around, it's slick with blood. Gunshots and shouting ring out from the front yard.

"Good. Your friends are here. I'll kill them all when I finish you."

He rushes forward and our swords clash. He is so much taller and wider than me as he presses his sword down toward my neck. My body strains with effort.

I hear Sicheii's voice again. "He underestimates you. Two arrows are stronger than one."

I smile.

"Why are you smiling?" he grumbles. "I'm going to kill you!"

I feel power flow toward my hand. I direct all my energy to the muscles in my arm. My strength multiplies. The sword stops moving toward me, and I bend it at him instead.

Fear jumps to his eyes. "This can't be."

He uses his other hand to push his sword against mine, but it's not enough. The edge of my blade cuts his cheek. He leaps backward, topples over the piano bench, and lands face first. I kick the bench away and stand over him.

"Stop! I'll give you anything." The violet swirls in his eyes pulse desperately.

"Can you bring Sicheii back from the dead?"

He shakes his head, and his eyes flutter to the side of the room. Using telekinesis, he pulls a mirror from a wall, and fires it at me. I see it coming and command it to stop. The mirror hovers for a moment and crashes to the ground and shatters.

He jumps to his feet and rushes me. I react just in time.

My hand moves on its own.

The tip of my blade punctures his stomach and the force of his body pushes it straight through to the hilt.

He stares at me, incredulous. "But you are only a little girl."

"I'm the Seeker Slayer."

He falls to his knees, drenched with blood. So much blood, a fountain of blood. His sword drops, and I yank mine free from his body.

He spits red sludge on the floor. I should be horrified. Maybe my hand moved because the fusion guided it. I'd like to think I didn't want him dead, but maybe I've inherited more from my father than I thought. I should feel remorse, but I only feel my cold anger over my grandfather. I have become the Seeker Slayer.

When he looks back at me, respect replaces the disdain in his eyes. "I underestimated you. That was my fault, but the other Seekers won't make the same mistake." His face goes blank. "I wish I could have seen Alpha, smelled the grass just once." He sputters and falls head first to the floor with a thud.

The front door flings open. Ayden and Troy race into the room, with Marlon a step behind them. They freeze when they see me. I toss my sword on the floor, and the blade disappears before it hits.

"Mom is in the back bedroom."

Ayden sprints past me.

"Are you okay?" Troy moves toward me, his steps hesitant.

I feel nothing as I stagger toward Sicheii. His face is still and lifeless. I could have sworn I heard his voice, but how could that be? His eyes are closed and he looks peaceful. He could be taking a nap, except he isn't sleeping. He isn't moving. He will never stir again.

Strange thoughts flood my mind. Sicheii was the one who took me to school on my first day of kindergarten. Mom was sick, but I wanted him anyway. I think she knew it. He held my hand as we walked through the double doors, and I felt like I could conquer the world. I always felt stronger when I was connected to him.

Odd, but I think about glazed donuts. It was his favorite food, and he could never have just one. He never drank alcohol. He wanted to be part of the world and could never understand how others wanted to dull their mind. "It makes no sense," he told me once. "Would I want to fish without a hook?"

I laugh out loud. I'd rather laugh than cry. He would want me to laugh. I thought he was immortal. Maybe that's why I never appreciated him the way I should have. He saved me, sacrificed his life for me, and now I realize he'd been doing that all along.

Lisa storms into the Villa. "Jake!" she cries.

Troy touches my shoulder. My head swims and I fall. I see nothing but blackness, sweet blackness.

CHAPTER

I wake in Sicheii's SUV with Ayden driving. Mom weeps next to me and Troy's arm hangs around my shoulders. "How did you guys find us?"

"When you didn't reply to my text, I called Katie. She hacked into the casino's reservation system. Only three Villas were occupied. She guessed right."

"But Gold Tooth and Slicked Back Hair were armed."

"I handled them, Juliet," Ayden answers from the front seat. "They were too busy looking in the windows to notice us sneaking up on them. Bloody careless of them."

I squeeze my mom's hand and she squeezes back.

Somehow, we end up in Dent's apartment. That's a blur,

but I remember the bathroom and the gross feeling of blood on my hands.

When I leave the bathroom, Mom sits in the living room in shock. Doctor Dan watches over her, so I talk with my father alone in the bedroom. Strange how I think of him as my father now, instead of "Ayden." We talk for a long time. Mom should know the truth, but she's not ready to hear it right now. She shakes, still suffering from shock as she twirls her hair, so we invent a temporary story for her.

When she returns from whatever dark place her mind had retreated to, I tell her the voices are gone, which is only partially untrue. I can control them and understand them, so they are no longer a problem, which is all that counts anyway. Ayden spins her a tale about Sicheii getting caught up in a Roundtree drug-selling scheme. He tells her Sicheii tried to stop Roundtree, but he failed. Slicked Back Hair and Gold Tooth were dealers who worked for the Seeker. They took her because they mistakenly believed he partnered with Roundtree.

All the pieces fit well enough. Mom heard us, or at least some of our story registered with her, because she nods her head at the right times.

We have to do something with Sicheii's body, so we decide to take him back to his apartment and make it look like he died after a fight with a burglar. Troy, Ayden and I wait until late at night, wrap him in a ceremonial burying shroud, and bring him to the gallery. I act as the lookout. Luckily, we don't run into anyone.

We return to my house. Sheriff Daniels shows up first thing in the morning with his Stetson in hand and a somber look on his face. Mom answers the door, and he walks into the foyer where he tells us that Sicheii is dead.

Mom immediately breaks out in combustible crying even though she knew what he was going to say. Tears rain down my face also. All of a sudden, Sicheii's death is real and irreversible. I spend the entire next day weeping in a dark room. I would like to believe all my tears belonged to Sicheii. There are many things I would like to believe, but some of those tears were for me.

Sicheii will be buried in two days, four days after his death, as tradition dictates. The entire tribe will likely go and so will half the town. I won't be there, and that hurts.

I've realized what he had tried to tell me all along. I don't have to choose between my heritage and Bartens. That was always a false choice. I just have to be Juliet Stone. It doesn't matter whether I'm rich or poor, beautiful or average, brown or white. Let others decide if Juliet Stone is good enough for them.

She's good enough for me.

The morning of my grandfather's funeral, I'm at the base of Devil's Peak with Troy, Marlon, Ella, and Katie. We sit in a loose circle on a dusty field littered with red rocks that look like they've come from Mars. The sun is out, and a hawk circles high over our heads. My eyes tear up when I see it. Sicheii is with me. I can feel him. He will help me do what I must.

I smile at my friends and try to memorize their faces, hoping to freeze this moment somewhere deep in my mind. I have just finished my story. I tell them the entire truth. Well, almost all the truth. I decide to leave out the part where Sicheii confessed to killing Baker and Brooks. Some secrets are worth keeping. Now that the truth hovers among us like a heavy fog, I have to do the really hard part.

"I'm leaving."

Katie's mouth drops, but no words come out.

"The Seeker said there were others who know about me and will come after me. I've stayed too long as it is. Everyone is in danger if I stay. I have to go." The choice is obvious, even though it will be hard.

"How will we get in touch with you?" Katie asks.

"We won't be able to," Ella says. "Any connection between us will put Juliet and ourselves in danger. She's leaving for good."

"I'm sorry I won't be around for your father's trial," I tell Katie. "Don't let them bother you. You're stronger than they are." By them, I mean the sharks at Bartens. I understand what true strength is now - strength to do what you think is right, to stand up for those who you love. Sicheii might have been misguided, but he taught me what sacrifice really is. I feel awful that I won't be able to protect Katie any more. She'll need a friend, but I see strength in her.

Katie smiles shyly. "You're not going to believe it, but Tyler sent me a text the other day. It turns out that he's into computers like me. We hung out together last night."

"When were you going to tell me?" I joke.

"Don't worry about me." Katie sighs. "I know dad's guilty. I've been fooling myself this entire time. Still, he's my father, and I love him no matter what."

"What are we supposed to do about these *Deltides*?" Marlon asks. "I mean... I don't know what comes next. There's no Snapple cap for this."

"Just because this Seeker said there will be an invasion, doesn't mean it's true," Ella says. She says this not only for Marlon, but for me also.

I nod. "That's right, and I have the feeling that whatever invasion or plan they have depends upon their leader's success. Maybe he'll fail. The Seeker said they age differently than we do, so who knows when they might show up, *if* they show up."

"They'll probably take one look at your ugly mug and be scared off," Troy adds.

Marlon gives him a hard shove, but he smiles.

"You'll give us some type of warning before space ships show up in town, won't you?" Ella asks.

"You all will be the first to know," I say. "I'm sure Mom will be missing me at the viewing by now, so I've got to go."

"Only you won't be going to the viewing," Ella says. "You're leaving now, aren't you?"

I nod and hug Ella and Marlon. When I face Katie, I remove a small paper swan from my pocket. I made it last night. It contains my last words for Sicheii. "Make sure you drop this in the casket for me."

Katie takes the paper swan from me, her eyes moist. "You're my best friend. If you ever need anything, you find me. I don't care about Deltites or Alphians or the rest of it. I'll always help."

"I know," I mutter and hug her. I try hard to keep the tears from my eyes, but they come anyway. When I let go, they pile into Ella's car, and I watch them drive away.

Troy squeezes my arm.

We are close, only inches apart. "You should be going also," I whisper. The last thing I want is to be alone. It takes all of my courage and newfound strength to utter those words.

"You know better. We're in this together. I never wanted to stay in this little town anyway." He whisks a loose hair from my eyes. His fingertips brush against my cheek. "Besides, you'll spend all this money too fast without me." Troy lifts an old leather satchel. The bag is stuffed with hundred dollar bills—a final gift from Sicheii.

I glance up at Devil's Peak. It is intimidating in the hot sun. "I'd better start then."

"Why not just tell me how to climb to the top. You're still hurt. I'll scoop up the Book of Wisdom and bring it down in a flash."

I grin at him. The location of the third and final book came to me in a dream last night. The dream showed me the way up Devil's Peak—a narrow trail to the top. *Did Roundtree know the book was hidden on the top of the rock formation? Maybe that was why he protested the original site of the casino.*

"I have to do this alone." He would never understand that the climb looks hard and that the new me is much stronger than he is. "It won't take me too long."

"I'll be waiting for you right here." He leans against the Honda.

"I know."

***

The climb was not as hard as it seemed. The trail from my dream was accurate. There is no way of knowing of the trail's existence from the ground or even on the rock formation itself, unless you know in advance where to find it.

Sicheii had taught me how to climb, so my footing was steady. He taught me many things. When I reach the top, I find the twisted arrows symbol carved into the rock in silver. There is no obvious opening. I rub my hand against the smooth rock face and hope for a seam. There's nothing but smooth rock. When I push against the stone, there is no give.

This has to be the right place, so I sit and think. *What would Sicheii tell me to do?* Whoever left this book behind would want to make sure only the Chosen retrieved it.

I hear Sicheii's voice in my head. "Your blood is special. Embrace your uniqueness."

Could it be that simple? I pull the Wind Catcher from under my shirt and look at the turquoise stone shaped like the Wind Spirit's symbol with the etching inside. A symbol within a symbol, the Wind Spirit inside of me. The inscription reads, "You are Chosen." I close my eyes and kiss the stone. He tried to tell me all along, but I would never listen.

I remove a small pocketknife from my back pocket, open the blade, prick my thumb, and smear the blood against the twisted arrows. The arrows glow and the rock face falls away, revealing a small hiding spot with an old leather journal that resembles the box from Roundtree's house.

I grab it and place it on the rocks next to me. The secrets in this "book" will only further complicate my life. I can run away with Troy, leave it behind, blend into the world, try to be average.

That future flashes in front of my eyes. We could have a normal life, only it's a false life. I can never be average. I was never average. I am Chosen, the Seeker Slayer. My life stopped being mine the moment Sicheii injected me with the Alphian DNA on the day of my birth. I should be angry with him, but I'm not. I miss him so much already.

"I do this for you, Sicheii. I will be a rock."

I cut the wax seal with my fingernail, open the book and find a small glass vial. The vial starts to pulse red, matching my rapid heart rate.

I know what I have to do. I take the vial in my hand and tip it back. The coldness comes and then the pain a moment later and then the knowledge.

My God... there are others like me.

ACKNOWLEDGEMENTS

Many people helped us to make this book a reality. Among them are our beta readers, whether they are young or just young at heart. Their insights were, as always, extraordinarily valuable. Karen spent countless hours carefully combing through the prose, finding ways to improve on it. The end product would not be nearly as good without her help. The extremely talented author, Ruby Standing Deer, deserves particular mention. Not only did she spend the time to authenticate our Native American themes, she went beyond that to help improve the writing and shape of the story.

The great folks at Evolved Publishing continue to show what a high quality small press can accomplish. We are honored that they agreed to publish this series. Megan Harris did a wonderful job editing the book and Mallory Rock proved, once again, that she's a true artist. We would also like to thank Lane Diamond who believed in this project from the beginning and whose support has proven invaluable in developing this trilogy.

ABOUT THE AUTHORS

Jeff Altabef lives in New York with his wife, two daughters, and Charlie the dog. He spends time volunteering at the Writing Center in the local community college. After years of being accused of "telling stories," he thought he would make it official. He writes in both the thriller and young adult genres. *Fourteenth Colony*, a political thriller, was his debut novel. *Shatter Point* is his second novel. As an avid Knicks fan, he is prone to long periods of melancholy during hoops season.

Jeff has a column on The Examiner focused on writing and a blog on The Patch designed to encourage writing for those that like telling stories.

You can find Jeff online at: www.JeffreyAltabef.com Also visit him on Goodreads, Facebook, Twitter, or email Jeff at JeffreyAltabef@gmail.com.

Erynn Altabef is an avid reader, dancer, and community activist. When she's not in High School, she loves Starbucks, performing in school musicals, baking, and watching movies with her friends.

Some of her favorite authors are Veronica Roth, Joelle Charbonneau, and her dad! (That would be Jeff Altabef.)

You can find Erynn online at: Facebook.com/ErynnAltabefAuthor.

WHAT'S NEXT FROM JEFF ALTABEF & ERYNN ALTABEF?

BRINK OF DAWN
(A Chosen Novel – 2)

Watch for the second book in this young adult fantasy
series, coming November 30, 2015.

~~~~~

Special Sneak Preview: Chapter 1

~~~~~

"You don't have to do this, Jules," Troy whispers. His
almond colored eyes are wide and piercing, and his long raven
hair falls past his shoulders in a tight braid. He's always looking
out for me. When younger, I got into fights, but even when it
was my fault, he would always stand up for me. Now I need
him more then ever. The stakes are as high as they could
possibly get, and he's still here beside me standing up for me.
He'll die protecting me if he has to, but I don't want that. I just
want him close to feel his friendship, to connect, to feel human.
Lately I've had a hard time feeling human without him.

He cocks his head to the side a little the way he does when
he's worried about me, and the warm expression in his eyes
melts my heart.

"When was the last time I did something I didn't want to
do?" I smirk, but after the words slip past my lips, I realize how
silly they are. It's one of those things that sounds cool to say.
You wish it were true, but once you think about it, it's not true
at all. At least not for me. Peer pressure doesn't easily bend me,
but I'm always stuck doing things I don't want to. And now

there's an entire destiny to fulfill that's been thrust upon me. I'd rather be normal and have nothing to do with this future, but we don't get a chance to pick our destiny. At least I don't.

Troy, on the other hand, is part of this mess by choice. A choice *he* made. He's always true to himself, to his Native American identity. He has no problem knowing what's right for him to do. I wish I could feel that way for a little while.

Life is often confusing and unclear to me. I see grays where he sees nothing but black and white. He knows me better than I know myself, so he understands I'm a reluctant participant in this story. Still, I'm resolved to follow this path to the end. There's no choice. I've already done too much to back out now.

"What's your mom going to say when she finds out?" he says.

"Since when are you worried about my mom? You've been getting me in trouble since kindergarten. Your name has been etched at the top of her *Undesirable List* since we were six. Besides, she's back home and we're here. She doesn't get a vote."

He frowns. "It's just that... once you do this, you can't undo it. It's forever."

"*Really.* I get the idea." I shove him lightly in the chest. I'm old enough to make up my own mind. He's just trying to protect me, so I can't get *too* angry with him.

"What are your classmates at that fancy private school going to think when they find out?"

I pause for a second and look at him. I mean, *really* look at him. When faced with change, we have a way of sorting events based upon our experiences. For example, the human eye doesn't actually see what we think it sees. There are huge gaps in our vision, but our minds fill in those gaps and we imagine one unbroken image based upon our experiences. Troy is doing the same thing. He's making believe things will go back to normal once I fulfill this destiny. *If* I fulfill this destiny.

He's hoping life will return to the way it was, but that's impossible. I've changed and will have to change even more to survive this journey. There will be no way to go back to normal. Normal has become a bad joke, but I can't tell him this. He needs to sort things into some pattern he understands and imagine a time when life returns to what it was for us. It's how he's coping with the situation. I need to be strong for him. I can't weaken his defenses, even if doubts and fears riddle my mind.

I straighten my back. "You know I don't care about what they think at Bartens. This is something I *want* to do. It's something I *need* to do." The wind kicks up and the cool night air brushes against my skin, leaving goosebumps in its wake.

The almost full moon lights the cloudless sky. We inch toward the store and hesitate at the door. A red neon sign reading *Tattoos* lights the front. I take a deep breath and shove the door open. A bell jingles above us.

No one's in sight. Pictures of various tattoos line the walls of the small rectangular store, creating a weird, colorful mosaic. Toward the front left is a glass case with a cash register on top and farther in the back is a flat massage table, some bright lights, and a rolling chair.

A woman strolls out from a back room. She's in her twenties, gaunt with sharp features, smoky gray eyes, short hair, one nose ring and small hoops that circle the edges of both of her ears. She's eating a wrap as she walks toward us. "What do you guys want?"

She's wearing a loose gray t-shirt and jeans. Brightly colored tats cover her left arm, mostly eagles and hawks. On the left side of her neck is a teardrop the size of the palm of my hand.

"I want a tattoo," I say casually, as if I'm ordering a cheeseburger at *McDonalds*.

The woman points to a sign taped on the cash register. "You've got to be 18 for me to give you a tattoo, and there's no way you're 18."

I'm almost sixteen. In the right light, I could pass for eighteen, but she probably has a lot of experience with under-aged teenagers asking for tattoos. Still, I feel a lot older than eighteen. "No one else is here. It's after eleven. this tattoo is really important to me." My voice whines slightly at the end.

"Why?" She crosses her arms against her chest and arches her eyebrows upward. Two gold rings, one in each eyebrow, bob up and down.

Her teardrop tattoo must mean something important. What happened to cause her to get this ink? I get the feeling she has suffered loss. It dulls the sparkle in her eyes and shows in the muscles that tighten her jaw. She'll relate to my story if it's truthful. "I need to remember someone who died recently. He was really important to me."

"Who?"

"My grandfather. I called him Sicheii. He died to protect me. He raised me like a father." Tears moisten my eyes. The tears are real. Sicheii's death is a fresh wound. Every time I think about him, pain flairs in my heart and salt water follows. People tell me the pain will get better with time, but they don't know what they're talking about. They mean well, but this pain will always be fresh. He'll always be gone, and it's partly my fault.

The woman's face softens when she sees the tears. "Just for the sake of discussion, what're you looking for?"

Troy drops the satchel looped over his broad shoulder, smiles, and lifts his t-shirt, which reveals his well-muscled chest and copper skin. Across his heart is a blue tat of two twisted arrows in a circle. Both arrows are different with different feathers and arrowheads.

The woman glides toward him and examines the ink on his chest. It's beautiful in its simplicity and symmetry. I can tell she admires it and wouldn't mind trying to copy it. Her eyes widen as she lingers over the details.

"What does it mean?"

I hesitate. What am I going to tell her, the truth—the symbol represents the ancient Order of the Twisted Arrows. Or that my grandfather unwittingly injected me at birth with alien DNA, which has changed me forever. That I'm one of four Chosen thrust into a battle for our world against a powerful enemy from a different planet.

None of those explanations will get me a tattoo. She'd probably chase us from the store, so I settle for something bland. "It represents an old society he belonged to. It meant everything to him. It was kind of a club." At least it wasn't a lie. She's probably used to people lying to her and would catch a whiff of one right away.

She traces the circle with her finger. "Is it some weird Native American thing?"

"You could say that." Native Americans use tattoos generally to identify with certain tribes or to honor their animal spirit guide. I'm half Native American on my mom's side. Sicheii was her father. I have long black hair, an oval face, coffee colored eyes and a long, pointy nose I unfortunately inherited from my Irish father. I look Native American except for the nose.

The tattoo artist leaves Troy, slides in front of me, and stands close. No more than a foot separate us. Traces of vegetable wrap linger on her breath. I'm taller than the average person and stand at least three inches higher than she does.

She studies my face for a long moment. I'm not sure what she's looking for. Maybe she's looking to see if I'm serious. "What's you name?"

"Juliet Wildfire Stone." I never used to tell people my middle name. It embarrassed me. Now, I realize it's who I am, part of my identity.

"Wildfire, huh? I can see that. Where do you want the tattoo?"

I roll up the right sleeve of my t-shirt. "My shoulder would be great."

She nods. "It'll cost you two hundred cash. And you can't tell anyone you got it here."

"Done." I hand her four fifty-dollar bills.

She guides me to the table in the back and places a pillow on one end. "You want it the same color?"

I jump on top of the table. "Yep."

She gestures for Troy to come close. "Keep your shirt up. I want to get it just right."

She's finished an hour later and wipes my arm with a towel. "That's so weird."

"What's wrong?" My heart jumps. *Did she just totally mess up my arm and leave me with some ugly circle thing?* Troy's smiling, so I can't imagine she did that bad of a job.

"Usually it takes a couple of weeks for the tat to heal. It always bleeds a little or gets puffy, but your arm already looks perfect, as if the ink had been on it forever."

She hands me a mirror so I can see the symbol. I smile. My tattoo is exactly the same as Troy's. Exactly the same as Sicheii's had been.

I shrug. "I've always been a fast healer."

I hop from the table. My DNA's been changed, so my body can regenerate itself almost instantly. I didn't know that before. It's just another one of my *abilities,* as Sicheii would say. I've started to think of them as *aberrations.*

I have four special *abilities* so far. I can hear other people's thoughts and read their emotions. I have increased strength and speed, can move things with my mind, and heal instantly. There will probably be more, but they scare me. With each new one, I become less human.

"We'd better get going," I say and head for the door.

She grabs my wrist. "Wait. I want to take a picture of the ink. For the wall."

"You can't do that." I yank my arm away from her.

"I won't take your face. Just the ink."

"Tough."

She scowls at me, but I ignore her and march outside. When we leave the store a sharp pain stabs through my head like someone has taken an axe to my skull and cleaved it in two. A wild rage burns through me and I see inside a villa—a piano and wooden floors. Breath catches in my throat and all the strength saps from my body. I slump to the ground when Troy catches me.

Air comes in bursts and then the pain vanishes. A cold sweat coats my back as I lean against him.

"Are you okay? What was that?" he asks.

I'm not okay and I suspect I'll never be okay again.

"They've found the Seeker I killed five days ago. They're in the villa. Now they're coming for us."

MORE FROM EVOLVED PUBLISHING

CHILDREN'S PICTURE BOOKS

THE BIRD BRAIN BOOKS by Emlyn Chand:
Courtney Saves Christmas
Davey the Detective
Honey the Hero
Izzy the Inventor
Larry the Lonely
Poppy the Proud
Ricky the Runt
Sammy Steals the Show
Tommy Goes Trick-or-Treating
Vicky Finds a Valentine

Silent Words by Chantal Fournier

Thomas and the Tiger-Turtle by Jonathan Gould

EMLYN AND THE GREMLIN by Steff F. Kneff:
Emlyn and the Gremlin
Emlyn and the Gremlin and the Barbeque Disaster
Emlyn and the Gremlin and the Mean Old Cat

I'd Rather Be Riding My Bike by Eric Pinder

VALENTINA'S SPOOKY ADVENTURES by Majanka Verstraete:
Valentina and the Haunted Mansion
Valentina and the Masked Mummy
Valentina and the Whackadoodle Witch

HISTORICAL FICTION

Circles by Ruby Standing Deer
Spirals by Ruby Standing Deer
Stones by Ruby Standing Deer

LITERARY FICTION

Carry Me Away by Robb Grindstaff
Hannah's Voice by Robb Grindstaff
Turning Trixie by Robb Grindstaff
The Daughter of the Sea and the Sky by David Litwack
The Lone Wolf by E.D. Martin
Jellicle Girl by Stevie Mikayne
Weight of Earth by Stevie Mikayne
Desert Flower by Angela Scott
Desert Rice by Angela Scott
White Chalk by Pavarti K. Tyler

LOWER GRADE (Chapter Books)

TALES FROM UPON A. TIME by Falcon Storm
Natalie the Not-So-Nasty
The Perils of Petunia
The Persnickety Princess

WEIRDVILLE by Majanka Verstraete
Drowning in Fear
Fright Train
Grave Error
House of Horrors
The Clumsy Magician
The Doll Maker

MEMOIR

And Then It Rained: Lessons for Life by Megan Morrison

MIDDLE GRADE

NOAH ZARC by D. Robert Pease:
Cataclysm (Book 2)
Declaration (Book 3)
Mammoth Trouble (Book 1)
Omnibus (Special 3-in-1 Edition)

MYSTERY / CRIME / DETECTIVE

Hot Sinatra by Axel Howerton

SCI-FI / FANTASY

Eulogy by D.T. Conklin
Shadow Swarm by D. Robert Pease
Two Moons of Sera by Pavarti K. Tyler

SHORT STORY ANTHOLOGIES

FROM THE EDITORS AT EVOLVED PUBLISHING:
Evolution: Vol. 1 (A Short Story Collection)
Evolution: Vol. 2 (A Short Story Collection)

All Tolkien No Action: Swords, Sorcery & Sci-Fi by Eric Pinder

SUSPENSE / THRILLER

Forgive Me, Alex by Lane Diamond
The Devil's Bane by Lane Diamond
Whispers of the Dead by C.L. Roberts-Huth
Whispers of the Serpent by C.L. Roberts-Huth

YOUNG ADULT

Farsighted by Emlyn Chand
Open Heart by Emlyn Chand
The Silver Sphere by Michael Dadich
The Sinister Kin by Michael Dadich
THE DARLA DECKER DIARIES by Jessica McHugh
Darla Decker Hates to Wait (Book 1)
Darla Decker Shakes the State (Book 3)
Darla Decker Takes the Cake (Book 2)

JOEY COLA by D. Robert Pease:
Cleopatra Rising (Book 2)
Dream Warriors (Book 1)
Third Reality (Book 3)
Anyone? by Angela Scott

THE ZOMBIE WEST TRILOGY by Angela Scott
Dead Plains (Zombie West #3)
Survivor Roundup (Zombie West #2)
The Zombie West Trilogy – Special Omnibus Edition
Wanted: Dead or Undead (Zombie West #1)

CPSIA information can be obtained at www.ICGtesting.com
Printed in the USA
BVOW08s0749010415

394245BV00005B/221/P